Humanity in Healthcare

The heart and soul of medicine

Peter Barritt
Family Physician
Shrewsbury

Foreword by
Iona Heath

Radcliffe Publishing
Oxford • Seattle

Radcliffe Publishing Ltd
18 Marcham Road
Abingdon
Oxon OX14 1AA
United Kingdom

www.radcliffe-oxford.com
Electronic catalogue and worldwide online ordering facility.

British Library Cataloguing in Publication Data

A catalogue record for this book is available from the British Library.

ISBN 1 85775 836 6

Typeset by Ann Buchan (Typesetters), Shepperton, Middlesex
Printed and bound by T J International, Padstow, Cornwall

Contents

Foreword

Peter Barritt suffers from a condition that I recognise. He is so steeped in his work as both general practitioner and teacher that in everything he reads he finds passages that resonate with his daily experience. He is trapped within a virtuous circle as his reading enriches his practice and his practice deepens and sensitises his reading.

The power of words to make us feel less alone is both astonishing and consoling. They are both the means and the ends of the human compulsion to search for meaning. They form the map that outlines our understanding and, at the same time, guides our search for more. The private reading of words opens us to a range of human experience far beyond the limitations of a single life. Words take us across space and time, invoking the capacity of the imagination to identify with the workings of other human minds. Skilled writers use words in ways that help us to see the world and our own place within it in a new light – a light that falls from a slightly different direction revealing subtly different detail. Words help us to make sense of our daily experience of joy and suffering and make it absolutely clear that those experiences are shared and that, to this extent, we are never truly alone.

Peter has read widely and deeply from the Dalai Lama to Aristotle and from John Donne to Susan Sontag. This book is suffused with quotations from his reading so that it becomes an anthology that sets healthcare squarely within its philosophical, cultural and political context. It gives the reader the chance to revisit and refresh the familiar and to make completely new discoveries. Every book leads the reader on to other books and this one leads in a multiplicity of directions. There is much to treasure but also much with which to disagree and it is this range that enables readers to take their own bearings within the map of understanding and to clarify, through their reactions, the nature of their own position. In so doing, the book orientates each reader within a particular philosophical, cultural and political context of his or her own and provides a firm base for further exploration and reflection.

Iona Heath
General Practitioner
Kentish Town
London
June 2005

Preface

This book is intended to present ideas and develop themes that will stimulate the reader. It is aimed at young health professionals with a particular gift, but hopefully it will resonate with experienced professionals who have remained young at heart. The gift is a desire to use humanity in our work, and the task is to develop this for the benefit of patients.

I hope that the ideas in this book are not seen as impracticable in the busy world of helping those who suffer. In truth, I don't believe that they are. Treating fellow humans with dignity, empathy, understanding and respect generally takes no more time, although it can be more demanding. The book includes an element of describing a counsel of perfection and how aiming to be good, rather than perfect, should be our aim.

The book covers religious and philosophical themes, and at times I have set out to be controversial but not hurtful. If personal prejudice or intolerance shines through and causes offence I would like to apologise, as this was not my intention. Health professionals will recognise black humour creeping into some sections of the book. This was introduced to encourage the poor reader who has a mountain of a book to climb, but not to sanction flippancy or lack of respect for patients. In a similar vein, I have written conversationally in order to lighten the text, but I accept that this may grate on some, particularly those of an academic disposition.

Readers will realise that this book is primarily a collection of ideas and thoughts of others. For this I make no apologies, as the intention is to illustrate how disciplines outside the health professions can enrich our daily experience. I believe that this is the key reason for studying humanities. In different chapters I have tried to illustrate how various arts can contribute to the understanding of issues relating to health. I have tried not to duplicate work that has already been well described in standard texts used in the training of health professionals, and for this reason there is scant mention of many important areas, such as patient-centred medicine, narrative-based medicine, the reflective practitioner and communication skills training.

Many of the books used during the preparation of the text are now out of print but can easily be purchased second-hand via the Internet. At the end of each chapter I have recommended some key texts that I have found interesting and well written. Many of these books were initially recommended by David Greaves and Martyn Evans, or by my friend Arvind Patel.

Clearly there is a conflict between the scope of this topic, which is huge, and the amount of time that a health professional can spare to read this book, which is not. I hope I have done justice to the discipline of medical humanities and provided an overview, but inevitably it can be no more than an introduction to the subject.

There is a long-running debate as to whether medicine is a science or an art. I hope to persuade the reader that it should become an inseparable combination of both. I would have no interest in being cared for by a health professional who was kind, considerate, caring and empathic but knew nothing about the science of my predicament. As circumstances have turned out, neither I, my wife nor my two children would be alive today without the benefits that modern science has bestowed upon us. Those to whom we owe our lives have shown not only mastery of science but also skill in the art of humanity. This book is about humanity in medicine, but it is in no way a diatribe against science. The intention was to strike a balance and to show how much the world outside medical science has to offer those of us within it.

The motivation for inflicting yet another book on the weary world was not to be proscriptive but to stimulate conversation, enthusiasm and ideas. I can do no better than quote from Descartes:[1]

> Let no one think I am here about to propound a method which everyone ought to follow in order to govern his reason aright; for I have merely the intention of expounding the method I have myself followed. . . . But no sooner had I finished the course of study at the conclusion of which one is ordinarily adopted into the ranks of the learned, than I began to think of something very different from that. For I became aware that I was involved in so many doubts, so many errors, that all efforts to learn were, as I saw it, of no other help to me than I might more and more discover my ignorance.

> (p. 263)

Peter Barritt
April 2005

Reference

1   Descartes R (1644) Dissertatio de methodo, pp. 2–3, quoted in Kierkegaard S (1843) *Fear and Trembling*, translated by Lowrie W (1941). Doubleday and Co., New York.

Acknowledgements

The idea for this book sprang from the teaching and learning I did as a course organiser for the Shropshire General Practice Vocational Training Scheme between 1992 and 2002. I was keen to try to encapsulate some of the experience and wisdom that was shared by young doctors and fellow course organisers about the humane practice of medicine. My educational guru at that time was Jonas Miller, and he pointed me in the direction of an MA Course in Medical Humanities at the University of Wales, Swansea. This course was set up by two luminaries of the medical humanities world, David Greaves and Martyn Evans. It has provided the stimulus for the bulk of this book, and I am very grateful to David and Martyn, who fostered enthusiasm and pointed out key texts.

Sympathetic support from the West Midlands Deanery, Shropshire County PCT and, most importantly, my partners Rob Laycock and Teresa Griffin, allowed me to write this book during a 12-month period of prolonged study leave.

Medical heroes may be a disappearing breed, particularly in hospital medicine where shift patterns mean that personal apprenticeship may no longer be viable. Nonetheless, I would like to pay homage to those clinicians who demonstrated humanity in medicine in my formative years. Professor John Malins and Dr Sadru Jivani are sadly no longer alive but my long-suffering trainer David McKinlay is, and so is my retired senior partner Keith Hodgson. My friend Simon Reid provided much appreciated support and enthusiasm during our 15 years together in medical education. In addition, most of the humanity I have learned in medicine has been taught by the many patients I have listened to since starting medical school in 1971.

Finally, I would like to thank my wife, who has supported and tolerated yet another madcap scheme with her usual fortitude and good humour. Curiously, like many women, she has no need for a book on theoretical humanity, as the practical form was presumably inserted at conception.

Reprint permissions for copyrighted material

Thanks are due to the following organisations that have kindly given permission for reproduction of copyrighted material.

Although we have tried to trace and contact all copyright holders before publication, this has not been possible in every case. If notified, the publisher will be pleased to make any necessary amendments at the earliest opportunity.

Isabel Allende, *Daughter of Fortune*. Copyright © 1999 by Isabel Allende. Reprinted by permission of HarperCollins Ltd and HarperCollins Publishers Inc.

Andrea Ashworth, *Once in a House on Fire*. Reprinted by permission of Macmillan Publishers Ltd, London.

W H Auden, *The Shield of Achilles*. Reprinted by permission of Faber and Faber Ltd.

W H Auden, *The Shield of Achilles*. Copyright 1952 by W H Auden. From *Collected Poems* by W H Auden. Reprinted by permission of Random House Inc.

W H Auden, *Musee des Beaux Arts*. Reprinted by permission of Faber and Faber Ltd.

W H Auden, *Musee des Beaux Arts*. Copyright 1940 and renewed 1968 by W H Auden. From *Collected Poems* by W H Auden. Reprinted by permission of Random House Inc.

John Berger and Jean Mohr. From *A Fortunate Man*. Copyright © 1967 by John Berger and Jean Mohr; copyright renewed 1995 by John Berger and Jean Mohr. Used by permission of Pantheon Books, a division of Random House Inc.

John Berger. From *Our Faces, My Heart, Brief as Photos*. Copyright © 1984 by John Berger. Used by permission of Pantheon Books, a division of Random House Inc.

Jean-Dominique Bauby, *The Diving Bell and the Butterfly*. Reprinted by permission of HarperCollins Ltd.

Leonard Cohen. *Ballad* from *Poems 1956–1968*. Published by Jonathan Cape. Reprinted by permission of The Random House Group Ltd.

The Dalai Lama. *The Art of Happiness*. Reprinted by permission of Hodder and Stoughton Ltd.

The Dalai Lama. From *The Dalai Lama's Book of Wisdom* published by Rider. Reprinted by permission of The Random House Group Ltd.

The Dalai Lama, *Ancient Wisdom, Modern World*. Reprinted by permission of Time Warner Book Group Ltd, London.

The Dalai Lama, *Ancient Wisdom, Modern World*. Copyright © Tenzin Gyatso, the Fourteenth Dalai Lama of Tibet, 1999. Reprinted by permission of Gillon Aitken Associates, London.

Roddy Doyle. From *The Woman Who Walked into Doors*. Published by Jonathan Cape. Reprinted by permission of The Random House Group Ltd.

The Silver Swan

The silver swan, who living had no note,
When death approached unlocked her silent throat,
Leaning her breast against the reedy shore,
Thus sung her first and last, and sung no more:
Farewell all joys, O death come close mine eyes,
More geese than swans now live, more fools than wise.

Anon. (c.1600)

May my book teach you to care more for yourself than
for it – and then more for all the rest than for yourself.

André Gide (1926), Fruits of the Earth.

PART ONE

Health and humanities

CHAPTER 1

The philosophy of healthcare

A good physician comes to thee in the shape of an Angell, and therefore let him boldly take thee by the hand, for he has been in God's garden, gathering herbs: and soveraine rootes to cure thee: A good Physician deals in simples, and will be simply honest with thee in thy preservation.

Thomas Dekker (1570–1641), *London Looks Backe*[1]

What is the use of studying philosophy if all that it does for you is to enable you to talk with some plausibility about some abstruse questions of logic, etc., and if it does not improve your thinking about the important questions of everyday life?

Ludwig Wittgenstein (1889–1951)[2]

'But that's medicine, the art of prolonging disease.'
'Jesus,' I said, with a laugh. 'Why would anyone want to prolong it?'
'In order to postpone grief.'

Peter DeVries (1969), *The Blood of the Lamb*[3]

Introduction

We live, dear reader, in strange times. Our cathedrals are shopping centres (once a week and twice on Sundays), our dreams are Disney, our reality is television and our ambition is material. I make no apology, therefore, for beginning with philosophy, the study of meaning. I warm to Wittgenstein, who detested professional philosophy and referred to it as 'a kind of living death.'[2] Wittgenstein worked in a hospital in World War Two and considered giving up philosophy to study medicine, so his thoughts are steeped in relevant experience. This book is not primarily about ethics in the usual sense. However, it does aim to raise awareness of the human dimension in our daily contacts with those who suffer, and to highlight the sanctity of the tasks associated with occupations that care for the ill. In this regard, I am with Wittgenstein, for whom ethics was an intensely personal and deeply serious affair. He believed that ethics was not simply about good conduct and good character, but about the sense of life, the state of one's soul or, as he often put it, about being decent.[2]

What do we mean by meaning? In *Philosophical Investigations* Wittgenstein had this to say:

> For a large class of cases – though not for all – in which we employ the word 'meaning' it can be defined thus: the meaning of a word is its use in the language.[5]
>
> (p. 43)

In my view, ethics should be our constant companion when we care for others. Youngsters who are employed as carers for those with advanced dementia, for example, face a constant stream of ethical challenges. So this book is very much about how we can develop understanding and compassion in our work and how we can maintain the dignity of those who suffer.

Terminology is a problem. Medicine has come to be associated primarily with doctoring, and I hope that this book will be of interest to anyone who works with the sick and suffering. In view of this, I have used 'healthcare' as the best of a bad bunch of terms which refer to the industry of caring for the sick, and 'healthcare professional' as the term that best incorporates all those who work within it. In fact I believe that our job should be primarily concerned with care for the sick, rather than interference with the healthy – but that is another chapter! Many of the references quoted refer to doctors or physicians, but apply equally to nurses, physiotherapists, counsellors and others involved in care for the sick.

The terms *illness*, *disease* and *sickness* need to be defined, and again I have gone with the meanings most commonly ascribed in current usage. Eric Cassell uses the following definitions:

> From this point on, let us use the word 'illness' to stand for what the patient feels when he goes to the doctor, and 'disease' for what he has on the way home from the doctor's office. Disease, then, is something an organ has; illness is something a man has.[6]
>
> (p. 48)

Using this definition, it is possible to have disease without illness (e.g. hypertension, hyperlipidaemia, HIV infection) and illness without disease (e.g. undiagnosed illness, chronic fatigue). Cecil Helman expands this concept:

> Illness is the subjective response of the patient, and of those around him, to his being unwell; particularly how he, and they, interpret the origin and significance of this event; how it affects his behaviour, and his relationship with other people; and the various steps he takes to remedy the situation. It not only includes his experience of ill-health, but also the *meaning* he gives to that experience.
>
> Illness therefore often shares the psychological, moral and social dimensions associated with other forms of adversity within a particular culture.[7]
>
> (p. 91)

What of sickness? Sickness is usually taken to mean the acceptance by others that a person is ill, even (as in some forms of mental illness) if that person is unaware of being ill. Marshall Marinker had this to say of sickness:

Sickness is a social role, a status, a negotiated position in the world, a bargain struck between the person henceforth called 'sick' and a society which is prepared to recognise and sustain him (or her). The security of that role depends on ... the possession of that much treasured gift, the disease. Sickness based on illness alone is a most uncertain status. But even the possession of disease does not guarantee equity in sickness. ... Best is an acute physical disease in a young man quickly determined by recovery or death – either will do, both are equally regarded.[8]

(pp. 81–4)

Scientific medicine is only comfortable with measurable phenomena. Humanities, arts and illness are based on individual experience of life and are therefore, by definition, anecdotal and unmeasurable. In *The Nature of Suffering*, Cassell writes:

The dominance and success of science in our time has led to the widely held and crippling prejudice that no knowledge is *real* unless it is scientific – objective and measurable. From this perspective, suffering and its dominion in the sick person are themselves unreal.[9]

(p. xi)

Healthcare demands that professionals use their humanity to apply the benefits of medical science wisely. Without humanity, medical science is in danger of becoming a headless monster. Here is Cassell again:

Since individual experience is inevitably anecdotal (one can have no other kind) and individual clinical judgements contain subjective elements (they are the product of a subject), banishing the subjective and anecdotal from medicine necessarily demotes the individuality of the physician to the level of the contaminant.[9]

(p. 19)

Scientific knowledge is crucial to healthcare, but it has limitations. The art of interpretation (or *hermeneutic inquiry*, as Western philosophers prefer to call it) is equally important, as McWhinney points out in *A Textbook of Family Medicine*:

Hermeneutic inquiry is inter-subjective. One person, in this case a physician, reaches an understanding of another's thoughts, feelings and sensations by entering into a dialogue in which the meaning of words and other symbols is progressively clarified. In an inter-subjective inquiry, neither party is unchanged by the process. In this case, the patient may gain a deeper level of self-knowledge as well as a resolution of her existential crisis; the physician also may learn something about the human condition and perhaps about himself.[10]

(p. 72)

This two-way dialogue is the fundamental means of learning about others (and ourselves), and we shall return to this in Chapter 2. Cassell expresses it thus:

> Physicians may remain objective; they may (in fact, must) retain their boundaries in order to remain private persons. But, as the sick are in bondage to them, they are in bondage to the sick, who provide the basis of their power and the source of personal reward and status. Physicians are also bound to their patients in another way, for it is from their patients that they learn, understand, and improve what they are and what they know.[9]
>
> (p. 72)

Let us start then with some philosophical inquiry. How should healthcare be viewed in the twenty-first century?

Healthcare as crisis

Many have argued that Western medicine faces Armageddon. Iona Heath perceives a crisis,[11] Ivan Illich perceives a nemesis,[12] and Bernard Lown moved from a 'profound crisis' to a 'meltdown' between editions.[13] It may be wise, as with the man carrying a billboard proclaiming the End of the World, not to hold one's breath until the event finally occurs.

After 30 years in medicine, the changes I notice are relatively slight. Patients continue to suffer and need our help. People are born, learn to love and to lose, become ill and die. The main changes I notice are longer consultation times, fewer prima donna specialists, more democracy in the consultation, much less on-call and an improved range of treatments on offer. Healthcare professionals have certainly lost some of the public's automatic trust and admiration, but there is plenty of gratitude and respect left for those who merit it. In my lifetime have come the prevention of congenital rubella and of rhesus incompatibility, immunisation against polio, diphtheria, measles, mumps, pneumonia, influenza, haemophilus A and hepatitis A and B, and the elimination of smallpox. The cure for peptic ulcer has been discovered, and well-tolerated treatments for asthma, depression, hypertension, hypercholesterolaemia, ischaemic heart disease and heart failure have been developed. Surgeons have developed open-heart surgery, joint replacement, cataract extraction, keyhole surgery and organ transplants. Gynaecologists have made great strides in the treatment of subfertility, paediatricians have saved many lives in special-care units, and anaesthetists have invented epidurals and pioneered intensive care. This is no mean achievement in a mere 50 years.

This is not to argue for smug satisfaction or the denial of important new problems to be confronted, but crisis may be overstating the case. There is and always has been change, and probably the rate of change is ever increasing as a result of man's inventiveness. Healthcare could be viewed as a victim of its own success. As treatments become increasingly skilled and the public expects the best possible results, increasing specialisation becomes inevitable. The challenge is somehow to coordinate and incorporate these technological advances in a way that preserves dignity and celebrates individuality.

Humans love to revel in past glories. Arcadian dreams of a lost Golden Age are as old as the Garden of Eden. Doctors dream of times when patients obeyed them without demur. Patients dream of times before avaricious multi-national pharmaceutical companies poisoned the population and of times when a handful of pulses and organic vegetables gave eternal life and freedom from suffering. We shall return to these themes in Chapter 3.

When mankind is not looking fondly backwards, it gazes wistfully forwards and dreams of Utopia. In *The Mirage of Health*, Rene Dubos argues that after Darwin, science moved centre-stage as the discipline to deliver the New Jerusalem.[14] Industrialisation in the nineteenth-century Western world created perfect conditions for generating disease. The problems of social inequality, poverty and squalor were alleviated by humanitarian and social reform which delivered pure air, clean water, good food and better housing. As the microscope arrived and germ theory got well under way, serums, vaccines and drugs became available to treat microbial diseases. The massive decline in deaths from infectious diseases in the latter half of the nineteenth century was attributed at the time to medical science, but we have since realised that it was in fact related to better social conditions. Improvements in life expectancy have resulted primarily from falling death rates due to infection in infancy and childhood. Indeed, as we shall see in Chapter 3, good health has almost nothing to do with good healthcare. All of these factors had a part to play in exaggerating the benefits of medical science to the population. The explosion of this myth caused much of the disenchantment with medical technology in the late twentieth century, epitomised by the railings of Ivan Illich in *Medical Nemesis*.[12]

Healthcare as models

There have always been two major conflicting views about health and illness. Characteristically the Ancient Greeks invented a God for each. Hygeia was a serene, benevolent maiden who was the guardian of health and symbolised the belief that men could remain well if they lived according to reason. This is the 'healthy mind in a healthy body' school of thought. Asclepius, on the other hand, was a handsome, self-assured, heroic young god who was the first physician according to Greek legend. Asclepius treated disease and restored health by correcting imperfections caused by accidents of birth or of life. Dubos argues that these two schools of thought have existed simultaneously in all civilisations in one form or another.[14] Alistair Campbell, writing in 1984, argued that these models led to the traditional roles of doctors and nurses:

> Doctors tend to have quite infrequent and fleeting contact with the bodies of their patients. ... The wish for cure dominates medicine, and the routine tasks of caring are delegated to nurses, who are regarded as more appropriate hourly companions for the patient. We might say that doctors tend to serve the male God of interventionist medicine, Asclepius. The more tranquil, nurturing role of Hygeia, the goddess of well-being, is seen as a lesser task, suitable for the womanly patience of nurses.[15]
>
> (p. 31)

These two models, of course, are not mutually exclusive and they may complement each other well, but tension between the extremes is inevitable. As Dubos observes:

To ward off disease or recover health, men as a rule find it easier to depend on healers than to attempt the more difficult task of living wisely.[14]

(p. 109)

Asclepius is represented in the drama of the operating theatre and the emergency room, and is the stuff of soap opera and television documentary. Hygeia, in her serene loveliness, is embodied in the yin and yang of Chinese medicine, physiology and homeostasis, epidemiology, public health, much complementary therapy, vegetarianism, whole/organic foodism, the gymnasium and the 'lofty hope that man can some day achieve a state of harmony within himself and with the surrounding world'.[14]

Hippocrates, in his wisdom, managed to incorporate both models and to be all things to all men. Dubos describes his legacy as follows:

> To the philosophically minded, Hippocrates stands for rational concepts based on objective knowledge and for the liberation of science in general, and of medicine in particular, from mystic and demonic influences. To the student of public health, the Hippocratic writings provide classical examples of the relation between the environments – physical and social – and the prevalence and severity of various diseases. To the physician, they offer objective description of symptoms, subtle methods of diagnosis, hints for dealing with the patient as a person and with his family – in short, all aspects of the art of medicine.[14]

(p. 112)

Nonetheless, not even Hippocrates escapes criticism altogether. As divine faith and demonic influence were replaced by scientific reason, Cassell believes that this eroded the importance of the individual in the scheme of disease.[6] The Spanish historian Pedro Lain Entralgo lays the blame for lack of communication between doctor and patient at Hippocrates' door:

> Hippocratic physicians were so eager to separate themselves from the superstitious and popular medicine they superseded that they disavowed the spoken or sung charms, chants and incantations that were formerly the primary modes of treatment. The use of the word in treatment was suspect, since it smacked of those earlier superstitions. The second source of silence was the fact that the Hippocratic school based its diagnosis and treatment on objective measurement. While objective measurement included the information of the senses, it decidedly did not include much of what the patient said, since this was merely opinion.[6]

(p. 56)

Hippocrates certainly helped to launch scientific medicine, albeit in a holistic framework. He taught that anyone living reasonably in an environment to which he was well adapted was not likely to fall ill, unless some accident or epidemic occurred. He believed in the natural ability of the sick body to restore the disturbed equilibrium, and he saw the physician's task as being to help the body to heal.

The balance between the Hygeian and Asclepian models was drastically altered by the arrival of the germ theory and the doctrine of specific aetiology of disease.

Edward Jenner could rightly claim to have ushered in this era. His experiments using cows to develop smallpox vaccination commenced in 1796. However, it was not until Robert Koch identified the tubercle bacillus in 1883 and Louis Pasteur identified the streptococcus, staphylococcus and pneumococcus in the period 1877–87 that the germ theory gained general credibility and widespread acclaim. Attention was switched to identifying a specific cause for each disease, and treatment involved attacking the causative agent or focusing treatment on the affected part of the body. As the realisation grew that therapeutic serums and prophylactic vaccines could not cure every disease, attention switched increasingly to the search for specific therapeutic drugs – the so-called 'Magic Bullet' approach. Perhaps the search for new drugs is about to be swept away by the latest revolution, namely genetic engineering and immunotherapy. Dubos reflects as follows:

> By equating disease with the effect of a precise cause – microbial invader, biochemical lesion, or mental stress – the doctrine of specific aetiology had appeared to negate the philosophical view of health as equilibrium and to render obsolete the traditional art of medicine.[14]
>
> (p. 99)

The public has become accustomed to miracles, and expectation of a 'cure for every ill' is widespread. A further nail was hammered in the coffin of holism by Descartes (1596–1650) with his theory of Cartesian dualism. He believed in a mechanical body inhabited by a non-material soul. Clearly Descartes was deprived of pets in childhood, because he argued that animals had no soul and were automatons. Consciousness and the mind were related to the brain but were, he believed, separate entities. His famous catchphrase 'I think therefore I am' was an idea that was first committed to paper around 1200 years before Descartes thought of it, by Augustine in his *City of God*:

> Without any delusive representation of images and phantasms, I am most certain that I *am,* and that I know and delight in this.[16]

Even dualism dates back to Ancient Greece. What is more, Descartes believed that the soul and mind interacted with the brain and the body via the pineal gland. Anyway, for reasons that are not immediately apparent, Descartes is considered to be the father of psychology, physiology and the biomechanical model of the human body. As secularism spread, his concept of soul was gradually dropped and the mind/body schism was complete. In medicine this has led to the separate disciplines of psychiatry (minds) and medicine (bodies). If patients fall ill but Western medicine can find no disease, the patient may be referred to a psychiatrist as a punishment. Alternatively, the family physician may talk of 'psychosomatic disease'. If successful treatments are found for psychosomatic diseases, the latter are immediately de-classified. In my professional career this fate has befallen duodenal ulcer, eczema, asthma, ulcerative colitis and epilepsy. The underlying text here is 'If I can't find anything wrong with you on my tests, you must be imagining it.' Patients are, in my experience, under-whelmed by the concept!

The body as machine has been termed the biomechanical or 'plumbing' model. This model involves regular checks for servicing, spare-part surgery and whole-body scans to detect faults that are not immediately obvious. Making the machine last for as long as possible, with as few breakdowns as is feasible, is part of the mission statement. The mechanic is a hero so long as he finds and fixes problems at the first attempt. Rewiring (pacemakers), pipe-cleaning (angioplasty), re-plumbing (vascular surgery), removal of blockages (bowel surgery, trans-urethral resection of the prostate) or new for old (hip replacement, heart transplant) may all be necessary. When the machines are no longer road-worthy, they are put in scrapyards (care homes) or are broken up for spare parts. Good engine oil is recommended (not too greasy) and may need thinning (aspirin). Quality control (audit and clinical governance) is imperative, and machines are tested under rigorous conditions (controlled clinical trials). The machine is a passive recipient in the hands of the skilled engineer. Profitability or, in a State-funded system, financial stringency is paramount.

The counterbalance to the biomechanical model has been termed by Peter Toon the 'humanist model'. The ethos here is well expressed by Cassell:

> The experience of the clinician produces knowledge tainted by emotion and passion. Science was meant to rescue medicine from this problem yet science cannot solve this problem. *There is no alternative to using this kind of experiential knowledge in medical care – understanding and accepting that fact is the beginning of the solution to the problem.*
>
> Only the physician as a person can empathically experience the experience of a sick person. *It must finally be accepted, therefore, that there can be no substitute for the physician as a person.*[9]
>
> (p. 227)

In this model the central figure is the sick person, and the healthcare professional is seen as a friend, witness or guide. Dialogue between the parties is human and interpretive, and feelings and emotions are valued and discussed. Human beings are helped to heal and their spirit or soul is carefully considered.[17]

As Toon reminds us, we need to sit lightly on our models. Each model has value in certain situations, and no one model is correct or complete. Rewiring is perfectly appropriate for a patient with complete heart block, whereas empathic witnessing may serve us well in a patient's dying moments.

Healthcare as capitalism

In *The Mirage of Health*, Dubos argues that technology has displaced religion and philosophy as the driving force in shaping the world and determining human fate. He also puts the onus of responsibility on scientists to become involved in the ethical debates that follow technological advances.[14] Human cloning is a particularly good example of the awesome ethical responsibility that can emanate from scientific advance. Medical technology has saddled every country in the world with intractable financial problems, as healthcare professionals find more and more expensive activities to perform. Jacob Needleman writes:

> The whole of our culture is having a reaction against a long-standing faith in the goodness of science and scientific technology, a kind of waking

up, a realisation that science has not lived up to what it promised. Throughout the world, people are having second thoughts about scientific technology, even as its influence and our dependency upon it continue to grow.[18]

(p.116)

The issue of dependence is crucial. The abstract thoughts of a taxpayer are often very different from the feelings of that same person some years later when their child with Down's syndrome needs open-heart surgery. One man's rationing is another man's manslaughter, so to speak. In a secular society where death means oblivion, medicine may be asked to preserve life whatever the cost and however bizarre the rest of that life may be. Feeding very elderly patients, who are semiconscious following severe strokes, via gastrostomy for years on end is an example of this. The patients I am thinking of here had decisions made for them by doctors and relatives because they had lost the use of meaningful communication. Ethically it is often easiest to 'do everything possible', and starting treatment is much easier than stopping it. Alfred Tauber rejects the concept of 'technology gone mad', arguing that humans invent technology and humans decide when and how machines and drugs are used.[19]

Of course, medical science is not just about technology. Clinical trials may question established dogma and lead to a reduction in unnecessary treatment – for example, routine episiotomy in childbirth and antibiotics for otitis media and tonsillitis. Medical science includes public health and epidemiology and, as we shall see in Chapter 3, these disciplines have uncovered fascinating insights into disease prevention that demand changes to fairness and democracy in society, rather than more money. Technology has raised expectations of health and happiness to unimagined heights, primarily because of a good track record. Subsistence farming may appeal to our notions of the 'Noble Savage', but most human beings cannot wait to escape from its clutches.

Rationing on some basis is inherent in all healthcare and always will be. Progress in sustaining the ageing or failing body, treating infections and cancer, and reconstructing after injury or mutilation will continue and comes at a cost. No society will be able to afford every treatment or procedure of which orthodox or complementary healthcare is capable. Our strivings and our aspirations are human, and limitless. Only spirituality, religion or philosophy can turn back that particular tide.

Certainly, materialism and capitalism stoke the public's desire for youth, beauty, happiness and immortality, because shifting commodities and making profit depend on it. On the other hand, if people choose to pay for a new nose or a slimmer bottom, who are we to object to this? Which of us accept the declines of old age with relish? This is the price of freedom and the cult of the individual. Campbell argues in *Health as Liberation* that our individualism leaves us only two ways of evaluating the goodness of our lives – the criterion of 'success' and the criterion of 'feeling good'. As he remarks, 'We live in a world in which each of us is the only significant inhabitant'. This contrasts with life before the Reformation, when class, occupation and religion defined us as people. Campbell writes:

> Through science and technology, we have achieved an ever-increasing mastery of the world around us. As a result, we no longer see suffering to be pre-ordained or inevitable.

We see freedom from pain, material comfort and personal fulfilment as part of our birthright, and we see failure to have these expectations met as a technical failure that must have a technical solution.

In summary, we find that the very individualism we treasure has become a primary source of our discontent.[20]

(pp. 55–9)

Healthcare as antithesis

The philosophy of healthcare can resemble a boxing ring, with opposing views defending their respective corners. This was emerging when healthcare as models was considered earlier. Much of the debate focuses around issues of whether subjective or objective factors are more important. Is the healthcare professional an innocent bystander or an integral part of illness and recovery? Is factual knowledge the crucial part of training for the professions (as most students are led to believe) or is examining emotion and developing intuition more important? At heart, is medicine a science or an art?

Philosophers, by their very nature, take nothing on trust. Toon tells us that attitudes to knowledge lie at two extremes. The radical sceptic doubts that anything can be known except one's own mental existence (the 'Descartes corner'), whereas the person who cherishes common sense takes everything at face value, with no doubts about the reality of appearances (the 'orthopaedic corner'). Storr argues that creative people are those who have recognised and bridged the gap between conscious and subconscious worlds, and perhaps this dichotomy is the most important of all. Both Iona Heath and David Greaves believe that mystery is a vital part of medicine. Greaves believes that the true art of medicine is that part which deals with matters which are inexplicable to orthodox science.[21] He also points out the conflict between openness and closure in our work:

> Medical systems of knowledge are therefore torn between the desire for 'closure' which will allow for diagnosis of disease, clinical research and technical control, and the 'openness' of experiential reality arising from an engagement with the patients' illnesses and suffering. However, attempts to integrate and so fully comprehend these two aspects can only be partially successful. Yet at the same time, in making the attempt to hold them together we engage with reality, and thereby alter it.[21]
>
> (pp. 142–3)

Greaves brings out a crucial point about models and antitheses, recognising that extremes can illuminate new ways of seeing the world but, as in the boxing ring, most of the action and interest takes place in the middle. This view is echoed by Cassell:

> To meet the challenge posed by the need to relieve suffering, medicine requires the introduction of a systematic and disciplined approach to learning from experience and the knowledge that comes from it, not

artificial divisions of medical knowledge into art and science or strained and unreal analyses of objectivity versus subjectivity.[9]

(p. 227)

What point, also, is there in our knowledge and experience if we are unable to use them practically and critically? This, according to the *Oxford Concise English Dictionary*, is the meaning of wisdom.[22] Wisdom requires inner reflection. Here is William Cowper's poem *Knowledge and Wisdom*:

> Knowledge and wisdom, far from being one,
> Have oftimes no connection. Knowledge dwells
> In heads replete with thoughts of other men;
> Wisdom in minds attentive to their own.
> Knowledge, a rude unprofitable mass,
> The mere material with which Wisdom builds,
> Till smooth'd and squar'd, and fitted to its place,
> Does not encumber what it means to enrich.
> Knowledge is proud that he has learn'd so much
> Wisdom is humble that he knows no more.[23]

(p. 101)

Graham Hills has even gone on to suggest that today we are struggling under the weight of far too much knowledge. Perhaps this is partly why computers have yet to replace healthcare professionals. Currently practical skills and wise judgement are hard to program into hard disks, but knowledge is certainly not a problem. Hills writes:

> The person who first said that a little knowledge is a dangerous thing could have gone on to say that more of the knowledge might be even more dangerous. Knowledge is fine in small doses. But generally speaking, knowledge is luggage, and it would be best to travel light.[24]

(p. 1578)

Isabel Allende describes the qualities of the good physician in her novel *Daughters of Fortune*, when a traditional Chinese doctor is instructing his apprentice:

> He said that knowledge was of little use without wisdom, and that there was no wisdom without spirituality, and that true spirituality always included service to others. As he explained many times, the essence of a good physician consisted of the capacity for compassion and a sense of the ethical, without which qualities the sacred art of healing degenerated into simple charlatanism.[25]

(p. 158)

Healthcare as virtue

In the latter part of the twentieth century there was a reassessment of the position of professions generally, and of medicine in particular. Tauber argues that doctors lost their previous status of demi-gods, which had been established in previous generations by personal sacrifice, uncommon intelligence, accomplishment and the authority of scientific power.[19] Personally I welcome the waning of the traditional roles of angels (nurses) and gods (doctors). The path is still open for healthcare professionals to display commitment, compassion, humility, skill, human understanding and kindness. In short, the pursuit of a virtuous life is still possible in medicine. However, listing virtues is, as Toon points out, a potentially tricky business:

> Virtue, like rights, can easily be little more than organised prejudice. Arbitrary lists of virtues can be invented to justify whatever the writer happens to wish to promote.[17]
>
> (p. 2)

However, as Stanley Hauerwas points out, it is important to remember that a society's decision to pay for some of its members to care for the sick is in itself no mean feat of virtue:

> ... what an extraordinary gesture it is for a society to set aside some to dedicate their lives to the care of the ill. That we do so, I think, is not primarily because we are self-interested and thus want to guarantee that when we are ill we will not be abandoned, but because we are unwilling to abandon others who need help. Therefore medicine as a moral practice draws its substance from the extraordinary moral commitment of a society to care for the ill.[26]
>
> (p. 13)

Hauerwas sees medicine as a tradition of wisdom concerning good care of the body which is shared by both patient and physician:

> ... a physician's authority derives from physicians' and patients' common moral beliefs and shared participation in a practice that embodies those beliefs. The physician's authority thus is based upon mastery of the moral and practical skills involved in that physician's commitment to care for and never abandon the ill and the dying.[26]
>
> (pp. 46–7)

Virtue and ethics are inextricably linked, and this brings us back to Wittgenstein's belief that ethics is a fundamental part of daily life. Ethics and virtue are both concerned with how personal conduct impinges on others and on the community at large. The ability to consider and feel for others is the basis of our humanity. The pinnacle of humanity is to treat the stranger in the same way as we treat those we love, and this endeavour in healthcare has much to recommend it. This is the central message in the parable of the Good Samaritan. Hauerwas sees medicine as:

> ... fundamentally an educational process for both doctor and patient, in which each is both teacher and learner. It is from patients that physicians learn the wisdom of the body.

By steadfastly identifying with the ill, physicians become teachers also for the healthy. Part of the physician's vocation, therefore, is to serve as a bridge between the world of the sick and the world of the healthy.[26]

(pp. 48–9)

The relationship between patient and healthcare professional is central to the virtue of the occupation. Ramsay emphasises this when he writes:

The moral commitment of the physician is not to treat diseases, or populations, or the human race, but the immediate patient before him or her.[27]

(p. 59)

If nothing else is possible, the moral commitment of the professional is to be a human presence in the face of suffering. Tauber argues that this moral commitment entails 'a sense of responsibility for those who suffer, and this responsibility must emanate from compassion'.[19] Tauber quotes a fifteenth-century Dominican visionary called Savonarola:

The physician that bringeth love and charity to the sick, if he be good and kind and learned and skilful, none can be better than he. Love teacheth him everything, and will be the measure and rule of all the measures and rules of medicine.[19]

(p. 112)

Tauber goes on to say:

The doctor does not solely serve as an objective observer, but partakes in a communion with the ill. Responsibility requires a personal *response*, one originating from the deepest recesses of the soul.[19]

(p. 113)

Working with the sick and suffering is a privilege in that it offers a meaningful and worthwhile occupation and the opportunity for spiritual growth and a virtuous life. Healthcare professionals are prone to feel sorry for themselves, and the world of illness can prove overwhelming at times. Healthcare offers us the chance to do good in the world, and for that we should be grateful. Maurice Nicoll, reflecting on the Good Samaritan, writes:

To act from compassion, to act from mercy, is to act from Good itself and not from any idea of reward. Truth alone has nothing to do with compassion, nothing to do with mercy. The most merciless and atrocious acts have been done in the name of Truth. For Truth divorced from Good has nothing real in it. It has nothing to check it, nothing to unite it and give it any real being.[28]

(p. 52)

References

1   Quoted in Scarlett E (1972) *In Sickness and in Health.* McClelland & Stewart, Toronto.
2   Quoted in Elliott C (ed.) (2001) *Slow Cures and Bad Philosophers.* Duke University Press, Durham, NC.
3   DeVries P (1969) *The Blood of the Lamb.* Little, Brown & Co., Boston, MA.
4   Allen W (1975) *Getting Even.* WH Allen & Co, London.
5   Wittgenstein L (1953) (trans Anscombe G) *Philosophical Investigations.* Basil Blackwell, Oxford.
6   Cassell E (1985) *The Healer's Art.* MIT Press, Cambridge, MA.
7   Helman C (1990) *Culture, Health and Illness.* Butterworth Heinemann, Oxford.
8   Marinker M (1975) Why make people patients? *J Med Ethics.* 1: 81–4.
9   Cassell E (1991) *The Nature of Suffering and the Goals of Medicine.* Oxford University Press, Oxford.
10 McWhinney I (1997) *A Textbook of Family Medicine* (2e). Oxford University Press, Oxford.
11 Heath I (1995) *The Mystery of General Practice.* Nuffield Provincial Hospitals Trust, Guildford.
12 Illich I (1975) *Medical Nemesis.* Calder & Boyars, London.
13 Lown B (1999) *The Lost Art of Healing: practicing compassion in medicine.* Ballantine Publishing, New York.
14 Dubos R (1960) *The Mirage of Health: utopias, progress and biological change.* George Allen & Unwin, London.
15 Campbell A (1984) *Moderated Love.* SPCK, London.
16 Augustine A (410) *De Civitate Dei* Book XI Chapter 26, translated by Dods M (1897) *The Works of Aurelius Augustine, Bishop of Hippo: The City of God.* T & T Clark, Edinburgh.
17 Toon P (1999) *Towards a Philosophy of General Practice: a study of the virtuous practitioner.* Royal College of General Practitioners, London.
18 Needleman J (1992) *The Way of the Physician.* Penguin Books, Harmondsworth.
19 Tauber A (1999) *Confessions of a Medicine Man.* MIT Press, Cambridge, MA.
20 Campbell A (1995) *Health as Liberation: medicine, theology and the quest for justice.* Pilgrim Press, Cleveland, OH.
21 Greaves D (1996) *Mystery in Western Medicine.* Avebury, Aldershot.
22 Thompson D (1995) *Oxford Concise English Dictionary* (9e). Clarendon Press, Oxford.
23 Cowper W (1731–1800) *The Task.* Quoted in *BMJ* (2001) 322: 101.
24 Hills G (1993) The knowledge disease. *BMJ.* 307: 1578.
25 Allende I (2000) *Daughters of Fortune.* Flamingo, London.
26 Hauerwas S (1986) *Suffering Presence.* T & T Clark Ltd, Edinburgh.
27 Ramsay P (1970) *The Patient as Person.* Yale University Press, New Haven, CT.
28 Nicoll M (1950) *The New Man: an interpretation of some parables and miracles of Christ.* Stuart & Richards, London.

Further reading

- Campbell A (1984) *Moderated Love.* SPCK, London.
- Campbell A (1995) *Health as Liberation: medicine, theology and the quest for justice.* Pilgrim Press, Cleveland, OH.
- Cassell E (1985) *The Healer's Art.* MIT Press, Cambridge, MA.
- Cassell E (1991) *The Nature of Suffering and the Goals of Medicine.* Oxford University Press, Oxford.
- Dubos R (1960) *The Mirage of Health: utopias, progress and biological change.* George Allen & Unwin, London.
- Elliott C (ed.) (2001) *Slow Cures and Bad Philosophers.* Duke University Press, Durham, NC.
- Greaves D (1996) *Mystery in Western Medicine.* Avebury, Aldershot.
- Hauerwas S (1986) *Suffering Presence.* T & T Clark Ltd, Edinburgh.
- Heath I (1995) *The Mystery of General Practice.* Nuffield Provincial Hospitals Trust, Guildford.
- Illich I (1975) *Medical Nemesis.* Calder & Boyars, London.
- McWhinney I (1989) *A Textbook of Family Medicine.* Oxford University Press, Oxford.
- Needleman J (1992) *The Way of the Physician.* Penguin Books, Harmondsworth.
- Tauber A (1999) *Confessions of a Medicine Man.* MIT Press, Cambridge, MA.
- Toon P (1999) *Towards a Philosophy of General Practice: a study of the virtuous practitioner.* Royal College of General Practitioners, London.

CHAPTER 2

The art of seeing

And he went back to meet the fox.
'Goodbye,' he said.
'Goodbye,' said the fox. 'And now here is my secret, a very simple secret. It is only with the heart that one can see rightly; what is essential is invisible to the eye.'

Antoine de Saint-Exupery, *The Little Prince*[1]

Things are not all so comprehensible and expressible as one would mostly have us believe; most events are inexpressible, taking place in a realm which no word has ever entered, and more inexpressible than all else are works of art, mysterious existences, the life of which, while ours passes away, endures.

Rainer Maria Rilke, *Letters to a Young Poet*[2]

I wanted to put this picture before your eyes, and your acceptance of this picture consists in your being inclined to regard a given case differently; that is, to compare it with this series of pictures. I have changed your way of seeing.

Ludwig Wittgenstein[3]

Introduction

One of the questions central to medical humanities is why studying art has merit in the education of healthcare professionals. Medicine in the twenty-first century has reached an important stage in its evolution. The advances and domination of scientific method have tended to marginalise the longer established disciplines of the care of those who are ill. The triumphs of technology have opened up new horizons in the treatment and relief of some diseases, but may engender false hope of triumph over illness, suffering, ageing and death. The illumination of the mysteries of life is an integral part of art and creativity. Art emphasises the individual nature of our perceptions and encourages us to distinguish between looking and seeing. In science there is a striving for *one truth*, whereas in art there are as many truths as there are points of view.

Imagination and creativity have an important part to play in helping healthcare professionals to understand, support and treat patients. We need to take time to consider how we see ourselves, and how others see us. Remaining unaware of strengths, virtues, weaknesses and prejudices can do a serious disservice both to patients and to fellow healthcare professionals.

Ways of seeing

All communication involves sending and receiving, and in that process there is considerable scope for misunderstanding. Images, spoken words or written words may mean different things to the sender and the receiver. Vocabulary is complicated by the many concepts that one word may encompass. Human communication can therefore be a risky affair, with misunderstandings being commonplace. This ambiguity adds richness to creative endeavour, as the audience may perceive new facets to a work that were not intended by the artist. Once created, a work of art takes on a life of its own.

The problem of how external stimuli are internally perceived is important. Dictionaries illustrate the variety of meanings that one word may have, and how important the context in which the word is set can be to its interpretation. For example, take the *Oxford Concise English Dictionary* and refer to the words *looking, seeing* and *understanding*. There are 12 meanings listed for the verb *look*. These include turn one's eyes in the same direction, contemplate, examine, consider, expect, ascertain and investigate. The word *see* can mean observe, watch, contemplate, find out, learn and understand. The verb *understand* can mean perceive the meaning of, believe or assume from knowledge, and be sympathetically aware of the character or nature of.[4]

The complexity of conceptual thought is apparent. Those who believe that there is only *one* way to see the world may be attracted to the notion that only scientific thought and knowledge are valid and true. The chemist Peter Atkins has been quoted as arguing as follows:

> Although poets may aspire to understanding, their talents are more akin to entertaining self-deception. They may be able to emphasise delights in the world, but they are deluded if they and their admirers believe that their identification of the delights and their use of poignant language are enough for comprehension. Philosophers, too, I am afraid, have contributed to the understanding of the universe little more than poets. ... They have not contributed much that is novel until after novelty has been discovered by scientists. ... While poetry titillates and theology obfuscates, science liberates.[5]
>
> (p. 123)

Clearly this author sees the world as one where science determines truth and humanities are a decorative diversion. The view that only scientific thought has validity may become less widespread as the limitations of science as a sole belief system become more apparent. In her book *Science and Poetry*, the moral philosopher Mary Midgley argues:

> We need somehow to value and celebrate knowledge without being dragooned into accepting propaganda which suggests it is the only thing that matters.[5]
>
> (p. 52)

When human thought becomes complex and confusing, visual imagery is often used to illustrate the dilemma. The word *reflection* is a good example of this. One of the most celebrated examples is contained in St Paul's first epistle to the Corinthians, and the image has stimulated poets, dramatists and film-makers. The concept has had to survive the oral tradition, the written word and the difficult process of translation. In the St James version of the *Holy Bible* the following account is given:

> When I was a child, I spake as a child, I understood as a child, I thought as a child: but when I became a man, I put away childish things.
> For now we see through a glass, darkly; but then face to face: now I know in part; but then shall I know even as also I am known.
> And now abideth faith, hope, charity, these three; but the greatest of these is charity.[6]

When ecclesiastical scholars returned to the original Hebrew, they discovered a mistake in the translation of the original text. This is one of many such mistranslations of the Bible which have led to curiosities such as Michelangelo's statue of Moses' head being adorned with horns rather than beams of light.[7] The *Revised English Bible* translates the same passage as follows:

> When I was a child I spoke like a child, thought like a child, reasoned like a child; but when I grew up I finished with childish things. At present we see only puzzling reflections in a mirror, but one day we shall see face to face. My knowledge now is partial; then it will be whole, like God's knowledge of me. There are three things that last forever: faith, hope and love; and the greatest of the three is love.[8]

To accept that there are numerous ways of seeing the world is also to accept that there is no absolute truth. The phrase 'seeing is believing' can equally be changed to 'believing is seeing', as two people may look at the same object but see something quite different. Our internal perceptions are never the same as those of other people. Our way of seeing is influenced by our knowledge, bias, prejudice, presumptions, experience, understanding, beliefs and dogma. In his book *Ways of Seeing*, John Berger writes:

> The way we see things is affected by what we know or believe. We only see what we look at. To look is an act of choice. ... Our vision is continually active, continually moving, continually holding things in a circle around itself, constituting what is present to us as we are. Soon after we can see, we are aware that we can also be seen. The eye of the other combines with our own eye to make it fully credible that we are part of the visible world. ... The reciprocal nature of vision is more fundamental than that of spoken dialogue. And often dialogue is an attempt to verbalise this – an attempt to explain how, either metaphorically or literally, 'you see things' and an attempt to discover how 'he sees things'.[9]
>
> (pp. 8–9)

Different individuals, different cultures, different periods in history and different core beliefs or philosophies will all influence the interpretation of events. I explored this theme in a poem called *Rainbow*:

They had gathered to gaze at the rainbow,
That stretched from the land to the sea,
The statesman, the singer, the thinker,
The poet, the painter, the priest.

The poet sharpened his pencil
And revelled in indigo rhyme,
His words were apt and prolific
His metre impeccably fine.

The painter was working on canvas
Frantically squeezing out paint,
Slapping it on to his vision
Before all the colours could fade.

The priest was bowed in obedience,
He fasted a day and a night,
He said God might be sending a message
It could be the coming of Christ.

The statesman commenced his oration
He lifted his arms to the sky,
He talked for close on one hour
Though no one gathered quite why.

The singer was singing his lyrics
A paint-box with magic acclaim,
He said rainbows were like our existence
Colourful, changing, insane.

The thinker had worked out a theory
He told them his feelings aloud,
Never mind if the rainbow should go soon
The time to enjoy it is now.

Peter Barritt

In St Paul's communication we have to accept that, *even if we had spoken directly to him at the time,* his exact meaning would remain contentious. Neither translation is right or wrong – both have merit. Our understanding of life can be likened to looking through dark glass or at an old mirror with some of the silver missing. In both situations we see not only through the glass but also our own reflection. Both give a combination of images – one of reality seen with difficulty, the other a reflection of ourselves. The same thing occurs when we look at the oldest of mirrors – the still pool of water that so fascinated Narcissus.

This combination of visions is particularly important in healthcare. Our realities are intensely personal, and good medical care involves reaching out to share the realities of others. Healthcare is enhanced if we value and celebrate the notion that ways of seeing the world are unique to each human being. Understanding and valuing another person's reality is crucial when that person is suffering or ill. As stated in the Book of Proverbs:

As someone sees his face reflected in water,
so he sees his own mind reflected in another's.[10]

More recently, Sylvia Plath wrote on the life of a mirror in her collection *Crossing the Water*:

> I am silver and exact. I have no preconceptions.
> Whatever I see I swallow immediately
> Just as it is, unmisted by love or dislike.
> I am not cruel, only truthful –
> The eye of a little god, four-cornered.
> Most of the time I meditate on the opposite wall.
> It is pink, with speckles. I have looked at it so long
> I think it is part of my heart. But it flickers.
> Faces and darkness separate us over and over.[11]

(p. 52)

The elusiveness of enlightenment has fascinated human beings since time immemorial. Other similes have been used to describe the problem. An unknown English priest who lived during the latter half of the fourteenth century used the metaphor of a cloud to illustrate the limits of man's understanding of God:

> When you first begin, you find only darkness, and as it were a cloud of unknowing. Do what you will, this darkness and this cloud remain between you and God, and stop you both from seeing him in the clear light of rational understanding, and from experiencing his loving sweetness in your affection.
>
> Reconcile yourself to wait in this darkness as long as it is necessary, but still go on longing after him whom you love. For if you are to feel him or to see him in this life, it must always be in this cloud, in this darkness.[12]

(pp. 61–2)

John Berger also stresses the importance of seeing:

> Seeing comes before words. The child looks and recognises before it can speak. ... It is seeing which establishes our place in the surrounding world; we explain that world with words, but words can never undo the fact that we are surrounded by it. The relation between what we see and what we know is never settled.[9]

(p. 7)

In *Art and Illusion*, Gombrich goes further:

> In order to apprehend an object visually, it is not enough just to look at it. What we know and have learned, and more especially what we have learned from other pictures, actually interferes with as well as facilitates our perception.[13]

(p. 251)

This theme is echoed in John Berger's account of a country doctor's life, *A Fortunate Man*. This book is illustrated by the photographer Jean Mohr and provides a fascinating combination of written and visual images, with two quite different ways of seeing. John Berger has a Marxist ideology that may have blinkered his vision of the villagers in the rural community that he studied. Pity for their poverty and lack of education may have hampered his appreciation of the humanity of the community and their doctor. The photographs do more justice to the struggle of John Sassall in trying to relieve suffering, but the text gives more clues to his subsequent suicide. Berger acknowledges early in the book the difficulty that an outsider may experience in seeing through the mask of appearances:

> Landscapes can be deceptive.
> Sometimes a landscape seems to be less a setting
> for the life of its inhabitants than a curtain behind which
> their struggles, achievements and accidents take place.
> For those who, with the inhabitants, are behind the curtain, landscapes are no
> longer only geographic but also biographical and personal.[14]
>
> (pp. 13–15)

Sighted people are able to look, but what is seen depends on numerous influences. What is understood by what is seen is even more ethereal and, by its very nature, will always be a limited version of personal reality.

The relevance of ways of seeing

How does the image of looking through dark glass help our work as healthcare professionals? Seeing through dark glass is difficult and gives a limited understanding of what we are looking at. Two machines may be strikingly similar but, apart from identical twins, no two human beings seem to be. It is the uniqueness and individuality of each human being that is at the heart of medicine's appeal.

Some groups of patients can prove particularly difficult for us to identify with or even understand. Diverse cultures and religions have different ways of interpreting health, illness, suffering and death. A culture interprets the world very differently as history proceeds. Healthcare professionals who do not share the mother tongue of the human beings they are looking after may struggle with nuances of speech or even a basic understanding of what is being said.

Unshakeable beliefs or prejudices held by either the healthcare professional or the patient may reduce the likelihood of a satisfactory encounter. Looking through dark glass is difficult enough without the extra handicap of wearing blinkers or earplugs. Any illness or disability that interferes with conceptual thought or its articulation is likely to further darken the way that healthcare professionals see their patients. Included in this category are those suffering from mental illness, learning disability, neurological insult or dementia. All of these illnesses may make verbal communication impossible.

In the complex task of understanding the perceptions of our patients we need to use all of the senses at our disposal. The smells of infection, alcoholism and diabetic ketosis may provide vital clues. Non-verbal communication is rightly given importance in the teaching of good consultation skills. Deaf doctors may adapt by using lip-reading and electronic stethoscopes and sphygmomanometers, but it is hard to envisage how a blind doctor would cope. Physical contact also has a crucial role in reaching out to our patients, and much of our physical examination may be more for the reassurance of the patient than for furthering our scientific understanding of their problems. Berger picks up on this transaction in his study of Dr Sassall:

> It is as though when he talks or listens to a patient, he is also touching them with his hands so as to be less likely to misunderstand: and it is as though, when he is physically examining a patient, they were also conversing.[14]
>
> (p. 77)

The magic ritual of the stethoscope enables us to listen *directly to the heart*. Patients might be surprised to learn that with the ophthalmoscope we can look *directly into the brain!* Medical technology also helps to illuminate the darkness, but to a lesser extent than patients might believe – we are like miners with lamps on our helmets. Nonetheless, the technology can be astonishing – the ultrasound detail of a woman's unborn child, the telescopic views through every known orifice and the precise detail of magnetic resonance imaging are but three examples. The effect on patients of these new ways of seeing can easily be underestimated. In Thomas Mann's era of the tuberculosis sanatorium it was the X-ray that reigned supreme. In his book *The Magic Mountain*, one chapter is fittingly entitled 'Sudden Enlightenment', and the patient Hans Castorp is allowed by the Hofrat to view his own hand through the X-ray screen:

> And Hans Castorp saw precisely what he must have expected, but what it is hardly permitted man to see, and what he had never thought it would be vouchsafed him to see: he looked into his own grave.
>
> With the eyes of his Tienappel ancestress, penetrating, prophetic eyes, he gazed at this familiar part of his own body, and for the first time in his life he understood he would die.[15]
>
> (pp. 218–19)

Earlier it was proposed that we not only believe what we see, but also see what we believe. For example, one could argue that every individual deserves compassionate healthcare. This sounds straightforward, but it becomes more complex when patients are known to be liars, rapists, murderers, abusers or paedophiles. Stereotyping, prejudice and enthusiasm for judging fellow human beings may suddenly challenge altruism. Reflections in dark glass appear. The professional's beliefs about pregnancy termination, single mothers, the homeless, homosexuals and the unemployed are bound to affect the consultation. Embodied in human form, our prejudices may confront us in an uncomfortable way. History, parental influence and previous experience will have fashioned our beliefs, and it is only a willingness to explore new ways of seeing those core beliefs that will prevent a slide towards dogmatism and intolerance. In *The Mystery of General Practice*, Iona Heath writes:

> All of us need our experience and, most of all, our sufferings to be acknowledged and given value; we need to tell our stories and have them heard.[16]
>
> (p. 28)

In situations where discomfort is sensed, there is an even greater need to reach out and share our humanity. If significant contact can be made, a fundamental change in view, a *paradigm shift*, may occur. This may result from fleeting views of personal reflection, a plumbing of the murky depths of our subconscious. There is merit in the phrase 'to understand is to forgive', particularly if forgiving is understood in the sense of ceasing to feel angry or resentful towards someone.

This willingness to reflect on prejudice and intolerance is what helps to distinguish the good professional from the average one. It involves discomfort and vulnerability. Mary Midgley goes further in *Science and Poetry*:

> Total ignorance about our own motives, habits and capacities is not excusable. Knowledge about these things is not an optional subject like Russian or trigonometry which we can drop if we are not very good at it. Failure to know ourselves can be a serious moral fault. And one reason why it is a fault is that it blocks our understanding of other people. The sort of basic sympathy and empathy that we need in order to understand others does not work unless we are attentive to our own motives and reactions as well. Unless we ask critically how we ourselves are behaving to them, we can't hope to understand how they are behaving to us. So, surprisingly enough, in the enterprise of understanding other people, *cognitive success depends on moral attitude*. To get far in this study, you need fairness, honesty, maturity and indeed generosity.[5]
>
> (p. 145)

Looking into our reflection is not always uncomfortable. Healthcare professionals are frequent visitors to the pain and despair that may only touch patients occasionally in their lifetimes. Experience of helping many people to die in peace and dignity, for example, can lead to compassion and confidence when caring for the terminally ill. The professional who comes to terms with mortality need not see death as a medical failure but as a natural and profound release from suffering and an exploration into the unknown. John Berger highlights this in *A Fortunate Man*:

> The doctor is the familiar of death. When we call for a doctor, we are asking him to cure us and to relieve our suffering, but, if he cannot cure us, we are also asking him to witness our dying. ... He is the living intermediary between us and the multitudinous dead. He belongs to us and he has belonged to them.[14]
>
> (p. 68)

The professional's perception of his personal worth and the worthiness of his patients will tend to become reality. Professionals who complain of being swamped by trivia or of being unappreciated by their patients may determine that reality. There is potential here for change. To work with heart and soul in healthcare, and to strive for continual improvement and self-knowledge may enable professionals to feel satisfied with their performance without becoming arrogant or boastful. Patients who express gratitude or show appreciation can be received with good grace. The ability to accept compliments and gratitude not only raises morale but also encourages expressions of appreciation.

Professionals need to see through dark glass clearly enough to witness the beauty and dignity of the human spirit. Patients and their families often bear suffering with acceptance, bravery and good humour. Once this has been clearly seen, is there any good reason not to tell these fellow human beings how much their courage is admired? In short, learning from patients and life is an essential part of professional fulfilment. It is easier as a healthcare professional to feel sorry for oneself, rather than to count one's blessings. As Iona Heath writes in the *Mystery of General Practice*:

> General practitioners are privileged to have a part in their patients' experience of family changes, retirement from work, move of home, illness, death and loss. This shared experience forms a bond of trust and respect which is mutual and earned over time. This trust allows the doctor and the patient to work together in their task of making sense of illness experience.[16]
>
> (p. 37)

Ways of seeing and the role of art

Creativity is not the sole preserve of art. The scientist's imagination is a crucial part of exploration and discovery. The difference between science and art has more to do with their aims. Science puts forward theories about causation and is interested in attempting to generalise about the world. Art, on the other hand, is about the experience of the individual and attempts to shed light on the meaning of that experience. Art is about our individuality and our uniqueness, although it does include an examination of common patterns of response to particular situations. Artistic creativity helps us to express ourselves and to understand others.

There are two sides to creativity, namely the effect on self and the impression on others. In *The Dynamics of Creation*, Anthony Storr writes:

> Discovering what one really thinks and feels is part of establishing one's unique identity; and producing creative work is one way of doing this.[17]
>
> (p. 309)

Speaking from the perspective of a psychiatrist, Storr sees creativity as a bridge between the conscious and the subconscious. Creative people are those with particular abilities to tap into their own subconscious:

> Man is a creature inescapably, and often unhappily, divided; and the divisions within him recurrently impel the use of his imagination to make new syntheses. The creative consequences of his imaginative strivings may never make him whole; but they constitute his deepest consolations and his greatest glories.[17]
>
> (pp. 332–3)

What is the relevance of art to healthcare? In *The Mystery of General Practice*, Iona Heath argues the case for studying art:

> As general practitioners, we need the ability to identify imaginatively with a wide range of individuals. To achieve this we need to avail

ourselves of as wide an experience of humanity as possible, and borrow skills from other disciplines. The skills of anthropology and biography help us with empathy and the use of continuity, and an awareness of poetry and myth can help us find the words to communicate our understanding to the patient. A grasp of philosophy and politics can show us how to be effective partisans on behalf of our patients.[16]

(p. 35)

Richard Holmes, the biographer of Shelley and Coleridge, highlights the need for human beings to tell their stories and have them valued and listened to:

... the lives of great artists and poets and writers are not, after all, so extraordinary by comparison with everyone else. Once known in any detail and any scope, every life is something extraordinary, full of particular drama and tension and surprise, often containing unimagined degrees of suffering or heroism, and invariably touching extreme moments of triumph and despair, though frequently unexpressed. The difference lies in the extent to which one is eventually recorded, and the other is eventually forgotten.[18]

(p. 36)

One of the difficulties for healthcare professionals is the ability to empathise with patients whose personal experiences are far from their own. Iona Heath argues:

Those of us lucky enough to lead lives of personal good fortune need writers to make us understand the reality of lives of privation and loss. Novelists can also help us across boundaries, take us into other cultures and provide us with insight into the experience of patients struggling to survive and communicate across barriers of language and culture.[16]

(p. 39)

Visual arts can also broaden our view within healthcare. What can be more enlightening than to survey a wall full of family photographs when visiting a patient at home? In *Ways of Seeing*, John Berger writes:

No other kind of relic or text from the past can offer such a direct testimony about the world which surrounded other people at other times. In this respect images are more precise and richer than literature. To say this is not to deny the expressive or imaginative quality of art, treating it as mere documentary evidence; the more imaginative the work, the more profoundly it allows us to share the artist's experience of the visible.[9]

(p. 10)

Writing more specifically about photography, Berger goes on to argue in *About Looking*:

A photograph is not only an image (as a painting is an image), an interpretation of the real; it is also a trace, something directly stencilled off the real, like a footprint or a death mask.[19]

(p. 54)

The metaphor of looking through dark glass has been used to illustrate the difficulty of communicating with each other and with the divine, as well as underlining the importance of confronting our personal weaknesses and prejudices. The art of seeing offers a useful way of challenging the dogma of scientific truth, and adds dimension to our work and our way of relating to our patients. Sanders, writing of psychoanalytic activity in *Nine Lives: the emotional experience in general practice*, argues:

> Psycho-analytic activity requires the courage and the imagination to permit a marriage between art and science. When they are separated, both remain sterile. In combination, they complement one another in an enhanced desire to find meaning in the experience of being alive.[20]
>
> (p. 3)

Nouwen is quoted by Cornette as follows:

> We are able really to care only if we are willing to paint and repaint constantly our self-portrait, not as a morbid self-preoccupation, but as a service to those who are searching for some light in the midst of darkness. To care one must offer one's vulnerable self to others as a source of healing.[21]
>
> (p. 13)

Cornette, a theological research assistant, writes:

> Caring for the spirit implies, primarily, caring for oneself. It relies on the ability to stay with all that is vulnerable and weak in the other ... and in oneself.... Every day we watch with patients, we listen to them and we want to accept them just as they are. The same is needed in our relationship with our colleagues ... and with ourselves.[21]
>
> (p. 13)

References

1 de Saint-Exupery A (1945) *The Little Prince*. William Heinemann, London.
2 Rilke RM (1934) *Letters to a Young Poet*. Norton, New York.
3 Quoted in Anscombe G and von Wright G (1967) *Zettel*. Blackwell, Oxford.
4 Thompson D (1995) *The Concise Oxford Dictionary* (9e). Oxford University Press, Oxford.
5 Atkins P (1995) The limitless power of science. In: J Cornwell (ed.) *Nature's Imagination*. Oxford University Press, Oxford.
6 *The Holy Bible, King James Version*. 1 Corinthians 13:11–13.
7 *Eyewitness Travel Guide: Rome* (1995) Dorling Kindersley, London.
8 *The Revised English Bible*. 1 Corinthians 13:11–13.
9 Berger J (1972) *Ways of Seeing*. BBC and Penguin Books, London.
10 *The Revised English Bible*. Proverbs 27:19.
11 Plath S (1971) *Crossing the Water*. Faber and Faber, London.

12   Anonymous (undated, reprinted 1961) *The Cloud of Unknowing.* Penguin Books, Harmondsworth.

13   Gombrich E (1962) *Art and Illusion.* Phaidon Press, London.

14   Berger J (1997) *A Fortunate Man.* Vintage Books, New York.

15   Mann T (1924, reprinted 1960) *The Magic Mountain.* Penguin Books, Harmondsworth.

16   Heath I (1995) *The Mystery of General Practice.* Nuffield Provincial Hospitals Trust, Guildford.

17   Storr A (1993) *The Dynamics of Creation.* Ballantine Books, New York.

18   Holmes R (1985) *Footsteps: adventures of a romantic biographer.* Hodder and Stoughton, London.

19   Berger J (1991) *About Looking.* Vintage Books, New York.

20   Sanders K (1991) *Nine Lives: the emotional experience in general practice.* Roland Harris Educational Trust, Oxford.

21   Cornette K (1997) 'For whenever I am weak, I am strong ...' *Int J Palliat Nurs.* 3: 13.

Further reading

*   Berger J (1972) *Ways of Seeing.* BBC and Penguin Books, London.
*   Berger J (1997) *A Fortunate Man.* Vintage Books, New York.
*   Heath I (1995) *The Mystery of General Practice.* Nuffield Provincial Hospitals Trust, Guildford.
*   Midgley M (2001) *Science and Poetry.* Routledge, London.
*   Storr A (1993) *The Dynamics of Creation.* Ballantine Books, New York.

CHAPTER 3

The politics of health

Look to your health; and if you have it, praise God, and value it next to a good Conscience; for health is the second blessing that we Mortals are capable of: a blessing that money cannot buy, and therefore value it, and be thankful for it.

Izaak Walton, *The Compleat Angler*[1]

Use your health, even to the point of wearing it out. That is what it is for. Spend all you have before you die, and do not outlive yourself

George Bernard Shaw, *The Doctor's Dilemma*[2]

There are on this earth such immensities of misery, distress, poverty and horror that the happy man cannot think of it without feeling ashamed of his happiness. But all happiness seems to me hateful which is obtained only at the expense of others and by possessions of which others are deprived.

André Gide, *Fruits of the Earth*[3]

Introduction

Although difficult to define, the concept of health and how it is measured is proving to be of crucial importance in assessing the success or otherwise of different models of social and political organisation. Despite this, political management of healthcare is usually resented by healthcare professionals, and governments rarely acknowledge that improving healthcare has little effect on improving the health of populations (more of this later in the chapter).

The levels of disease in a society seem to depend primarily on social organisation and economic distribution, and as such may turn out to be the most sensitive indicator of the well-being of the community in which we live. In these circumstances it seems reasonable for healthcare professionals to show an interest in the political, economic and social factors that have so much influence on the generation of illness in the community.

Understood in these terms, the concept of health takes on a special quality. Inequality in health becomes linked to inequality in social structures, in the distribution of wealth and in the quality of our environment. Ignoring the importance of these issues as healthcare professionals would be akin to fiddling while Rome burns. On an individual level we are confronted by challenges to human virtue and justice. In other words, if causes of inequality in health are now well understood, what do we plan to do about them? As the reality sinks in that social and economic factors actually generate illness, what is the healthcare professional's role in influencing the causes of disease? Is our task merely to pick up the pieces, or do we have a responsibility to influence the organisation of society to reduce morbidity?

The evidence that improving healthcare has little effect on reducing inequality in health poses a major challenge to the vested interests of orthodox medical care. In a Western consumer society there is more to gain from selling MRI scanners, health checks and jogging shoes than from increasing minimum wages, overseas aid and levels of personal taxation. Furthermore, the effectiveness of encouraging personal responsibility for health is challenged by much of the evidence available, and the obsession of pursuing a healthy lifestyle in affluent societies could be viewed as a bourgeois affectation designed to deny the reality of illness, suffering, ageing and death.

Before we look at inequalities in health, we need to examine how health is defined and measured.

Definitions of health

As we discussed in Chapter 1, perfect health and happiness have been a dream of mankind since time immemorial. In the fourth century BC, the Yellow Emperor wrote in his *Classic of Internal Medicine* that in ancient times 'people lived to a hundred years, and yet remained active and did not become decrepit in their activities.'[4]

The word 'health' is thought to derive from the Old English word 'haelth', the condition being 'hal' – that is, safe and sound. Earle Scarlett defines health as essentially another name for human harmony – harmony not only among our several parts, but also between our environment and ourselves.[5] When Katherine Mansfield was dying of tuberculosis, she wrote in her journal:

> By health I mean the power to live a full, adult, living, breathing life in close contact with what I love – the earth and the wonders thereof … I want to be all that I am capable of becoming.[6]
>
> (p. 351)

Mark Twain was rather less prosaic when he complained that the only way to keep your health was to 'eat what you don't want, drink what you don't like, and do what you'd rather not.'[7] In 1947, the World Health Organization weighed in with a fulsome definition of health, perhaps reflecting the heady optimism following the end of hostilities:

> Health is a complete state of physical, mental and social well-being and not merely absence of disease. … The health of all peoples is fundamental to the attainment of peace and security and is dependent upon the fullest cooperation of individuals and states.[8]
>
> (p. 13)

This definition may be rather prosaic for some, but it does highlight the idea that health involves not only the individual but also the state. This idea is expanded by Alistair Campbell, who writes:

> I shall argue that to speak properly of health we need to describe the place where the personal and the communal intersect. The freedom that is health cannot be found in solitude: it is a freedom found when we humans learn to cooperate ... to reach a common goal.[9]
>
> (p. 5)

Thus Campbell sees health as a communal achievement rather than a private possession, based on our ability to show care and respect for all as we face a common fate.[9] Ivan Illich, writing in 1975, takes this theme further:

> [Health] designates the ability to adapt to changing environments, to growing up and to ageing, to healing when damaged, to suffering and to the peaceful expectation of death. Health embraces the future as well, and therefore includes anguish and the inner resources to live with it.[10]
>
> (p. 167)

It soon becomes apparent that the concept of health is philosophically diverse and has historical, political and cultural influences. The biomedical definition usually revolves around the absence of demonstrable disease, but diseases vary between cultures, particularly with regard to conditions like drug addiction, and with variations outside the so-called normal range in biological measurement (e.g. low blood pressure, high cholesterol levels, etc.). As Illich pointed out in his book *Medical Nemesis*,[10] each civilisation makes its own diseases: 'What is sickness in one might be crime, holiness or sin in another' (p. 57). Homosexuality, heroin addiction and alcoholism are ready examples of this.

In a study of elderly patients in Aberdeen, people regarded themselves as healthy, despite the diagnosis of disease, if they felt that they had the strength and the will to prevail over disease. Conversely, they regarded themselves as unhealthy if they lacked such a feeling of fitness, even in the absence of a medical diagnosis of disease.[9] Alistair Campbell goes further in his definition of health when he states:

> A full account of human health must allow for forms of personal and social life in which those made vulnerable by incurable disease, permanent disability or imminent death remain full members of our human community, with opportunities to continue exercising their personal freedom.[9]
>
> (p. 20)

Since health has such a diversity of meanings, how can we measure it? The usual answer has been to resort to the biomedical model, and most comparisons between populations have used life expectancy or the prevalence of diseases with relatively well-defined criteria for diagnosis, such as myocardial infarction, tuberculosis or cancer. In the light of the wider meanings of health discussed above, it is important to understand that these measurements are only a proxy measure of health, and that they measure quantity rather than quality. Despite these limitations, studies of longevity and disease rates have led to fascinating insights into the differences that occur within societies and between different cultures. Indeed it was the study of historical patterns of morbidity and mortality that led McKeown in the 1970s to explode the myth that scientific medicine had been primarily responsible for the improvements in health that had occurred during the twentieth century.[11]

Inequalities in health

The idea that the external environment influences health and disease is a very ancient one. Once this concept is accepted, it becomes inevitable that equality of health is impossible. The only way to achieve health equality would be to exterminate the current world population and replace it with identical clones all born on the same day. Thereafter the clones could all eat identical food, breathe the same air, perform the same work, have the same social standing, earn similar economic privileges, perform the same amounts of exercise while following identical pursuits, partake in identical harmful habits, avoid aggression and war, and when illness arose, attend the same medical services and take identical treatment so that iatrogenic disease could be equally shared. As the clones would have to be of the same gender, the experiment would draw to a timely end after one generation. This is the prescient nightmare of Aldous Huxley's *Brave New World* and of WH Auden's poem *The Shield of Achilles*:

> She looked over his shoulder
> For vines and olive trees,
> Marble well-governed cities
> And ships upon untamed seas,
> But there on the shining metal
> His hands had put instead
> An artificial wilderness
> And a sky like lead.[12]

(p. 78)

This is why issues of humanity, liberty and justice are so deeply ingrained in the concept of health. The essence of humanity is the very individuality that makes equality of health unattainable. Forcing a population to become healthy necessarily impinges on the basic human freedom to enjoy harmful activities, and has been a cornerstone of most totalitarian or extremist philosophies. It seems highly likely that Aryan cloning might have been an attractive option to Hitler once Jews, homosexuals, gypsies, the learning disabled and the other flotsam and jetsam of humanity had been finally 'solved'. This is an extreme example, of course, but issues of personal liberty are at the heart of objections to the juggernaut that rumbles ever onward under the banner of health promotion. Similarly, screening for and terminating pregnancies affected by Down's syndrome is a policy that makes some uncomfortable. There is also a problem with screening for conditions such as prostate cancer, where early detection raises anxiety but has not been shown to improve the long-term outcome.

If equality of health is both impossible and undesirable, one can still argue convincingly that reducing health inequality is a noble pursuit. The enormous socio-economic gap between rich and poor in the world, with its attendant effect on health, is an affront to fairness and justice.[13] On the other hand, it is not necessary to invoke health as a rationale for reducing poverty, as poverty is itself considered by most to be a demeaning state.

Whitehead has drawn a distinction between equitable and inequitable distributions of health. He defines inequitable distributions of health as those that are avoidable, unnecessary and unfair. For example, illness arising from natural biological variation or from freely chosen health-damaging behaviour would be perceived as 'fair'. Differences resulting from socio-economic disadvantage, health-damaging behaviour that was not freely chosen, exposure to health hazards in the environment, or impaired access to healthcare services would be perceived as 'unfair'.[13] This may sound reasonable, but few illnesses are caused by a single factor, and there is a strong danger in this approach that patients will then be judged as 'responsible' or 'not responsible' for their particular misfortune. Smoking is perhaps the commonest injurious behaviour that leads to a blame culture among healthcare professionals, with patients' suffering being perceived as 'their own fault'. There are clearly factors that influence smoking behaviour, such as parental example, peer pressure, social milieu, etc., for which individuals are not accountable. Special financial arrangements have been proposed for health costs associated with dangerous sports. But what about cyclists who do not wear safety helmets? And should pedestrians wear them, too? Discussions could become arcane.

It is time now to look more specifically at the causes of inequalities in health and why progress in reducing them has so far had only limited success.

Socio-economic factors

The major influence on the health of populations is related to social and economic factors. This reality was brought to modern consciousness as a result of diseases associated with poor living conditions generated by the Industrial Revolution in the nineteenth century. The determination to improve social conditions for the workforce sprang partly from altruism and partly from economic necessity. In Prussia, Rudolf Virchow was employed to investigate the causes of a typhus outbreak in the industrial area of Upper Silesia. He concluded that poverty was the breeder of disease, and that it was the responsibility of physicians to support social reforms that would reconstruct society according to a pattern which was favourable to human health.[4] The improvements in nutrition, sanitation, water supplies, air quality and housing that resulted from humanitarian and economic concerns for the workforce led to a large reduction in epidemic disease in the industrial world. Ironically, many developing countries have still not achieved these crucial improvements. War, pestilence and famine are still the major killers in developing countries.

Socio-economic inequalities in health were first discovered in the nineteenth century on the basis of mortality statistics. The availability of national population statistics permitted the calculation of varying mortality rates by, for example, occupation or city district.[13] Since the nineteenth century there has been a steady decline in mortality, largely as a result of a reduction in death rates at a young age, particularly in the first year of life.[14] The increasing proportion of the elderly in developed countries is primarily due to the fact that more people survive child-hood. There have only been modest increases in the age to which an old person may expect to live beyond the 'three score and ten' allocated since Biblical times. Recent estimates of the contribution of all medical procedures (including immunisation and screening) to modern life expectancy put it at no more than about five years.[14] In 1635, a man called Thomas Parr, who lived in Shropshire in England, was believed to be 152 years old. This remarkable achievement was brought to the attention of the King, who invited him to London. After being presented to the King he ate and drank well and promptly died. A post-mortem performed by William Harvey found all the man's organs to be healthy, and death of a surfeit was declared before he was buried in Westminster Abbey.[4]

Although death rates have generally declined, it is less clear whether relative inequalities in mortality have declined. It appears that the relative risk of dying for those in a low rather than a high socio-economic position has remained remarkably stable, and in the latter part of the twentieth century there was a definite increase in relative mortality in many developed countries.[13] Rates of morbidity show a similar pattern. A comparative study covering 11 countries in Western Europe showed that in the mid- and late 1980s the risk of ill health was 1.5–2.5 times higher in the lower half of the socio-economic distribution than in the upper half.[13]

As the important effect of socio-economic factors on health became apparent in the late 1970s, the results of studies by epidemiologists and sociologists were brought to the attention of politicians. In England, Richard Wilkinson wrote an open letter to the Secretary of State for Health and Social Security, and this led to the formation of a working group under Sir Douglas Black. In 1980 this working party produced a report known as the Black Report.[15] In the interim, the Government had changed from a socialist to a right-wing Conservative Government. The report was released in a way that was designed to minimise its impact, with only 250 copies made available and no press release or conference organised.[15]

The Black Report concluded that the poorer health experience of lower occupa-tional groups applied at all stages of life. If the mortality rates of occupational class I (professional workers and members of their families) had applied to classes IV and V (partly skilled and unskilled manual workers and members of their families) during 1970–72, a total of 74 000 lives of people aged under 75 years would not have been lost. This estimate included nearly 10 000 children and 32 000 men aged 15 to 64 years. The working group concluded that social and economic factors such as income, work (or lack of it), environment, education, housing, transport and what are today called 'lifestyles' all affect health and all favour the better off.[15]

The report made 37 recommendations, which included improvements in information, research and organisation so that better plans might be drawn up, and redressing the healthcare system so that more emphasis was given to prevention, primary care and community health. Most important of all, it recommended radi-cally improving the material conditions of life of poorer groups, especially children and people with disabilities, by increasing or introducing certain cash benefits, such as child benefit, maternity grant and infant care allowance, and a comprehen-sive disablement allowance, and developing new schemes for day nurseries, antenatal clinics, sheltered housing, home improvements, improved conditions at work and community services.[15]

The Government of the day baulked at the likely cost of these recommendations, and instead emphasised the role of personal rather than social responsibility for health. In 1992, another report was commissioned to re-examine the situation and assess progress, and it was published as *The Health Divide*. Apart from political indifference, one problem remained with the evidence in that all causes of death showed a marked class difference that could not be fully explained by lifestyle differences (e.g. alcohol consumption, smoking, or any other known factor).[15]

As research progressed in the 1980s and 1990s it became increasingly apparent that one of the crucial factors in explaining the health gap between rich and poor in different societies was the scale of the difference between rich and poor in that society. Studies from many countries have confirmed that life expectancy is dramatically improved where income differences are smaller and societies are more socially cohesive.[14] The quality of the social life of a society is one of the most powerful determinants of health, and is closely related to the degree of income inequality.[14] This finding clearly has a dramatic impact on ways of considering how to tackle health inequality. Effectively it appears that making the rich less rich and the poor less poor is the best way to address the root cause of health inequality in society.

Healthcare interventions can only 'patch up' those who have become ill as a result of social and financial inequality.[13] A number of influential reports on this issue have now been produced, notably those published by the World Health Organization in 1992, by the King's Fund in 1995, by Sir Donald Acheson in 1998 and by the Dutch Programme Committee in 2001. All of these reports stress the importance of reducing inequalities in income, employment, housing, nutrition and education, and of strengthening the social fabric of the community.[13] Different national social policies have had varying degrees of success in reducing levels of poverty in developed countries. The most successful countries are those such as Denmark, Finland, Norway and Sweden, which have encompassing systems of income maintenance, where universal flat-rate benefits are combined with benefits related to past income and labour-market participation. These are also the countries with some of the smallest health inequalities in the world. Those countries with means-tested and low flat-rate benefits intended to target the poor, such as the UK, the USA and Australia, have higher poverty levels, greater income inequality and greater health inequality.[13]

Efforts have been made to increase levels of employment and to make work pay. In the UK in 1999 the first ever national minimum wage was introduced and, despite predictions that it would cause unemployment, no increase in unemployment appears to have resulted.[13] Nonetheless these are relatively early days in determining particular strategies that can be guaranteed to reduce health inequalities. In Europe there is a concerted effort to compare results using different strategies. In some countries health inequalities are largely class based (e.g. the UK), whereas in others they may show strong racial links (e.g. the USA, New Zealand and Australia), and these factors can influence the political willingness to take action.[13]

The strength of the association between socio-economic factors and disease is dramatic, particularly with regard to the most important causes of death, including ischaemic heart disease, stroke, hypertension, obesity, lung cancer and suicide.[14] Income distribution has particularly strong links with homicide, violent crime, alcohol-related deaths, traffic accidents and deaths from all accidents. Death rates in Harlem, New York are higher at all ages except infancy than in rural Bangladesh.[14] In almost all the rich developed countries death rates among the lower social classes are two to four times higher than those among the top social classes.[14]

Wilkinson argues that studies by a large number of researchers in eight different countries show that the quality of the social life of a society is one of the most powerful determinants of health, and that this in turn is very closely related to the degree of income equality.[14] The qualities that the healthiest countries (e.g. Sweden, Norway and Japan) share are social cohesion and egalitarian culture. Individualism and the market economy are restrained by social morality. There is a strong sense of community, and inhabitants are more likely to be involved in social and voluntary activities outside the home.[14]

This situation has important repercussions for efforts to reduce inequality. Providing expensive services such as social services, police and prisons, family therapy, health services and so on is doomed to producing marginal benefits (or none at all) if we fail to alter the environment that establishes the high levels of risk to health. International studies show large differences in the scale of social problems, with countries like the USA and the UK showing high crime rates, large prison populations, low educational standards, high health inequalities and relatively poor overall standards of health. In contrast, in the 1980s Sweden and Japan had low crime rates, low health inequalities, high educational standards and the highest life expectancy in the world.[14]

Socio-economic inequality leads to societies that are divided and dominated by status, prejudice and social exclusion, and this leads to aggressive subgroups alienated from society, in which crime, addiction and self-abuse become common. As Wilkinson points out, those at the bottom of the social hierarchy also suffer the greatest social, psychological and emotional deprivation, and this may well have a greater impact on their health than the more direct effects of material deprivation.[14]

The social and health effects of income inequality provide a powerful argument for reducing it. Society stands to benefit from lower crime rates, better health, smaller prison populations and less emphasis on service provision. Previously this important area has been dominated by political prejudice and populist rhetoric. The harsh light of epidemiological and sociological evidence may make it harder to argue the case for more doctors, more policemen, more prison officers, more social workers and less welfare for the disadvantaged in society.

International economics

Having dealt in some detail with the impact of economic and social factors in health, it should become easier for us to examine one of the other great health divides, namely that between the developed and developing world. The evidence also highlights the importance for countries of striving for economic improvement to protect the social cohesion of their cultures. The materialist market economy rests on individuality, competitiveness, a lust for personal possessions, social escapism (particularly television) and a profound disinterest in those without money. Work in industrialised countries usually involves travel away from the home (and often out of the country) and this does not help to create a close-knit community. The spread of communication technology means that time with the family is easily interrupted. The employment opportunities for women outside the home tend to increase as countries develop, and this may lead to a situation where neither parent sees much of their children. When parents are at home, they may be exhausted by commuting, long hours and the frenetic work rate that is typical of the consumer society.

As Wilkinson points out, money only assumes a dominant role in society once subsistence farming ceases to become the norm. In traditional societies, food sharing and gift exchange are the dominant forms of distribution.[14] The Western style of development tends to lead to increasing urbanisation with consequent weakening of social cohesion, and to worsening levels of poverty. One of the challenges for developing countries is whether they can achieve economic success without the social failure that often accompanies it.[14] However, there are many examples of ways to improve equality without sacrificing social cohesiveness. Land reform and redistribution, universal education, increased employment opportunities and provision of low-cost housing have all been successfully employed by some developing countries, although these methods have also caused major injustice and bloodshed in others, particularly when racial or tribal prejudice has determined who is to be more equal than others. The evidence to date suggests that narrowing socio-economic differences in society tends to improve growth.[14] The rich and powerful in both developed and developing countries may prefer to hold on to their fortunes and live in enclaves safe from the social discord created by socio-economic inequality. Since the world's media is controlled by a small number of magnates, there may be little interest in widely publicising the causes of health inequality. Levels of literacy and political perception can be relatively low in young democracies, and this can enable institutional corruption that diverts resources away from the needy.

There are clearly levels of poverty, often associated with war, famine or infectious disease (particularly AIDS), that are directly life-threatening. As national income increases there is a resultant improvement in health and longevity, but this levels off at a certain threshold, and beyond this point further increases in national wealth produce little further improvement in health. This point in economic development has been termed the 'epidemiological transition', and thereafter the diseases of affluence, such as ischaemic heart disease and obesity, start to predominate, and death from infectious disease becomes less common.[14]

Once through the epidemiological transition, health inequalities relate to the social and economic factors discussed previously. This means that a developing country can improve the health of its inhabitants by striving for an egalitarian culture rather than by trying to become as rich as possible. In 1976, the International Labor Organization defined the satisfaction of basic needs as follows:

> the minimum requirements of a family for personal consumption: food, shelter, clothing: it implies access to essential services, such as safe drinking water, sanitation, transport, health and education; it implies that each person available for and willing to work should have an adequately remunerated job. It should further imply the satisfaction of needs of a more qualitative nature: a healthy, human and satisfying environment, and the popular participation in the making of decisions that affect the lives and livelihoods of the people, and individual freedoms.[16]
>
> (p. 7)

This statement has proved far-sighted, and it encapsulates much of the sound logic that follows on from sociological and epidemiological research. It wisely uses the concept of needs rather than rights. Ignatieff expands on this concept in his book *The Needs of Strangers*:

> It is because money cannot buy the human gestures which confer respect, nor rights guarantee them as entitlements, that any decent society requires a public discourse about the needs of the human person. It is because fraternity, love, belonging, dignity and respect cannot be specified as rights that we ought to specify them as needs and seek, with the blunt institutional procedures at our disposal, to make their satisfaction a routine human practice.[17]
>
> (p. 13)

If we know the job that needs to be done in order to reduce health inequalities, what are the factors that impede progress? Perhaps little has changed since Gloucester addressed his son in *King Lear:*

> Let the superfluous and lust-dieted man,
> That slaves your ordinance, that will not see
> Because he does not feel, feel your power quickly:
> So distribution should undo excess,
> And each man have enough.[18]

Ignatieff points out that by the time mankind had passed from the stage of hunter-gatherers to farmers, mankind was already split between landowners and labourers, so that the history of human labour is one of economic inequality.[17] Our needs are also part of our nature, and caring for the needs of strangers is the essence of humanity. Care of strangers within our particular society, culture or nation has been termed *communitarianism,* where citizens or state boundaries properly limit justice and other moral concerns. Those who believe that we have obligations not only to those nearby but also to distant strangers, and that justice extends beyond borders, have been called *cosmopolitans.*[19] Communitarians may care for fellow citizens but not 'foreigners' or 'immigrants', whereas cosmopolitans have concerns for international change, cooperation and justice. A communitarian approach could reduce health inequalities in a community, society or nation, but it will require a cosmopolitan view of justice for health inequality to be tackled on a global scale.

O'Neill argues that it is the human qualities of vulnerability, dependency and selfishness that create the need for justice:

> Since human beings are not always compassionate and considerate to each other, justice requires institutions that unavoidably curtail human freedom. Injustice can be prevented or minimised both by prohibiting, policing and penalising those who might inflict it and by empowering, educating and supporting those who may be exposed to it.[19]
>
> (pp. 138–9)

We shall now consider the impact of globalisation and of international institutions in the arena of health and economic inequality.

International inequality

It is clear that one of the major causes of health inequality is the massive inequality between the rich industrialised countries and the poor agricultural ones. Globalisation is seen by some observers as the spread of Western enlightenment (Disney, Coke, McDonald's etc.), and by others as the relentless destruction of traditional cultures for economic gain. In their book *Culture and Development*, Schech and Haggis refer to globalisation as:

> the intensification of global interconnectedness, particularly the spread of capitalism as a production and market system. It also refers to innovations in technologies of communication and transportation, which are reconfiguring social relationships spatially, temporally, and in terms of speed.[20]
>
> (p. 58)

It is reasonable to say that globalisation favours the urban rich and disadvantages the rural poor.[21] Some feel that globalisation represents the triumph of uncontrollable global capitalist forces dominated by trans-national corporations that are responsible only to their rich shareholders. Others feel that the new technologies are shrinking time and space so that we are beginning to appreciate the 'global village' in which we live.[21]

It is certainly true that trans-national corporations play a crucial role in the world economy. The top 37 000 corporations employ 73 million people and account for a third of world output, four-fifths of global investment and two-thirds of world trade.[21] On the other hand, very few (about 5%) of the trans-national corporations are genuinely global, and the rest are primarily national companies with foreign operations. This is important when it comes to the issue of how these companies are taxed and regulated in areas such as consumer protection, market control, environmental regulation, occupational health and safety and competition.[21] The health and skills of a nation's workforce are still a critical factor in economic success, and this makes reduction in health inequality and improvement in education an important role for the State.

Key players in the international economy and in the continuation of world inequality and poverty are the World Bank, the International Monetary Fund (IMF) and the World Trade Organization (WTO). They operate as bastions of neo-liberalism with their mantra of international competitiveness, free markets and free trade.[21] The G8 countries hold more than half the votes on the IMF Executive Committee, and the USA controls nearly a fifth of the votes as well as a right of veto over any decision.[21] Nicola Yeates, in her thoughtful book *Globalization and Social Policy*, states that:

> These institutions, in conjunction with trans-national development banks and institutes and bilateral aid agencies, have sustained the major economic and social inequalities that characterise contemporary globalisation; they have overseen the accumulation of unprecedented levels of wealth in the advanced industrialised countries and mass impoverishment in, and indebtedness of, developing countries.[21]
>
> (p. 104)

The creation of loans, debts and the restructuring forced by these institutions on developing countries is generally disastrous. What are known as *structural adjustment programmes* (SAPs) affect the livelihood of more than 4 billion people, or 80% of the world's population.[21] Yeates continues:

> Indeed, SAPs have been associated with, if not contributed directly to, widening inequalities, both nationally and internationally. Between 1970 and 1989, countries with the richest 20% of the world population increased their share of global GNP from 73.9 to 82.7%, while countries with the poorest 20% of the world population saw their share of global GNP fall from 2.3 to 1.4%. The world's 358 billionaires possess as much wealth as the poorest 45% of the world's population.[21]
>
> (p. 107)

There is clearly a need for international institutions. Problems such as marine pollution, whaling, overuse of fisheries, acid rain, ozone depletion, deforestation and greenhouse gas emission cannot be solved by nations acting alone.[22] MacIntyre has argued that institutions are essential as a means of regulating the activities (or practices) of individuals:

> Institutions are characteristically and necessarily involved with what I have called external goods. They are involved in acquiring money and other material goods; they are structured in terms of power and status, and they distribute money, power and status as rewards. Nor could they do otherwise if they are to sustain not only themselves, but also the practices of which they are the bearers. For no practices can survive any length of time unsustained by institutions. Indeed so intimate is the relationship of practices to institutions – and consequently of the goods external to the goods internal to the practices in question – that institutions and practices characteristically form a single causal order in which the ideals and the creativity of the practice are always vulnerable to the acquisitiveness of the institution, in which the cooperative care for common goods of the practice is always vulnerable to the competitiveness of the institution. In this context the essential function of the virtues is clear. Without them, without justice, courage and truthfulness, practices could not resist the corrupting power of institutions.[23]
>
> (p. 194)

The question about the major international monetary institutions is not whether they are necessary, but whether they are just. Are they virtuous in trying to improve the lot of poorer countries or are they morally corrupt? This is of crucial importance to the attempt to reduce global health inequalities. The care of distant strangers is by nature political. Ignatieff emphasises this point:

> This was the first question I began with: when is it right to speak for the needs of strangers? Politics is not only the art of representing the needs of strangers; it is also the perilous business of speaking on behalf of needs which strangers have had no chance to articulate on their own.[17]
>
> (p. 12)

If international institutions are robbing the poor, could individual or state charity fulfil the role? Ignatieff thinks not:

> Woe betide any man who depends on the abstract humanity of another for his food and protection. Woe betide any person who has no state, no family, no neighbourhood, no community that can stand behind to enforce his claim of need.[17]
>
> (p. 53)

This reliance on politics to protect the needs of the vulnerable is echoed by Adam Smith:

> In civilised society [a man] stands at all times in need of the co-operation and assistance of great multitudes, while his whole life is scarce sufficient to gain the friendship of a few friends.[17]
>
> (p. 105)

What is more, the rich and powerful can always find good reasons not to give to the poor:

> Whether on grounds of concealed wealth, idleness or self-neglect, beggars can always be found wanting. The claim of need has nothing to do with deserving; it rests on people's necessity, not on their merit, on their poor common humanity, not on their capacity to evoke pathos.[17]
>
> (p. 34)

International trade includes organised crime, tourism, the sex industry, spare organ sales and 'mail-order brides'. It also includes the active promotion of harmful Western habits such as bottle-feeding and smoking. International trade needs justice and those with the courage to insist on it. Ultimately there will be a need to shed nationalism and embrace cosmopolitanism, otherwise the sense of helplessness and injustice will fuel extremism and terrorism. The United Nations Research Institute on Social Development concludes:

> In the last analysis, action depends on people's interpretation of what is possible and right. Thus the longer-term nature of mobilisation for sustainable development depends not only on activism, but on dominant views about where the world could – and should – be going. . . . Questioning extreme individualism and the unbridled power of money – reasserting the value of equity and social solidarity, and reinstating the citizen at the centre of public life – is a major challenge of our time. The 'invisible hand' of the market has no capacity to imagine a decent society for all people, or to work in a consistent fashion to attain it. Only human beings with a strong sense of the public good can do that.[24]
>
> (p. xix)

Environmental stress

As individuals, much of our success in avoiding disease has more to do with luck and genetic make-up than with any personal merit associated with immaculate behaviour. Once populations are studied the effects of genetic variance and luck become less important, although fate still governs those affected by war, famine and infectious disease. Given the strong link between socio-economic factors and the health of populations, how does the environment in which we live generate illness? The importance of good nutrition, clean water and safe sanitation has been obvious since the Industrial Revolution, as has that of occupational health and safety. Pollution, exposure to toxic chemicals at work and the risk of domestic, occupational and traffic accidents will vary from one society to another. However, as previously discussed, the effect of low socio-economic status on health cannot be accounted for by well-known behavioural or material risk factors for disease. This particularly applies to cardiovascular disease, where risk factors such as smoking, high serum cholesterol levels and high blood pressure account for less than half the socio-economic gradient.[13] The missing factor appears to be stress.

The concept of stress was first described in 1936 by Hans Selye, who defined it as an inherent physiological mechanism which prepares the organism for action and which comes into play when demands are placed on it. The environmental influence may be physical, psychological or socio-cultural, and was named a *stressor*. He described three stages of the response to stress. The first stage is the alarm reaction, in which the organism becomes aware of the stressor. The second stage is that of resistance or adaptation, where the organism recovers to a functional level superior to that before the stressor appeared. The third stage is exhaustion, where prolonged exposure to stressors causes failure of recovery processes to cope or to restore homeostasis. In other words, a moderate level of stress improves performance, but too much causes exhaustion and worsens it. Stressors in humans work on the hypothalamic–pituitary–adrenocortical (HPA) axis.[25]

Sapolsky describes how bodies used for teaching anatomy during the period 1830–1930 mainly came from the poorhouses, and when post-mortems were performed on wealthier clients it was noticed that they had curiously small adrenal glands. A medical condition termed *idiopathic adrenal atrophy* was then invented. The rich also appeared to have enlarged thymic glands, and these were treated with irradiation that later caused thyroid cancer. Subsequently it was realised that it was chronic poverty that had caused adrenal enlargement and thymic atrophy. Sapolsky proposes that chronic stress causes elevated levels of corticosteroids, central obesity, insulin resistance, poor lipid profile and an increased tendency to blood clotting.[26] In addition to effects on the HPA axis, chronic stress causes changes to behaviour, including increases in smoking, alcohol and drug use and decreases in physical activity. Giving up smoking is difficult when your self-esteem is low, you feel pessimistic about life and smoking is one of your few sources of relaxation and luxury. Similarly, alcohol is used throughout society to help people to relax, to ease social contact, to drown sorrows and to escape stressful circumstances.[27]

Those interested in the effects of poverty on the soul could do worse than read John Steinbeck's *The Grapes of Wrath*. Wilkinson, too, writes with passion in his book *Unhealthy Societies:*

> To feel depressed, cheated, bitter, desperate, vulnerable, frightened, angry, worried about debts or job and housing insecurity; to feel

devalued, useless, helpless, uncared for, hopeless, isolated, anxious and a failure: these feelings can dominate people's whole experience of life, colouring their experience of everything else. It is the chronic stress arising from feelings like these which does the damage.[14]

(p. 215)

Stress can be fatal. Rosengren found death rates to be three and a half times higher in middle-aged men who had experienced at least three stressful life events.[28] Parkes studied death rates in widowers aged 55 years or older, and found a 40% increase in death rates in the first 6 months of bereavement, with the death rate from ischaemic heart disease 67% above that expected. Mortality rates dropped to normal after the first year.[29] Following the coal-mine tragedy in Aberfan in south Wales, close relatives of children who had been killed had death rates seven times higher than those of controls during the following year.[30]

In the developed world the social organisation of work is now likely to be the most important occupational health hazard. Studies in Sweden, the USA, Germany and the UK have shown that having little control over one's work, low levels of social support from managers or colleagues and a fast pace of work have all been linked to cardiovascular symptoms and other health problems.[14] In the Whitehall study, the lowest-grade administrators had a three-fold higher mortality rate from ischaemic heart disease and from a range of other causes than the highest-grade administrators.[31] Repeating the study 20 years later showed no diminution in social-class difference morbidity, and the authors concluded that more attention should be paid to social environment, job design and the consequences of income inequality.[32] Wilkinson points out that companies might find changes in office practice more effective than employing counsellors in reducing sickness absence and improving productivity.[14] More recently, atherosclerosis of the carotid arteries has been shown to progress more rapidly over a period of 4 years in men aged 42–60 years who have a stressful work environment.[33]

For those fortunate enough to be in work, the threat of losing their job is real for many. In 1994 a MORI poll in the UK showed that even in the 'middle classes' around 35% of respondents were worried about impending job loss in the next 12 months, and 20% of families had recent experience of unemployment.[34] Unemployment brings financial difficulties, housing insecurity, worsening interpersonal relationships and an increased risk of depression. Lack of money, lack of choices and lack of space for children to play all contribute to conflict between different family members' needs and demands. The top three contributory causes noted by case workers in child abuse cases are marital problems, debts and unemployment. Rates of hyperactivity in children were three times as high, and conduct disorders four times as high, in social class V (unskilled manual occupations) as in social class I (professional occupations).[14] Even childhood accidents have a strong relationship with class difference. Brown showed that accidents among children in social class V were also closely related to psychiatric morbidity, and the risks doubled if the mothers were depressed. Rates of depression were four times higher (28%) among working-class compared with middle-class mothers. Accident rates were only higher in mothers who were actually depressed. Before and after depression the children had similar accident rates to those of women who did not suffer depression.[35]

Lack of a confiding relationship with a close friend, relative or partner is associated with poorer health, but so also is less involvement with wider social networks, community activities, and so on. Health-related behaviour is closely linked to social milieu, with social gradients in smoking, dietary composition and leisure time. It is hard to change behaviour without altering the social circumstances. This was the conclusion reached by Syme in his study of the Multiple Risk Factor Intervention Trial (MRFIT) in the USA:

> Even when people do successfully change their high-risk behaviours, new people continue to enter the at-risk population to take their place. For example, every time we finally helped a man in the MRFIT project to stop smoking, it is probable that, on that day, one or two children in a schoolyard somewhere were for the first time taking their first tentative puffs on a cigarette. So even when we do help high-risk people to lower their risk, we do nothing to change the distribution of disease in the population because ... we have done nothing to influence those forces in the society that caused the problem in the first place.[36]
>
> (p. 22)

Culture and gender

Cultural factors have an important influence on the generation of or protection against disease. The division of labour between the sexes, who works out of the home, who looks after the children and who prepares the food can all influence patterns of disease. Cultural norms concerning marriage, sexual behaviour, use of contraception and termination, infanticide and population policies are all important. The degree of medicalisation of female physiology and childbirth varies between different cultures, and idealisation of bodily form can lead to eating disorders and a proliferation of cosmetic surgery. In many countries women are isolated, secluded and excluded from education or wage earning. O'Neill touches on gender injustice in her book *Bounds of Justice*:

> Family structures always limit independence, and usually limit women's independence more; women who have no adequate entitlements of their own and insecure rights to a share in family property or income will not always be coerced, but are always vulnerable to coercion.[19]
>
> (p. 165)

The influence of gender and culture on health merits a book in itself, and there is not space here to do this topic justice.

Healthcare

Since the levels of disease in society are largely determined by economic and social factors, it is not surprising that medical services have little impact on health inequalities. This is not to say that what we do as healthcare professionals is a waste of time, but rather that we primarily influence the quality of life of those with disease. At one time the inequalities in medical provision were thought to be crucial to health inequalities. In 1971 Tudor Hart achieved fame by inventing the

Inverse Care Law, according to which the availability of good medical care tends to vary inversely with the need for it in the population served.[37] In the UK, where there is a National Health Service, research suggests that the distribution of medical care favours the poor.[38] A similar cross-European study of equality of access to primary and secondary care reached similar conclusions, with distribution close to the needs-expected requirement and levels of utilisation much higher in the lower-income groups in all countries.[39]

Individual perceptions

At the start of this chapter the various definitions of health were considered and it became clear that individuals have different ways of interpreting whether or not they are healthy. Campbell develops this theme in detail in his book *Health as Liberation*:

> So the freedom that is health is not a life without pain or disability or mortality.... It lies not in 'freedom from,' but in 'freedom to' – freedom to create and inhabit a space we can still call our own. ... Health entails the self in positive action when faced with threats to its survival.[9]
>
> (pp. 40–1)

Campbell is firm in his conviction that health must be seized by individuals, and that suffering or disease is very much part of health:

> If health is to be found when the self retains its sense of dignity and worth, even in the face of death, then we can see the inadequacy of our current attempts to promote health in our modern world. All around us there are people whose lives are emptied of meaning, who fear the end of life yet find little fulfilment or sense of pride in being alive, who have been left with no route for the transcendence of life's testing times and no sense of community that cares for them or will notice how their lives end up. ... Health is not to be found by a grasping for advantage over others in an effort to insulate oneself against life's maladies; it is those who risk their own security to protect the neediest and most vulnerable that may hope to find some ways of living with their own vulnerability and finitude.[9]
>
> (pp. 42–4)

Campbell sees our wish to be independent as part of the problem:

> We cannot feel secure so long as we are valued only for our strength and competitiveness. We have tried to use medicine to bolster this strength, but in doing so we have merely uncovered the futility of seeking to build into our bodies a permanency they can never have. ... In all this, we seem to have lost the art of being healthy in our determination not to be sick.[9]
>
> (pp. 58–9)

It may come as no surprise that Illich goes further, seeing the banishment of all things medical as the major route to health:

> Healthy people are those who live in healthy homes on a healthy diet, in an environment equally fit for birth, growth, work, healing and dying, sustained by a culture which enhances the conscious acceptance of limits to population, of ageing, of incomplete recovery and ever imminent death. Healthy people need no bureaucratic interference to mate, give birth, share the human condition and die.[10]
>
> (p. 169)

Wilkinson feels that the discovery of the causes of health inequality may bring changes as dramatic and beneficial as the public health changes that resulted from the Industrial Revolution:

> Just as the benefits of those reforms extended beyond health into the quality of life, so the social reforms necessitated by recognition of the social determinants of health will improve the quality of life as well as health.[14]
>
> (p. 25)

Understanding of the causes of inequality in health is relatively recent, and there is potential for real progress to be made. There are grounds for optimism that encouraging an egalitarian and socially cohesive world may lead to economic and social benefits that make sense from both humanitarian and pragmatic points of view. Wilkinson makes a sound argument for adopting health indices as the most reliable indicator of the quality of life, rather than using the various economic indices:

> In terms of the quality of life, which is ultimately a matter of people's subjective sense of well-being, the psychosocial processes round inequality, social cohesion and its effect on health are overwhelmingly important. They are important not only from the point of view of those down the social scale who suffer them most, but also because the deterioration in public life, the loss of a sense of community, and particularly the increase in crime and violence, are fundamentally important to the quality of life for everyone.[14]
>
> (p. 215)

References

1 Walton I (1676, reprinted 1915) *The Compleat Angler.* Clarendon Press, Oxford.
2 Shaw GB (1913, reprinted 1946) *The Doctor's Dilemma.* Penguin Books, Baltimore, MD.
3 Gide A (1949, reprinted 1970) *Fruits of the Earth.* Penguin Books, Harmondsworth.
4 Dubos R (1960) *Mirage of Health.* George Allen & Unwin, London.

5 Scarlett E (1972) *In Sickness and in Health.* McClelland & Stewart, Toronto.

6 Mansfield K (1927) *Journal of Katherine Mansfield.* Constable, London.

7 Twain M (1907) *Following the Equator. Volume II.* Harper & Brothers, New York.

8 World Health Organization (1947) *Chronicle of the World Health Organization. Volume 1.* World Health Organization, Geneva.

9 Campbell A (1995) *Health as Liberation.* Pilgrim Press, Cleveland, OH.

10 Illich I (1975) *Medical Nemesis.* Calder & Boyars, London.

11 McKeown T *et al.* (1975) An interpretation of the decline in mortality in England and Wales during the twentieth century. *Population Stud.* 29: 391–422.

12 Auden WH (1968) *Selected Poems.* Faber & Faber, London.

13 Mackenbach J and Bakker M (eds) (2002) *Reducing Inequalities in Health.* Routledge, London.

14 Wilkinson R (1996) *Unhealthy Societies.* Routledge, London.

15 Townsend P and Davidson N (eds) (1988) *Inequalities in Health: the Black Report.* Penguin Books, Harmondsworth.

16 International Labor Organization (1976) *Employment, Growth and Basic Needs.* International Labor Organization, Geneva.

17 Ignatieff M (1994) *The Needs of Strangers.* Vintage, London.

18 Shakespeare W (1608) *King Lear.* Act Four, Scene One.

19 O'Neill O (2000) *Bounds of Justice.* Cambridge University Press, Cambridge.

20 Schech S and Haggis J (2000) *Culture and Development.* Blackwell, Oxford.

21 Yeates N (2001) *Globalization and Social Policy.* Sage, London.

22 McCormick J (1995) *The Global Environmental Movement.* John Wiley & Sons, Chichester.

23 MacIntyre A (1985) *After Virtue.* Duckworth, London.

24 United Nations Research Institute on Social Development (UNRISD) (2000) *Visible Hands: taking responsibility for social development.* UNRISD, Geneva.

25 Helman C (1990) *Culture, Health and Illness* (2e). Butterworth-Heinemann, Oxford.

26 Sapolsky R (1991) Poverty's remains. *Sciences.* 31: 8–10.

27 Action on Smoking and Health (ASH) (1993) *Her Share of Misfortune.* ASH, London.

28 Rosengren A, Orth-Gomer K, Wedel H *et al.* (1993) Stressful life events, social support and mortality in men born in 1933. *BMJ.* 307: 1847–51.

29 Parkes C, Benjamin B and Fitzgerald R (1969) Broken heart: a statistical study of increased mortality among widowers. *BMJ.* i: 740–43.

30 Conduit E (1992) If A–B does not predict heart disease, why bother with it? A clinician's view. *Br J Med Psychol.* 65: 289–96.

31 Marmot M, Shipley M and Rose G (1984) Inequalities in death-specific explanations of a general pattern? *Lancet.* 1: 1003–6.

32 Marmot M, Davey Smith G, Stansfield S *et al.* (1991) Health inequalities among British civil servants: the Whitehall II study. *Lancet.* 337: 1387–93.

33 Everson S, Lynch J and Chesney M (1997) Interaction of workplace demands and cardiovascular reactivity in progression of carotid atherosclerosis: population-based study. *BMJ.* 314: 553–7.

34 Smith D (1994) Despairing middle class fearful about the future. *Sunday Times.* 26 June.

35 Brown G (1978) Social class, psychiatric disorder of mother, and accidents to children. *Lancet.* 1: 378–80.

36 Syme S (1996) To prevent disease: the need for a new approach. In: D Blane, E Brunner and R Wilkinson (eds) *Health and Social Organization.* Routledge, London.

37 Tudor Hart J (1971) The Inverse Care Law. *Lancet.* i: 405–12.

38 O'Donnell O and Propper C (1989) *Equity and the Distribution of National Health Service Resources.* Welfare State Programme Paper No. 45, London School of Economics and Political Science, London.

39 van Doorslaer E, Wagstaff A, Van der Burg H *et al.* (2000) Equality in the delivery of healthcare in Europe and the US. *J Health Econ.* 19: 553–83.

Further reading

- Campbell A (1995) *Health as Liberation.* Pilgrim Press, Cleveland, OH.
- Dubos R (1960) *Mirage of Health.* George Allen & Unwin, London.
- Illich I (1975) *Medical Nemesis.* Calder & Boyars, London.
- Mackenbach J and Bakker M (eds) (2002) *Reducing Inequalities in Health.* Routledge, London.
- Marmot M, Shipley M and Rose G (1984) Inequalities in death-specific explanations of a general pattern? *Lancet.* 1: 1003–6.
- Marmot M, Davey Smith G, Stansfield S *et al.* (1991) Health inequalities among British civil servants: the Whitehall II study. *Lancet.* 337: 1387–93.
- O'Neill O (2000) *Bounds of Justice.* Cambridge University Press, Cambridge.
- Wilkinson R (1996) *Unhealthy Societies.* Routledge, London.
- Yeates N (2001) *Globalization and Social Policy.* Sage, London.

PART TWO

Suffering: the heart of medicine

CHAPTER 4

Suffering and spirituality

How long, Lord, will you leave me forgotten,
how long hide your face from me?
How long must I suffer anguish in my soul,
grief in my heart day after day?

Psalm 13[1]

What miserable revolutions and changes, what down-falls, what break-necks and precipitations may we justly think ourselves ordained to, if we consider, that in our coming into this world out of our mothers womb, we do not make account that a child comes right, except it come with the head forward, and thereby prefigure that headlong falling into calamities which it must suffer after.

John Donne, *Sermon III*[2]

About suffering they were never wrong,
The Old Masters: how well they understood
Its human position; how it takes place
While someone else is eating or opening a window or just walking
dully along.

WH Auden, *Musée des Beaux Arts*[3]

It is such a secret place, the land of tears.

Antoine de Saint-Exupery, *The Little Prince*[4]

Introduction

Man is a reasoning animal. When suffering or disaster strikes, much thought is given to identifying the cause. This is the basis of superstition and magic, where special rituals are performed to stave off misfortune or to placate the causative force. Religions also have their origins based firmly in the struggle to make sense of suffering and death. Complex rules of personal behaviour, sacrifice and mental training are an integral part of most religions. Rules may grow from tradition or be transmitted by prophets or the founders of a new faith. Those who diligently follow the prescribed code may be disappointed when adversity affects them. This disappointment is at the heart of the Book of Job in the Old Testament, but is equally tangible today in those who become ill or old despite following a healthy lifestyle. Those who believe in immortality have the consolation that matters may improve in the next life, if not in this one.

Eric Cassell has defined suffering as:

> a state of severe distress associated with events that threaten the intact-
> ness of person. The perception of impending destruction causes suffering
> which persists until the threat of disintegration has passed or until the
> integrity of the person can be restored in some other manner.[5]
>
> (p. 33)

Our personal experience of suffering, and the sense that we can make of it, is a
crucial part of our integrity and humanity. The ability of each individual to cope
with suffering will vary. The capacity to reach out to others who suffer may be
limited if we have no personal framework for understanding suffering, or if we fail
to take time to consider the spiritual beliefs of those we are trying to help. Even if
willingness is present, lack of personal experience of suffering may limit the understanding of those who are in anguish.

Cassell believes that spiritual decline in a community leads to a reduction in the
power of belief and an increase in the importance of the individual self as a legitimate entity separate from a God or Gods.[5] However, it is important not to confuse
religion and spirituality. Religion reflects a belief in a superhuman power that
must be obeyed and worshipped. Spirituality is more a state of awareness or mind
that contemplates the soul of the universe and the sanctity of a moral and virtuous
life, rather than its more material aspects. Spirituality may involve thoughts of
immortality but not necessarily of the individual. It might involve moral progress
or the passage of love from one generation to the next. Therefore a decline in
religious faith does not necessarily lead to a corresponding fall in spirituality.

This chapter is an attempt to briefly outline the response to suffering of the
major world religions, as well as the attitudes to suffering in an atheist capitalist
society. Examining the meaning of suffering is not a traditional part of the training
of healthcare professionals. Cassell laments this situation when he writes:

> Without system and training, being responsive in the face of suffering
> remains the attribute of individual physicians who have come to this
> mastery alone or gained it from a few inspirational teachers – which is
> where we are today. The separation of the disease that underlies the
> suffering from both the person and the suffering itself, as though the
> scientific entity of the disease is more real and more important than the
> person and the suffering, is one of the strange intellectual paradoxes of
> our times.[5]
>
> (pp. viii–ix)

As Cassell points out, healthcare is concerned with individuals who suffer, and this
makes the professions associated with healthcare personal. The success of medical
science rests on the special relationship between the healthcare professional and the
patient.[5] Our task may become easier if we can reach some understanding of suffering and help patients *within their own spiritual beliefs* to make sense of their suffering.

Modern Western society is increasingly one that incorporates people of many
different religious faiths, or none at all. I believe that healthcare professionals need
to understand and honour the individual beliefs of their patients and avoid
inflicting their own spiritual viewpoint on another's suffering, unless specifically
requested to do so by the patient as part of ongoing friendship. Naturally, healthcare

professionals also have a right to practise according to their own faith, and to opt out of procedures such as abortion, but generally they do not have the right to block access to procedures that society has sanctioned or to perform those that their society has outlawed (e.g. female circumcision or euthanasia). This view is expressed more eloquently by Hauerwas:

> In order to care for Christians, Jews, Muslims and atheists alike, medicine has had to fashion or conform to a secular morality that accents respect for freedom. It does this by focusing more on procedures such as free and informed consent than on substantive moral convictions dealing with such matters as abortion or suicide. The latter must now be regarded as matters of private choice, not to be made by the profession or the community.[6]
>
> (p. 9)

The attempt to understand or make sense of suffering should not detract from the reality or validity of the lived experience. Personal suffering will alter and probably enrich the abilities of healthcare professionals, and this is encapsulated in the age-old concept of the *wounded healer*, a concept that we shall return to in Chapter 11. The experience of suffering is a lifelong memory, if not in the conscious mind then in the subconscious one. Bowker writes:

> To talk of suffering is to talk not of an academic problem but of the sheer bloody agonies of existence, of which all men are aware and most have direct experience.[7]
>
> (p. 2)

There will be limits to our understanding of suffering, and individual variations in how well we cope with that which is sent in our direction. This is perhaps the central message of the Book of Job. In order to survive hardship, a leap of faith may be required and the ultimate meaning of suffering is probably, like the nature and purpose of our existence, mysterious.

The meaning of suffering

One of the major shortcomings of technological medicine is that, in the relentless search for cures for disease, the suffering of humans is relatively neglected. If suffering is perceived as serving no useful purpose, there is a temptation either to ignore it or to abolish it altogether. Speaking as a Christian, Hauerwas argues:

> I have always thought it odd that anyone should think it possible or even a good thing to eliminate all suffering. Suffering, I have been taught, is not something you eliminate, but something with which you must learn to live. ... without allowing ourselves and others to suffer we could not be human or humane. For it is our capacity to feel grief and to identify with the misfortune of others which is the basis for our ability to recognise our fellow humanity.[6]
>
> (pp. 24–5)

The search for meaning in suffering was highlighted by Viktor Frankl, a Jewish psychiatrist who endured years of dehumanising horror in Nazi death camps. Writing in 1946 about his experiences, he says:

> man's main concern is not to gain pleasure or to avoid pain, but rather to see a meaning in his life. That is why man is even ready to suffer, on the condition, to be sure, that his suffering has a meaning.
>
> But let me make it perfectly clear that in no way is suffering *necessary* to find meaning. I only insist that meaning is possible even in spite of suffering – provided, certainly, that suffering is unavoidable.[8]
>
> (p. 136)

Frankl found comfort in turning a predicament into a human achievement, particularly the challenge of bearing suffering bravely:

> When a man finds that it is his destiny to suffer, he will have to accept his suffering as his task; his single and unique task. He will have to acknowledge the fact that even in suffering he is unique and alone in the universe. No one can relieve him of his suffering or suffer in his place. His unique opportunity lies in the way in which he bears his burden.[8]
>
> (p. 99)

The bravery with which one has borne suffering becomes a source of pride:

> Instead of possibilities, I have realities in my past, not only in the reality or work done and of love loved, but of sufferings bravely suffered. These sufferings are even the things of which I am most proud, though these are things which cannot inspire envy.[8]
>
> (p. 144)

There is certainly a paradox which most healthcare professionals must have encountered in that those who have suffered most are often the most thoughtful and cheerful of patients. There is a feeling that suffering somehow deepens and strengthens the personality. In Ancient Greece, Herodotus is quoted as having written 'my sufferings have been my lessons.'[9] Certainly a serious illness can change a person's perspective on what is important in life; sometimes the quest for material wealth is abandoned. As Job succinctly expresses it:

> Naked I came from the womb,
> naked I shall return whence I came.
> The Lord gives and the Lord takes away;
> blessed be the name of the Lord.[10]

Job also recognised that life is marked by ageing, illness, suffering and death. Could we appreciate joy without experiencing sorrow, or happiness without knowing suffering? Even love, the most dizzying of human pleasures, is eventually replaced by hate or grief.

> Every being born of woman is short-lived and full of trouble.
> He blossoms like a flower and withers away;
> fleeting as a shadow, he does not endure.[11]

The Dalai Lama has pointed out that although suffering may strengthen some of us, at times it can have the opposite effect. Suffering may make us more gentle and sensitive, less arrogant and proud:

> The vulnerability we experience in the midst of our suffering can open us and deepen our connection with others.[26]
>
> > (p. 169)

The lesson we learn may be that of accepting the help of others with grace, as expressed in the poem *My Love Stood By My Side*:

> My love stood by my side
> In the harsh and bleakest time,
> When flesh was cut to ribbons
> And my heart ebbed with the tide.
>
> My God had pronounced sentence
> In the mortal wood and nail,
> When bones were crushed to bloody pulp
> And my inner spirit failed.
>
> When deception howled derision,
> Spat the naive with contempt,
> When I was all for giving up
> My love stood by my side.
>
> > Peter Barritt

Suffering and religion

Religion is irretrievably linked to the sufferings of humanity. In times of hardship there is increased interest in all things divine. As we discussed earlier, the need to explain misfortune and take precautions against future suffering underpins superstition, magic and most religions. In his study of gurus, the psychiatrist Anthony Storr found that many spiritual leaders (including the Buddha, Jesus, Ignatius of Loyola and Jim Jones) had found enlightenment following a period of intense mid-life suffering.[12] Suffering may strengthen faith and bring individuals closer to their God, although this is not invariable. My grandmother, for one, relinquished her devout and lifelong Methodist faith after nursing my grandfather through years of strokes, double incontinence and dementia. She felt that she could no longer believe in an all-powerful and all-loving God who would put a good soul through that intensity and duration of personal suffering for no obvious purpose. This dilemma is a very real one for both Christianity and Islam, and is well summarised by Hauerwas in his book *God, Medicine and Suffering*:

> Formulating the problem of suffering in its conventional statement revolves around the seeming contradiction between the divine power and the divine love. If God is *loving* and at the same time *all-powerful*,

then why is there so much suffering in the world? The assumption is that the deity *could,* if the deity *would,* simply eliminate suffering.[13]

(p. 47)

We move on now to touch very briefly on some of the ideas about suffering in different world religions, most of which come from John Bowker's excellent book *Problems of Suffering in Religions of the World.* I hope that the brief descriptions that follow will not cause offence, as the intention was to stimulate interest in different faiths, not to denigrate them. In particular I hope that the reader may be encouraged to read the wisdom and poetry of unfamiliar scriptures.

Judaism

The classical interpretation of the cause of suffering in the Old Testament comes from events in the Garden of Eden. God created man and woman in perfect form, but a moment of indiscretion with the tree of knowledge of good and evil led to their fall from grace. A life of hard labour, painful childbirth and suffering was their punishment for original sin. Suffering results either from personal sin or from that committed by ancestors. However, this rationale for suffering still leaves a problem with regard to the distribution of suffering on earth.[7] The Psalms in particular are full of lament for the tribulations of the faithful and the flourishing of the wicked. Why do children, the innocent and the faithful suffer? The distribution of suffering is a recurrent theme in Ecclesiastes:

> Food does not belong to the wise, nor wealth to the intelligent, nor success to the skilful; like fish caught in the destroying net, like a bird taken in a snare, so the people are trapped when misfortune comes suddenly upon them.[14]

The author of Ecclesiastes proposes that life is a test:

> In dealing with human beings it is God's purpose to test them and to see what they truly are. Human beings and beasts share one and the same fate: death comes to both alike. They all draw the same breath. Man has no advantage over beast, for everything is futility. All go to the same place: all came from dust and to the dust all will return. Who knows whether the spirit of a human being goes upward or whether the spirit of a beast goes downward to the earth? So I saw there is nothing better than all should enjoy their work, since that is their lot. For who will put them in a position to see what will happen afterwards?[15]

This theme is also taken up in the Book of Job. Satan picks one of God's most faithful servants and tests him with misfortune and illness. Satan is convinced that if the suffering is sufficiently dire, Job will lose his faith or cry out against God. Job not only retains his faith (if not his good humour), but also accepts his suffering stoically and prays for his misguided friends. This is perhaps the first Biblical reference to the idea of personal suffering bringing benefit to others.[7] God's answer to the question of why Job should suffer when he has led a blameless life is that man knows far too little about the creation to understand the full picture. The idea of suffering as a punishment for sin appears to be rejected, and the concept of an afterlife as a consolation for suffering in this life is not mentioned.[7] The reward for Job is a return of his considerable personal fortune, a further ten children and another 140 years of earthly life.

Reference to a life after death becomes more prominent as the Jewish faith develops:

> The souls of the virtuous are in the hands of God,
> No torment shall ever touch them.
> In the eyes of the unwise, they did appear to die,
> their going looked like a disaster,
> their leaving us, like annihilation;
> but they are in peace ...
> Those who are faithful will live with him in love;
> For grace and mercy await those he has chosen.[16]

Bowker argues that belief in an afterlife became stronger as a result of increasing Jewish martyrdom in the second century BC, and later the fall of Jerusalem to the Romans. Visions of a catastrophic end to the earth begin to appear where good and evil part ways for ever, though many Jews in the post-Biblical period refused to accept the validity of these apocalyptic visions. Rabbinic discussions on suffering have widened to include the suffering of animals and to distinguish between different types of suffering. Bowker feels that the Jewish ability to understand suffering as a means of attaining grace has been of crucial importance in their survival:

> 'He who gladly bears the sufferings that befall him brings salvation to the world.' Without this sense of commitment to the totality of God's creation and purpose, the tenacious survival of Jewish communities under at times intense and relentless persecution would be almost inexplicable.[7]

(pp. 29–37)

Christianity

Suffering is at the very heart of the Christian faith. The crucifixion of Jesus is taken as a graphic illustration of the sacrifice that God was prepared to make for his chosen people, akin to Abraham preparing to sacrifice his son Isaac. Christ is said to have suffered and died in order for our sins to be forgiven:

> It is your vocation because Christ himself suffered on your behalf, and left you an example in order that you should follow in his footsteps. When he was abused he did not retaliate, when he suffered he uttered no threats, but delivered himself up to him who judges justly. He carried our sins in his own person on the gibbet, so that we might cease to live for sin and begin to live for righteousness. By his wounds you have been healed.[17]

Mortal suffering may thus be viewed as an opportunity to identify with Jesus, who made the ultimate sacrifice on our behalf. Peter writes of 'undeserved suffering':

> It is a sign of grace if, because God is in his thoughts, someone endures the pain of undeserved suffering.[18]

Paul develops the theme of using the personal experience of suffering to help to comfort others:

> He consoles us in all our troubles, so that we in turn may be able to console others in any trouble of theirs and to share with them the consolation we ourselves receive from God. As Christ's suffering exceeds all measure and extends to us, so too it is through Christ that our consolation has no limit.[19]

The Christian church has created its own academic discipline, *theodicy*, to defend the justice and righteousness of God in the face of evil and suffering. The suffering of the innocent remains a problem for a religion with an all-loving, all-powerful God, as discussed previously. An afterlife is a firm tenet of Christianity, although whether this will be found in heaven or on earth is uncertain. Christ appears to have thought that the Kingdom of God would appear on earth within the lifetime of his disciples, in apocalyptic form. He asked his disciples to proclaim this message to Jews, but not to Samaritans or Gentiles.[20]

There is disagreement about the last words of Christ on the cross. Matthew and Mark record his last words as 'My God, my God, why have you forsaken me?', whereas Luke quotes Jesus as saying 'Father. Into your hands I commit my spirit' and John quotes him as saying 'It is accomplished!'. The last words according to Matthew and Mark certainly sound more human than divine, but that is the dilemma for the non-Christian. Was Jesus a heavenly being or a good man who thought he was?

Islam

Although the Quran has strong literary and theoretical links to the Judaeo-Christian tradition, its revelation of God's message via the prophet Muhammad is unique. The words of the Quran are believed by Muslims to have absolute and timeless importance. Indeed the Quran describes itself as 'the Book in which there is no doubt.'[7] The fact that the Jewish and Christian holy books differ both in their form of expression and in the substance of their message is taken as proof, as far as the Quran is concerned, that Jews and Christians have corrupted the revelation entrusted to them by God through their prophets. In the Quran the omnipotence of God is emphasised as well as his mercy and compassion. Suffering, like the whole of creation, is under the direct control of God and is seen as a fact of life:

> Do you reckon that you will enter the garden
> without there coming upon you the like of those
> who have passed away before you?
> Evils and griefs afflicted them, and they trembled so much

that the apostle and those that were with him said,
'When will the help of God come?'
Oh, truly, the help of God is near![21]

The Quran provides examples of suffering being inflicted on the sinful as punishment from God:

> To God belongs everything in the heavens and in the earth:
> he forgives whom he wills,
> he punishes whom he wills,
> and God is forgiving, compassionate.[21]

As in the Bible, there is recognition in the Quran that not all suffering is related to sin. The concept of suffering as a test or trial of faith is also proposed:

> Surely we will test you with something of fear, and of hunger,
> and of loss of wealth and lives and produce;
> yet give good tidings to the patient,
> who, when calamity afflicts them, say,
> 'We belong to God, and to him we are returning.'[21]

Although acceptance of personal suffering is a tenet of Islam, the formation of a compassionate Muslim society that reduces poverty and injustice is a major part of instruction within the Quran. Giving alms to the poor is one of the 'five pillars of Islam'.[7]

> It is not piety that you turn your faces to the East and West, but piety is belief in God, and in the last day, and in the angels, and in the book, and in the prophets, and to give of your substance, however dear to you, to your family, to orphans, to those in need, to travellers, to beggars, for the ransom of slaves, for establishing prayer, and for the giving of regular charity; and those who fulfil whatever agreements they have undertaken, and are patient in evil and misfortune and peril, those are the ones who are sound, and those are they who are god-fearing.[22]

The promise of an afterlife in paradise is central to Islam, and the trials of earthly life are accepted as 'the will of Allah'.

Hinduism

The essence of Hinduism is that there are many ways to view life, all of which are valid but none of which provide the complete answer. The oldest Hindu scriptures, the *Vedas,* are thought to have developed in the second and first millennia BC. The *Vedas* contain hymns to gods who generally represent the forces of nature or the universe, as well as verses and instruction on rituals, ceremonies and sacrifices to the gods that will help to ward off evil and bring good fortune in life. Suffering in Hinduism is part of the essence of the universe, since it is seen as part of the cycle of killing and being killed, devouring and being devoured. Sacrifice can be viewed

as identification with this process and an attempt to bring influence to bear.[7]
Suffering is seen as a result of conflict between forces:

> Cosmic process is one of universal and unceasing change and is patterned
> on a duality which is perpetually in conflict, the perfect order of heaven
> and the chaos of dark waters. Life creates opposites, as it creates sexes, in
> order to reconcile them.[7]

(p. 203)

Viewing the world as consisting of conflicting opposites – of evil and good, of pain
and of pleasure, of suffering and healing – means that people who isolate one part
of the duality as though it were the whole truth are led into unbalanced action.

The Hindu scriptures were extended and developed in the *Brahmanas,* the
Aranyakas and finally in the *Upanishads.* The teaching in these various scriptures
overlaps and merges, and is difficult to date. In Hindu teaching, suffering may be
beneficial if it cuts humans off from attachment to unworthy objects. Giving up
life's pleasures – that is, asceticism – is an important means of getting suffering into
perspective:

> He who is beyond hunger, thirst, delusion, sorrow, decay, death. When
> saints know that Self, they conquer desire for children, wealth,
> companions, live the life of the mendicants. Desire for children is desire
> for wealth; desire for wealth is desire for companions; therefore let a
> spiritual man transcend all book-learning, and live like a child. When he
> transcends book-learning and childlike simplicity, let him meditate.
> When he transcends meditation and lack of meditation, he becomes a
> saint.[23]

(p. 138)

The *Upanishads* clarify that the divine is to be found within us and all other beings.
The concept of *karma* explains the apparent injustice in the world. Our inner spirit
was never born and never dies, so reincarnation will occur when the spirit leaves our
current body. Sins in this life and in our previous lives will cause suffering, whereas
good deeds and lack of attachment to transitory pleasures will lead to joy.[24]
Meditation (the practice of clearing the conscious mind while awake) and yoga are
important disciplines within Hinduism for achieving enlightenment:

> When the wise rests his mind in contemplation on our God beyond
> time, who invisibly dwells in the mystery of things and in the heart of
> man, then he rises above pleasures and sorrow.[24]

(p. 59)

Those who are wedded to the desires of the flesh and attachment to transitory
objects are doomed to endless reincarnations, rather than achieving *nirvana*:

> O Revered One, in this foul-smelling, unsubstantial body, a conglomer-
> ate of bone, skin, muscle, marrow, flesh, semen, blood, mucus, tears,
> rheum, faeces, urine, wind, bile and phlegm, what is the good of the
> enjoyment of desires? In this body which is afflicted with desire, anger,
> covetousness, delusion, fear, despondency, envy, separation from what is

desired, union with the undesired, hunger, thirst, old age, death, disease, sorrow and the like, what is the good of the enjoyment of desires? And we see that all this is perishing, as these gnats, mosquitoes and the like, the grass and the trees that grow and decay.... In such a world as this, what is the good of enjoyment of desires? For he who has fed on them is seen to return [to this world] repeatedly.[7]

(p. 216)

The correct approach to personal suffering in Hinduism involves inner peace and detachment, although compassion for the suffering of others is also advocated:

Happiness and misery, prosperity and adversity, gain and loss, death and life, in their turn, wait upon all creatures. For this reason the wise man of tranquil self would neither be elated with joy nor depressed with sorrow.[25]

(p. 124)

Buddhism

Suffering lies at the heart of Buddhism. The Four Noble Truths as defined by the Buddha are the existence of suffering, the causes of suffering, the cessation of suffering and the path that leads to the cessation of suffering. Not only is suffering acknowledged and accepted, but the way to transcend or eliminate suffering is also taught. The Buddha believed that thirst, striving and greed for attachments to possessions, relationships and life are the root cause of suffering. The Pali word for suffering is *dukkha*, but it has a range of other meanings that include impermanence, emptiness, and lack of wholeness or perfection. Three forms of suffering are recognised by the Buddhist.

1 *Dukkha-dukkha.* This is the suffering that is inevitable in life, such as the suffering involved in birth, illness, ageing and death.
2 *Viparinama-dukkha.* This is the suffering that is associated with the consciousness of sentient beings who understand that happiness does not last and who perceive a gap between what they have and what they desire. The process of unwanted change can also cause suffering.
3 *Samkhara-dukkha.* This is the suffering that arises from the actual nature and constitution of human beings, which is composed of bodily matter, sensations, perceptions, mental awareness and consciousness. Awareness of our inevitable decay and death is one example of this form of suffering.

Complete freedom from suffering is experienced in *nirvana,* a state which the Buddha reached via the process of enlightenment, and which he then devoted his life to teaching others to attain. The path to enlightenment is via the Noble Eightfold Path, which consists of right view (understanding), right thought, right speech, right action, right livelihood, right effort, right mindfulness and right concentration. These eight factors form the three foundations of Buddhist life, namely wisdom, ethical conduct and mental discipline. Right view and right thought constitute wisdom; right speech, right action and right livelihood constitute ethical conduct; and right effort, right mindfulness and right concentration constitute mental discipline.[7]

The spiritual teacher has a crucial role with regard to the attainment of wisdom. Buddhism has grown as a faith alongside Hinduism – the concepts of rebirth and *karma* are shared. However, Buddhists do not believe in a God or even in a human self as such. Heaven is attainable for each one of us to find within ourselves. Personal conduct in life and spiritual preparation for death are crucial aspects of advantageous rebirth. The six personal perfections of personal conduct are generosity, morality, even disposition, constant endurance, concentration (or meditation) and wisdom. Life is seen as eternal and universal, and is not confined to the body.[7] By good personal conduct, an even temperament, regular meditation and thought and compassion for others, the Buddhist not only minimises their own personal suffering but also strives to avoid inflicting suffering on others.

Suffering, capitalism and atheism

Suffering in a materialist culture can be a great market opportunity, as the pharmaceutical industry clearly demonstrates. Western society has been successful in reducing levels of suffering (e.g. by reducing perinatal mortality and helping to prolong life expectancy). Prosperous capitalist countries have reduced levels of poverty, conflict and hunger, although probably by helping to generate them elsewhere. As levels of suffering have fallen, the individual's ability to cope with suffering also seems to have diminished. The Dalai Lama writes:

> as suffering becomes less visible, it is no longer seen as part of the fundamental nature of human beings – but rather as an anomaly, a sign that something has gone terribly wrong, a sign of 'failure' of some system, an infringement on our guaranteed right to happiness!
>
> This kind of thinking poses hidden dangers. If we think of suffering as something unnatural, something that we shouldn't be experiencing, then it's not much of a leap to begin to look for someone to blame for our suffering.
>
> … the refusal to accept suffering as a natural part of life can lead to viewing oneself as a perpetual victim and blaming others for our problems.[26]
>
> (pp. 121–4)

Campbell agrees with this formulation:

> Those of us who have lived all our lives in a Western society of this type can barely imagine the insecurity, lack of freedom and sheer physical suffering our forebears experienced and which is an ever-present reality in many societies today. Who would want to return to being trapped by rank or social status, to having no real choice of occupation or marriage partner, and to being at the mercy of famines, droughts, uncontrolled territorial aggression and myriad untreated diseases? To have dignity,

freedom and safety in our ordinary lives is no mean inheritance. Yet it is clear that despite all these gains, we feel far from sure that we have achieved a life that is satisfying, even in a narrow hedonistic sense.[27]

(pp. 56–7)

We discussed earlier the need for meaning in suffering, and Campbell feels that this lack of meaning in an atheist materialist world is a major problem:

All around us there are people whose lives are emptied of meaning, who fear the end of life yet find little fulfilment or sense of pride in being alive, who have been left with no route for the transcendence of life's testing times and no sense of community that cares for them or will notice how their lives end up.[27]

(p. 42)

As healthcare professionals we need no reminding of the propensity for blame when suffering strikes, or for cash consolation for those affected. Blaming others for our misfortunes means that we fail to take responsibility for our own lives. Endless retelling of past injustice perpetuates suffering. Following misfortune or illness, the person who judges their present life in terms of what they used to be able to do is forcing him- or herself to dwell on what might have been rather than on what can be.[5] Once suffering becomes pointless, there is no merit in accepting it. Epidurals for every childbirth and euthanasia for every severe illness seem logical. (Incidentally, as a natural-born coward, I am not suggesting that there is anything wrong with epidurals, and I would have headed up that particular queue had the need arisen.)

The Dalai Lama has pointed out that religion is not essential for human spirituality to develop and, of the two, he feels that the latter may have more to offer the future of the planet.[28] What sense, then, can human spirituality make of suffering outside of a particular religious framework?

Suffering and human spirituality

There seems to be no doubt that suffering affects our personal development. Suffering may foster growth and love and it may bring out the best in us. Hauerwas feels that suffering is more a test of character than a teacher:

[Suffering] may reveal us as better or worse than we had thought ourselves to be. Suffering can just as easily destroy us as it can make us more resolute.[6]

(p. 26)

Clearly there are many who have felt strengthened by their experience of suffering, including Nietzsche, who wrote 'that which does not kill me, makes me stronger'.[8] The achievement of bearing suffering bravely is one that we commonly witness in our daily work, the importance of which has been emphasised by Frankl:

> In accepting this challenge to suffer bravely, life has a meaning up to the
> last moment, and it retains this meaning literally to the end.[8]
>
> (p. 137)

Many people who suffer find perspective by considering others whose suffering is
worse than theirs. Suffering may open our eyes to tragedy both inside and outside
our own communities. I have a particular problem with those in ripe old age who
become consumed with relatively trivial suffering (why me, doctor?). Have they
worn blinkers for the past 80 years? I have heard it said that God only gives
each person as much suffering as they can cope with, so perhaps this is the answer.
One spiritualist patient told me that those who do not suffer enough in their first
life have to come back for a second dose – an interesting echo of reincarnation
theory.

Suffering can certainly clarify or change our priorities in life. Ignatieff writes:

> we learn what we need by suffering. We learn how much is enough by
> learning what it is like to have less than enough. Our education in need
> is a tragic passage from blindness to sight.[29]
>
> (p. 20)

The Dalai Lama calls this the 'loosening of bonds with the material world'. As well
as dampening materialism and workaholism, suffering can reduce pride, arrogance
and conceit. Even those who have spent their lives dedicated to the suffering of
others have to learn the lesson of dependency, and of asking for and gracefully
receiving the help of others. Furthermore we all need this experience of relying on
help from others:

> What matters to a person is the subjective feeling of being 'loved, wanted,
> valued, esteemed and able to count on others should the need arise'.[30]
>
> (p. 50)

Increasing our consideration for others is a major benefit that suffering may endow
upon us:

> When you are aware of your pain and your suffering, it helps you to
> develop your capacity for empathy, the capacity which allows you to
> relate to other people's feeling and suffering.[26]
>
> (p. 173)

This then is perhaps one of the greatest benefits of personal suffering, that of
fostering the growth of compassion:

> our experience of suffering reminds us of what all others endure, it serves
> as a powerful injunction to practise compassion and refrain from causing
> others pain. And to the extent that suffering awakens our empathy and
> causes us to connect with others, it can serve as the basis of compassion
> and love.[28]
>
> (p. 148)

This may explain the anomaly of those patients who suffer the most and yet display great humanity and generosity of spirit. It might also explain why the hale and hearty elderly have missed the plot. Suffering seems to rescue human beings from being self-centred, selfish and indifferent to the trials of others.[26] It is not only human beings who suffer, and the religions that stemmed from India (Buddhism, Hinduism and particularly Jainism) have far more to offer other living organisms than Judaism, Christianity and Islam. The Western tenet that any suffering which is inflicted on animals for human benefit (particularly medical advance) is allowable is not universally shared. The Dalai Lama writes:

> It is our suffering that is the most basic element that we share with others, the factor that unifies us with all living creatures.[26]
>
> (p. 177)

Using personal suffering to foster compassion for others is a central feature of Buddhism, but love for others who suffer is central to all of the major world religions. We shall return to the topic of compassion in Chapter 13. For those of us who have opted to earn our living by sharing the suffering of others, personal misfortune can be enlightening. Hauerwas writes:

> By learning to live as embodied beings, that is, as people subject to disease and ultimately death, we learn how significant it is that we be capable of caring for one another through the office of medicine. For through our bodies we are forced to face our need for one another, and through learning to acknowledge that need we discover our 'control' comes only through trust in others.[6]
>
> (p. 50)

Following a severe illness resulting from imprisonment as an enemy alien in World War One, Albert Schweitzer wrote:

> Whoever amongst us has learned through personal experience what pain and anxiety really are must help to ensure that those out there who are in physical need obtain the same help that once came to him. He no longer belongs to himself alone; he has become the brother of all who suffer. It is this 'brotherhood of those who bear the mark of pain' that demands humane medical services.[31]
>
> (p. 35)

Sharing suffering is a demanding task, as Frank has emphasised:

> One of the most difficult duties as human beings is to listen to the voices of those who suffer. The voices of the ill are easy to ignore, because these voices are often faltering in tone and mixed in message, particularly in their spoken form before some editor has rendered them fit for reading by the healthy.[31]
>
> (p. 25)

Personal suffering is a complex experience to share, and is at the root of some of the most sublime human achievements. As Hauerwas points out, it is the artist who has 'the gift as well as the burden' of illuminating suffering for others.[13] In his novel *The Third Man*, Graham Greene observes:

> In Italy for thirty years under the Borgias, they had warfare, terror, murder and bloodshed – but they produced Michelangelo, Leonardo da Vinci and the Renaissance. In Switzerland, they have brotherly love, five hundred years of democracy and peace, and what did they produce? The cuckoo clock.[26]
>
> (p. 169)

Would the symphonies of Beethoven, the late quartets and piano sonatas of Schubert, the writings of Woolf and Kafka, the paintings of Goya and van Gogh, and the poetry of Milton, Donne and Plath have been possible without the personal suffering they had experienced? I think not. As André Gide wrote in the preface to his hymn of recovery, *Fruits of the Earth*:

> In the very flights of its poetry there is an exuberance of someone to whom life is precious because he has been on the point of losing it.[32]
>
> (p. 11)

I shall let John Berger have the final word:

> From where does Pain come to us?
> From where does he come?
> He has been the brother of our visions
> from time immemorial
> And the guide of our rhymes.[33]
>
> (p. 98)

References

1 *The Revised English Bible*. Psalms 13:1–2.
2 Quoted in Bowker J (1970) *Problems of Suffering in Religions of the World*. Cambridge University Press, Cambridge.
3 Auden WH (1979) *Selected Poems*. Faber and Faber, London.
4 de Saint-Exupery A (1991) *The Little Prince*. Mammoth, London.
5 Cassell E (1991) *The Nature of Suffering and the Goals of Medicine*. Oxford University Press, New York.
6 Hauerwas S (1988) *Suffering Presence*. T and T Clark, Edinburgh.
7 Bowker J (1970) *Problems of Suffering in Religions of the World*. Cambridge University Press, Cambridge.
8 Frankl V (1985) *Man's Search for Meaning*. Washington Square Press, New York.
9 Spiro H (ed.) (1993) *Empathy in the Practice of Medicine*. Yale University Press, New Haven, CT.

10   *The Revised English Bible.* The Book of Job 1:21.

11   *Ibid.* The Book of Job 14:1–2.

12   Storr A (1996) *Feet of Clay.* Harper Collins, London.

13   Hauerwas S (1990) *God, Medicine and Suffering.* Eerdmans, Grand Rapids, MI.

14   *The Revised English Bible.* Ecclesiastes 9:11–12.

15   *The Revised English Bible.* Ecclesiastes 3:18–22.

16   *The Revised English Bible.* Wisdom of Solomon 3:1–5,9.

17   *The Revised English Bible.* The First Letter of Peter 2:21–24.

18   *The Revised English Bible.* The First Letter of Peter 2:19.

19   *The Revised English Bible.* The Second Letter of Paul to the Corinthians 1:4–5.

20   *The Revised English Bible.* Matthew 10:5–8.

21   Quran ii.210 (214).

22   Quran ii.172 (177).

23   Swami S and Yeats WB (1937) *The Ten Principal Upanishads.* Faber and Faber, London.

24   Mascaro J (1965) *The Upanishads.* Penguin Books, Harmondsworth.

25   *Mahabharata Santiparva* 141.102.

26   HH Dalai Lama and Cutler H (1998) *The Art of Happiness.* Hodder & Stoughton, London.

27   Campbell A (1995) *Health as Liberation: medicine, theology and the quest for justice.* Pilgrim Press, Cleveland, OH.

28   HH Dalai Lama (2001) *Ancient Wisdom, Modern World: ethics for the new millennium.* Abacus, London.

29   Ignatieff M (1994) *The Needs of Strangers.* Vintage, London.

30   McWhinney I (1989) *A Textbook of Family Medicine.* Oxford University Press, Oxford.

31   Quoted in Frank A (1997) *The Wounded Storyteller: body, illness and ethics.* University of Chicago Press, Chicago.

32   Gide A (1949, reprinted 1970) *Fruits of the Earth.* Penguin, Harmondsworth.

33   Berger J (1991) *And Our Faces, My Heart, Brief as Photos.* Vintage Books, New York.

Further reading

- The Bible.
- Bowker J (1970) *Problems of Suffering in Religions of the World.* Cambridge University Press, Cambridge.
- Campbell A (1995) *Health as Liberation: medicine, theology and the quest for justice.* Pilgrim Press, Cleveland, OH.
- Cassell E (1991) *The Nature of Suffering and the Goals of Medicine.* Oxford University Press, New York.
- HH Dalai Lama (2001) *Ancient Wisdom, Modern World: ethics for the new millennium.* Abacus, London.
- HH Dalai Lama and Cutler H (1998) *The Art of Happiness.* Hodder & Stoughton, London.
- Frankl V (1985) *Man's Search for Meaning.* Washington Square Press, New York.

- Gide A (1949, reprinted 1970) *Fruits of the Earth.* Penguin, Harmondsworth.
- Hauerwas S (1988) *Suffering Presence.* T and T Clark, Edinburgh.
- Ignatieff M (1994) *The Needs of Strangers.* Vintage, London.
- Mascaro J (1965) *The Upanishads.* Penguin Books, Harmondsworth.
- The Quran.

CHAPTER 5

The illness experience in literature

We study health, and we deliberate upon our meats, and drink, and air, and exercises, and we hew and we polish every stone that goes to that building; and so our health is a long and a regular work: but in a minute a cannon batters all, overthrows all, demolishes all; a sickness unprevented for all our diligence, unsuspected for all our curiosity; nay, undeserved, if we consider only disorder, summons us, seizes us, possesses us, destroys us in an instant.

John Donne, *Devotions*[1]

At Tierra del Fuego, all my teeth fell out.
On the Congo, a cayman devoured one of my feet.
In India, a wasting disease attacked me
And my skin turned beautifully green and as it were transparent;
And my eyes grew large and sentimental.

André Gide, *Fruits of the Earth*[2]

Illness is the night-side of life, a more onerous citizenship. Everyone who is born holds dual citizenship, in the kingdom of the well and in the kingdom of the sick. Although we all prefer to use only the good passport, sooner or later each of us is obliged, at least for a spell, to identify ourselves as citizens of that other place.

Susan Sontag, *Illness as Metaphor*[3]

I had fallen into an abyss, with the breaking apart of my tissues, my perceptions, the natural unities of body-soul, body-mind. And I had been lifted from the abyss, reborn, reaffirmed, by powers beyond my understanding and reason. I had been shaken and foundered – but mysteriously saved.

Oliver Sacks, *A Leg to Stand On*[4]

Introduction

Definitions of illness, disease and sickness were discussed in Chapter 1. In this chapter we shall explore the human experience of illness – both that of the sufferer and that of their friends and family. This exploration has been well summarised by Kleinman in his excellent book *The Illness Narratives*:

> By invoking the term illness, I mean to conjure up the innately human experience of symptoms and suffering. Illness refers to how the sick person and the members of the family and wider social network perceive, live with, and respond to symptoms and disability.[5]
>
> (p. 3)

This chapter will primarily concentrate on the initial impact of illness. Chronic illness and disability will be examined in Chapter 6.

Understanding the human reaction to the onset of illness is a crucial part of our ability to facilitate healing. The importance of making sense of suffering as a means of alleviation has already been discussed. Unfortunately, the orthodox medical conception of disease is fundamentally different from the lived experience of illness. This is wonderfully illustrated by the author and neurologist Oliver Sacks in his book *A Leg to Stand On*.[4] If the reader wants one book to read in order to gain a better understanding of this conflict, they should start here. McWhinney suggests four ways for us to gain a better understanding of illness:

> We can learn, first of all, by paying attention to their [the patient's] experience, by practicing the very difficult art of listening, by reading the appropriate literature, and by reflecting on our own experience.[6]
>
> (p. 85)

As we discussed in Chapter 3, good health is usually taken for granted and only appreciated in hindsight. It could be argued that this is sensible. Human beings show ability in planning for future adversity (the storing of surplus food being an early example), but spending life worrying about what could go wrong with the body and mind might be of little evolutionary advantage, although sickness insurance makes a lot of sense. This state of affairs is well summarised by Eric Cassell in *The Healer's Art*:

> The healthy have confidence in themselves and in their bodies, a confidence built on experience and fed by the sense of invulnerability.[7]
>
> (p. 125)

On the other hand, many cultures and religions have encouraged the healthy to anticipate and come to terms with illness, suffering, ageing and death. Buddhism is probably the best example of this. Determination to ignore the suffering of others throughout life may be interpreted as a sign of selfishness, personal weakness and fear. Waiting until misfortune strikes may mean that the lessons to be learned from illness arrive far too late for us, or those around us, to benefit from them. Tolstoy's short story *The Death of Ivan Ilyich* is a classic example of this. Tolstoy, in typical sardonic style, describes Ivan's approach to mortality:

> The example of a syllogism which he had learned in Kiezewette's *Logic,* 'Caius is a man, men are mortal, therefore Caius is mortal,' had seemed to him all his life to be true as applied to Caius but certainly not as regards himself. That Caius – man in the abstract – was mortal, was perfectly correct; but he was not Caius, nor man in the abstract: he had always been a creature quite, quite different from all others.[8]
>
> (p. 54)

The lessons of illness come in the form of personal answers to the questions that illness poses, foremost among which is the question 'What has my life been about?'. Kleinman again finds apt words:

> Disability and death force us to reconsider our lives and our world. The possibility for human transformation, immanent or transcendent, sometimes begins with this disconcerting vision.
>
> For the seriously ill, insight can be the result of an often grim, though occasionally luminous, lived wisdom of the body in pain and the mind troubled.[5]

(p. 55)

Illness as questions

When illness strikes there seem to be some basic questions that all of us will ask, either of ourselves, our family and friends or our healthcare professionals.

What is wrong?

The first question is usually 'What is wrong with me? Am I ill?'. Rudebeck described physical illness as 'a sense of bodily unease, an experience of the functioning of the body as being not quite right.'[9] Symptoms may be sudden and dramatic, but if they start gradually they can be difficult to perceive. Tiredness, in particular, is an early symptom that commonly occurs in the healthy as well as in the sick. The sophistication of our sensory equipment is such that, without symptoms, illness is unlikely. This explains why health checks are largely an expensive waste of time. However, symptoms without disease are commonplace. Consultations with family, friends, neighbours and the media are used to check the significance of symptoms before professional help is sought.

Can I be treated?

If an illness is confirmed by the healthcare professional, the sufferer will usually want to know whether there is a cure or treatment available. Failing that, the patient may want to know whether their suffering can be relieved. Not every patient, of course, wants to know 'the whole truth and nothing but the truth'.

What will happen to me?

Predicting the likely course of illness is a fundamental part of the healthcare professional's role, even if intuition or inspired guesswork is often flawed. Some patients want to know if their condition is going to be fatal. Sentiments from the professional along the lines of 'life is an incurable disease' are unlikely to be warmly received.

Why me?

As previously noted, man's reasoning nature is an inherent part of consciousness. Those of the Ivan Ilyich school may be dumbfounded when personal illness strikes. Those with fear in their hearts may believe that a virtuous life on this earth can last for ever. Only those who transgress (the smokers, the slothful or the obese) will be punished. Sontag feels that there is an underlying sentiment here that 'Life is not fair'.[3] Those who have been aware of the suffering of others through their own times of relative good fortune may ask the more pertinent question 'Why not me?'.

Illness as loss

Reaction to illness has been compared by some professionals to bereavement, and there are certainly losses to accept when illness strikes. However, bereavement is a reaction to an irrevocable event, and there are important differences between this and the continuing lived experience of being ill (more of this in Chapter 6). What are the losses that illness brings?

Loss of confidence

Illness strikes fear in the heart. This sense of foreboding permeates Thomas Mann's account of life in an alpine TB sanatorium in *The Magic Mountain*:

> This world of limitless silences had nothing hospitable; it received the visitor at his own risk, or rather it scarcely even received him, it tolerated his penetration into its fastnesses in a manner that boded no good: it made him aware of the menace of the elemental, a menace not even hostile, but impersonally deadly.[10]

Oliver Sacks, too, described his fear:

> I cannot call it the dread of death, though doubtless that was contained in it. It was rather a dread of something dark and nameless and secret – a nightmarish feeling, uncanny and ominous.[4]
>
> (p. 27)

John Berger argues that it is the uniqueness of our experience that generates fear:

> As soon as we are ill we fear that our illness is unique. We argue with ourselves and rationalise, but a ghost of the fear remains. And it remains for a very good reason. The illness, as an undefined force, is a potential threat to our very being and we are bound to be highly conscious of the uniqueness of that being. The illness, in other words, shares in our own uniqueness. By fearing its threat, we embrace it and make it specially our own. That is why patients are inordinately relieved when doctors give their complaint a name. The name may mean very little to them; they may understand nothing of what it signifies; but because it has a name,

> it has an independent existence from them. They can now struggle or complain *against* it. To have a complaint recognised, that is to say defined, limited and depersonalised, is to be made stronger.[11]
>
> (pp. 73–4)

The fear that accompanies illness can paralyse action and banish reason. This underlies the delay in presentation of patients with ominous symptoms, such as breast lumps and drastic weight loss. When reason deserts us, a return to a state of childlike dependency follows. Eric Cassell argues that 'The sick person, as stripped and helpless as an infant, has to be brought back.'[7] As confidence dwindles, the ill may become confused in their encounters with the medical system. Even a neurologist may struggle:

> There were some difficulties about 'the history', because they wanted to know the 'salient facts', and I wanted to tell them everything – the entire story. Besides, I wasn't quite certain what might or might not be 'salient' in the circumstances.[4]
>
> (p. 29)

Loss of control

All illness causes interference with function in some way, whether it be with self-care, work, leisure or interpersonal relationships. The loss of control of personal function (e.g. with urinary or bowel incontinence) can be devastating, and Cassell believes it to be 'the aspect of illness that is most destructive to the sick.'[7] There are important differences in the value that control is given by individuals, and loss is likely to be more traumatic for those who value it most highly. Tasks that were previously automatic, such as toileting or washing, may become impossible hurdles. The changed body needs constant vigilance to anticipate what can and cannot be done. Society expects those who have lost control to try to regain it as soon as possible. If this is not possible, then this loss of control should be hidden from others.[12] Illnesses associated with fluctuating impairment, such as arthritis or multiple sclerosis, cause unpredictability, so that planning for tomorrow becomes especially difficult.[13] Ultimately illness may rob us of our ability to lead an independent life, and adjusting to the necessity for constant help from others can be difficult.

Loss of innocence

In Chapter 1 we discussed how society may endorse an individual as sick. The nature of the particular society in which we live will determine the rules for sickness and whether or not the individual should be judged guilty of the misdemeanour of falling ill.

The historical and literary profile of different diseases has been examined by Susan Sontag in her essay *Illness as Metaphor*. She demonstrates how tuberculosis (TB) was perceived, like the Grim Reaper himself, as mysterious, dark and full of dread. TB was seen to 'consume' the body, causing pallor but increasing beauty, libido, soulfulness and the ability to write poetry (e.g. Keats, Shelley) or music (e.g. Chopin, Paganini). TB was thought to stem from too much sensual passion, which was unduly repressed or thwarted.[3] As the incidence of TB has declined, cancer has taken over as the silent killer that stalks abroad. As with TB, those prone to cancer are thought to show insufficient passion, and to be repressed. Sontag argues that in today's culture insanity has taken the place of TB, with the sufferer being portrayed as a 'hectic reckless creature of passionate extremes, someone too sensitive to bear the horrors of the vulgar, everyday world.'

If blame is not forthcoming from the way we handle our passions or nature, then lifestyle will certainly win the day. Governments are keen on promoting this knowledge under the guise of health promotion, and blameworthy behaviour can include diet, dress, hygiene, lifestyle, relationships, work, physical exercise, smoking and drinking habits.[14] Woe betide the smoker who develops lung cancer who dares to ask 'Why me?'. The AIDS sufferer would obviously know better. Clearly those who have caused their disease deserve it.[3] Addictions and obesity are conditions that share this sense of stigma. There is, of course, nothing new under the sun, and the idea of disease as divine retribution for personal transgressions or sins is as old as history itself.[14]

The general public, on the whole, prefers to blame external agents such as mercury dental fillings, immunisations, mobile phone masts or the medical profession in general.

Loss of omnipotence

Illness often brings a realisation that good health and life do not go on for ever. Suffering, sickness, ageing and death may no longer be viewed as processes that happen exclusively to others.

Illness as experience

As well as being aware of the questions posed and the losses incurred by illness, healthcare professionals need to understand the reality of the lived experience and be aware of the various ways in which people learn to cope. The world of life-threatening illness is a strange landscape to step into, and those who return are irrevocably changed. Virginia Woolf, writing possibly the longest sentence in the history of the English language, believed that the experience of illness had been sadly neglected by writers:

> Considering how common illness is, how tremendous the spiritual change that it brings, how astonishing, when the lights of health go down, the undiscovered countries that are then disclosed, what wastes and deserts of the soul a slight attack of influenza brings to view, what precipices and lawns sprinkled with bright flowers a little rise of temperature reveals, what ancient and obdurate oaks are uprooted in us by the act of sickness, how we go down into the pit of death and feel the waters of annihilation close above our heads and wake thinking to find ourselves in the presence

of angels and the harpers when we have a tooth out and come to the surface in the dentist's arm-chair and confuse his 'Rinse the mouth – rinse the mouth' with the greeting of the Deity stooping from the floor of Heaven to welcome us – when we think of this, as we are so frequently forced to think of it, it becomes strange indeed that illness has not taken its place with love and battle and jealousy among the prime themes of literature.[15]

(p. 9)

Once again, Oliver Sacks comes to our rescue:

Outwardly, then, there was soundlessness and noise, and inwardly, simul-taneously, a deadly inner silence – the silence of timelessness, motionlessness, *scotoma,* combined with the silence of non-communica-tion and taboo. Incommunicable, *incommunicado,* the sense of excommunication was extreme. I maintained an affable and amenable surface, while nourishing an inward and secret despair.[4]

(p. 78)

The sense of disconnection from the world is emphasised if admission to a hospital or asylum occurs, particularly if the institution is distant and remote (as in *The Magic Mountain*). Cecil Helman describes how depersonalisation is encouraged by institutional procedures, shared by prisons and the armed forces:

clothing is removed, and replaced by a uniform of bathrobe and slippers. In the ward they are allocated a number, and transformed into a 'case' for diagnosis and treatment. When they have recovered they regain their own clothes and rejoin their community.[14]

(p. 203)

This process of depersonalisation is also described by Sacks:

One's own clothes are replaced by an anonymous white nightgown, one's wrist is clasped by an identification bracelet with a number. One be-comes subject to institutional rules and regulations. One is no longer a free agent; one no longer has rights; one is no longer in the world-at-large. It is strictly analogous to becoming a prisoner and humiliatingly reminiscent of one's first day at school. One understands that this is protective, but it is quite dreadful, too.[4]

(p. 28)

The experience of the passage of time becomes distorted in illness. The metaphysi-cal poet, John Donne, suffered a severe illness in 1623 and published his reflections on this illness, *The Devotions,* in 1624:

When we must pant through all those fiery heats, and sail through all those overflowing sweats, when we must watch through all those long nights, and mourn through all those long days (days and nights, so long as Nature herself shall seem to be perverted, and to have put the longest day, and the longest night, which should be six months asunder, into one natural, unnatural day).[1]

(pp. 152–3)

Jean-Dominique Bauby suffered a catastrophic stroke in his forties which left him paralysed, speechless and only able to move one eyelid. He dictated his account of illness, *The Diving-Bell and the Butterfly*, using his one functioning eyelid:

Sunday. The bell gravely tolls the hours. The small Health Department calendar on the wall, whittled away day by day, announces that it is already August. Mysterious paradox: time, motionless here, gallops out there. In my contracted world the hours drag on but the months flash by.[16]

(pp. 108–9)

Sacks also noticed time behaving strangely:

'How long is it since you were testing the leg out with me?'
She glanced at her watch. 'Not ten minutes,' she said. 'Does it seem longer?'
Not ten minutes! I could hardly believe my ears. In that ten minutes, it seemed to me, I had been through a lifetime's experience. I had voyaged round a whole universe of thought. I had travelled so far – and they were still serving lunch![4]

(p. 57)

The family experience

The lived experience of illness is felt acutely by family and friends, who usually have the prime responsibility for care. The losses and limitations that illness imposes on the individual will also affect the carers. Restriction on physical abilities often means extra work for other family members to perform. Financial losses resultant on the illness impinge on the whole family. People of a certain age have expectations about what levels of physical activity they should be able to enjoy. The sick person may no longer be able to travel or take part in holidays that the family used to enjoy together. Family members have a choice between giving up these activities or feeling the guilt of leaving their loved ones out. Chronic illness can catapult a person and their close family into virtual old age. Referring to families with children who have profound neurological damage, Carl Elliott writes:

Their parents often look like war veterans, exhausted and shell shocked.... The lives of entire families are often structured around the care of such children and are marked by a special kind of grace and tragedy. Often the parents and siblings of such children have made personal sacrifices of heroic proportions, but they are still haunted by guilt for what they have not done, or for the things they have secretly wished for.[17]

(pp. 89–90)

The philosopher Gorovitz has listed four good reasons not to be ill and all of these impinge directly on family and friends:

1   Illness causes discomfort and dysfunction.
2   Illness results in an undesirable egocentricity that shrinks a sick person's view of the world.
3   This state of egocentricity and shrunken worldview is in turn boring and constraining.
4   Illness, unless trivial, is an unwelcome, implicit affirmation of human vulnerability and mortality.[18]

(pp. 60–1)

Acquaintances and the general public find chronic illness in particular boring. This is strikingly obvious when the meaningless greeting 'How are you?' is used. The ill quickly learn to lie when asked this question, as a truthful answer will either be ignored or regarded as bad form. Good friends, good colleagues and humane healthcare professionals can all play a vital part in listening to the troubles of the sick person. Otherwise the burden will fall entirely on the immediate family. In general, illness *is* boring and it usually makes us miserable and hard to live with. All serious illness, but perhaps mental illness in particular, puts great stress on other family members.

Egocentricity alters the family dynamic, and problems of dependency, selfishness and unreasonable demands can make life difficult. The sick person may envy the well, become stuck in their anger at the injustice of illness, or deny that they are ill at all. These are all understandable and justifiable stages to pass through in the illness experience, but they can be destructive to the family if they become enduring. Watching someone you love suffering from a problem you can do little about is itself an upsetting experience. However, human beings seem to have a well of sympathy that is not bottomless, and chronic illness may drain the well dry. Hauerwas acknowledges this problem:

> We may initially be quite sympathetic with someone with a chronic disease, but it seems to be asking too much of us to be compassionate year in, year out. Thus the universal testimony of people with chronic illness that their illness often results in the alienation of their former friends.[19]
>
> (p. 77)

Woolf was dismissive of sympathy:

> About sympathy, for example – we can do without it. That illusion of a world so shaped that it echoes every groan, of human beings so tied together by common needs and fears that a twitch at one wrist jerks another, where however strange your experience other people have had it too, where however far you travel in your own mind someone has been there before you – is all an illusion. We do not know our own souls, let alone the souls of others. Human beings do not go hand in hand the whole stretch of the way. There is a virgin forest in each, a snowfield where even the print of birds' feet is unknown. Here we go alone, and like it better so.[15]
>
> (pp. 13–14)

The ability to think about and care for others varies between individuals. Traditionally, caring has been viewed as a feminine characteristic, probably because women honed their nurturing skills looking after children, but this is a broad generalisation about a world that is rapidly changing. As materialistic capitalism breaks up the extended family and encourages both partners in a relationship to work, institutional care for severe illness may become more likely. The willingness of the family to care for an ill member may reflect their experience of that person before illness struck. A loving person who has spent their life giving to others is more likely to engender a sympathetic response when their need arises.

Another of literature's great invalids is Franz Kafka, who spent much of his life in and out of the TB sanatorium. His allegorical tale *Metamorphosis* describes the family reaction to a disfiguring change of health when the son of the family, Gregor Samsa, wakes unexpectedly one morning to find that he has turned into a giant beetle, six feet long. Initially he is concerned with learning to walk with many legs, how to get out of bed and whether he can get to the office on time. The family are dismayed because they cannot understand insect-speak, and he has a disconcerting habit of scurrying under the furniture for scraps of food. They lock him in his bedroom and only his sister shows some kindness in taking food to him. One day he escapes into the living room and his father throws an apple at him which gets stuck in his back, rots and causes infection. Gregor pines away and dies, and is promptly thrown in the rubbish bin by the cleaning lady. Kafka's metaphor raises important issues about the nature of chronic disability, disfigurement, stigma and family shame. He also illustrates how being stripped of a bread-winning role and becoming dependent on others can alter power structures within a family.[20] As Howard Brody writes:

> Self-respect and the possession of a rational plan of life presuppose a set of reciprocal relationships among a group of peers.[21]
>
> (p. 99)

Severe illness forces both the individual and the family to rethink life plans and interpersonal relationships. The family may, of course, fail to cope with or adjust to the changes that illness brings, and unrealistic expectations of what the sick person can achieve may arise. Sick people are expected to get better as soon as possible, and to be cheerful but not to enjoy themselves.[21]

Illness as change

We have looked at illness in terms of the questions it poses, the losses incurred and the feelings experienced. Another way of considering illness is to view it as yet another example of the continuous and unavoidable change to which the universe is subject. This is the Buddhist perspective. The advantages of accepting illness as a manifestation of inevitable change are as follows.

1   Illness, suffering, ageing and death are accepted as unavoidable, and questions about fairness and 'Why me?' become less relevant. Blame and retribution are less likely as suffering is expected.

2   If illness is accepted as inescapable, less time is spent bemoaning one's fate, and the task of adjusting to changed circumstances can begin. Fighting against old age and death no longer becomes necessary.
3   Once accepted, the art of life becomes a matter of making the best of whatever fate throws at one.
4   Wearing blinkers throughout life in order to avoid seeing the suffering of others becomes unnecessary, and compassion may result.
5   Illness, suffering, ageing and death are unavoidable.

This approach is demonstrated in Reynold Price's account of his spinal tumour, *A Whole New Life*. He argues that as a result of his cancer, surgery and radiation-induced paralysis, his body has changed and he has therefore become a different person. He offers advice to 'become someone else, the next viable you – a stripped-down whole and clear-eyed person, realistic as a sawed-off shotgun and thankful for air.' Loved ones 'will be hard at work in the fierce endeavour to revive your old self, the self they recall with love and respect.' He argues that a new body calls for a new self, and the efforts of loved ones to turn the clock back must be resisted.[22] This link between self and body goes one step further than that described by McWhinney, who argued that illness divorces the body from self:

> In health, the body and the self are one: we *are* our bodies. In sickness, the body becomes something other than the self, something alien, over which the self has limited control.[6]
>
> (p. 87)

Howard Brody also argues in *Stories of Sickness* that life plans have to be altered, and that this should be done without damaging self-confidence:

> The successful accomplishment of a life plan depends on a good deal of luck; and if one is prevented from accomplishing a life plan owing to illness or some other major factor outside of one's control, then no diminution of self-respect is warranted.
>
> The point to be taken is that even radical revision in one's life plan occasioned by illness need not in the end lead to loss of self-respect, however difficult emotionally the transition phase may be.[12]
>
> (p. 56)

Accepting the inevitability of change does not stop feelings of grief being aroused, with the attendant emotions of shock, anger, denial and depression. Nor does the receiving of illness mean passive or fatalistic inaction. The process becomes one of positive and conscious adjustment. For the sick person, therefore, there is work to be done. Kelly has described four major tasks:

1   technical management of the illness … taking medication, coping with colostomies, etc.
2   managing thoughts and feelings and maintaining self-respect
3   maintaining interpersonal relationships … renegotiation of roles and responsibilities may be required
4   making sense of the illness … so the person can adjust and move on.[13]

(p. 53)

Time for reflection in illness is often not hard to find. Woolf describes her experience as follows:

> Directly the bed is called for, or sunk deep among pillows in one chair, we raise our feet even an inch above the ground on another, we cease to be soldiers in the army of the upright; we become deserters. They march to battle. We float with the sticks on the stream; helter-skelter with the dead leaves on the lawn, irresponsible and disinterested and able, perhaps for the first time for years, to look round, to look up – to look, for example, at the sky.[15]
>
> (p. 14)

Energy for reflection is often lacking while the worst of the discomfort of illness persists, although those with a terminal illness have no other option. In the thick of illness, hope is frequently lost:

> The posture, the passivity of the patient lasts as long as the doctor orders, and its end cannot be envisaged until the very moment of rising. And this moment cannot be anticipated, or even thought of, even hoped for. One cannot see, one cannot conceive, beyond the limits of one's bed. One's mentality becomes wholly that of the bed, or the grave.[5]
>
> (pp. 54–5)

Kleinman acknowledges this problem, but offers the possibility of transcendence:

> The moral lesson illness teaches is that there are undesired and undeserved pains that must be lived through, that beneath the façade of bland optimism regarding the natural order of things, there is a deeper apprehension of a dark, hurtful stream of negative events and troubles. Change, caprice and chaos, experienced in the body, challenge what order we are led to believe – need to believe – exists. Disability and death force us to reconsider our lives and our world. The possibility for human transformation, immanent or transcendent, sometimes begins with this disconcerting vision.[4]
>
> (p. 98)

Energy for reflection is more likely if recovery takes place. Sacks writes:

> I had no idea what to make of these effects, and entertained fears that I might never recover. I found the abyss a horror, and recovery a wonder; and I have since had a deeper sense of the horror and wonder which lurk behind life and which are concealed, as it were, behind the usual surface health.[4]
>
> (p. vii)

The sense of recovery is an uplifting experience, and even if suffering itself is not ennobling, recovery from it certainly is. Sacks describes the first stirrings:

> Not only was there some lifting of the hopelessness that weekend, but a

curious sort of lightness and gaiety of spirit. There was the sense of a possible convalescence. A sense of renewal grew in me.[4]

(p. 87)

Music was a critical factor in Sacks' recovery:

And there was music, a new radio, when I returned to my room – wonderful Purcell, *Dido and Aeneas* – and this too, like the wind and the sun and the light, came like a heavenly refreshment to my senses. I felt bathed in the music, penetrated by it, healed and quickened through and through: divine music, spirit, message and messenger of life!

I suddenly fell into a deep blissful sleep: sleeping in trust, cradled in God's arms. A deep, deep, and in itself healing, sleep – my first proper rest since the day of the accident – my first sleep uninterrupted by hideous nightmares and phantoms. The sleep of innocence, of forgiveness, of faith and hope renewed.[4]

(p. 94)

Recovery may be an experience of great joy, worthy of a grateful hymn:

I felt aflame with amazement, gratitude, joy – aflame with love, worship, praise.

... I was flying with joy – a joy which was to last, and deepen, for six weeks, which transformed, and transfigured the world, and made everything a new wonder and festivity.

I was no longer the only one in the world, as perhaps every patient thinks in the ultimate solitude of illness.

A pure and intense joy, a blessing, to feel the sun on my face and the wind in my hair, to hear birds, to see, touch and fondle the living plants.

I closed my eyes and murmured a prayer of thanksgiving and praise. Who cared if there was really any Being to pray to? What mattered was the sense of giving thanks and praise, the feeling of a humble and grateful heart.

This peacefulness had a quality of thanksgiving and praise, a kind of silent, holy intensity; but a silence which was also thanksgiving and song. I felt the grass, the trees, the heath all round me, the whole earth, all creatures, issuing forth in praise. I felt all the world itself was one vast hymn – and that my own peaceful soul was part of it.

We had known sickness as one knows evil or terror, and now sought for health, the restored balance of being, as one seeks for goodness or truth.

For myself, now, liberated, released, emergent from the dark night and abyss, there was an intoxication of light and love and health.[4]

(pp. 118–44)

There are many creative hymns of recovery, and both André Gide's *Fruits of the Earth* and John Donne's *Devotions* fit within this category. Gide writes:

From that day onward every moment brought me its freshness as an ineffable gift, so that I lived in an almost perpetual state of passionate wonder.[2]

(p. 28)

This euphoria and ecstasy cannot last unchanged for ever, and return to the land of the healthy can be a delicate affair, where life picks up its rhythm if not its complete rhyme:

> *Hallowed Be Thy Name*
> Rays of winter sun,
> Songs of wind,
> The absolution of rain ...
> A cheek with no tears.
> Balm of trodden peat,
> Harmony of leaves,
> The forgiveness of mist ...
> A psalm with no grief.
>
> Clouds of unknowing,
> Trespass of will,
> The head without vice ...
> A sonata with no form.
> Words of straight comfort,
> A painless soul,
> The kingdom of glory ...
> A poem with no rhyme.
>
> Peter Barritt

Illness causes us to change, and this change can prove threatening to the healthy. Sacks was lucky enough to go into that vanishing commodity, the convalescent ward:

> If we, freshly sick, could not face the world, the world could not face us, with our lineaments of sickness and affliction. We inspired horror and fear – I saw this quite clearly – and for the world's sake, no less than our own, could not be let out. We had been stamped, with the stigmata of patients, the intolerable knowledge of affliction and death, the intolerable knowledge of passivity, lost nerve, and dependence – and the world does not care to be reminded of such things.[4]
>
> (p. 127)

Healthcare professionals who become ill are changed, too, usually for the better as far as their patients are concerned. As a neurologist, Sacks was more impressed by the wisdom of patients about their illness than by that displayed by their doctors:

> There is among doctors, in acute hospitals at least, a presumption of stupidity in their patients. And *no one* was 'stupid', no one is stupid, except the fools who take them as stupid. Working in a chronic hospital with the same patients for years, one gains a greater respect for them – for their elemental human wisdom, and the special 'wisdom of the heart'.[4]
>
> (p. 132)

Sacks considered illness a great opportunity for the healthcare professional:

I saw that one must oneself *be* the patient, a patient among patients, that one must enter both the solitude and the community of patienthood, to have any real idea of what 'being a patient' means, to understand the immense complexity and depth of feelings, the resonances of the soul in every key – anguish, rage, courage, whatever – and the thoughts evoked, even in the simplest practical minds, because as a patient one's experience *forces* one to think.[4]

(p. 132)

Sacks has had an extraordinary career as a neurologist and writer, and perhaps his early misadventures have contributed to the keenness of his observation and the warmth of his heart:

My adventure was ending. But I knew that something momentous had happened, which would leave its mark, and alter me, decisively, from now on. A whole life, a whole universe, had been compressed into these weeks: a density of experience neither given to, nor desired by, most men; but one which, having happened, would refashion and direct me.[4]

(p. 152)

References

1   Donne J (1624, reprinted 1959) *Devotions Upon Emergent Occasions and Several Steps in My Sickness.* Ann Arbor, University of Michigan Press, MI.

2   Gide A (1949, reprinted 1970) *Fruits of the Earth.* Penguin, Harmondsworth.

3   Sontag S (1983) *Illness as Metaphor.* Penguin, Harmondsworth.

4   Sacks O (1986) *A Leg to Stand On.* Pan Books, London.

5   Kleinman A (1988) *The Illness Narratives: suffering, healing and the human condition.* Basic Books, New York.

6   McWhinney I (1989) *A Textbook of Family Medicine.* Oxford University Press, New York.

7   Cassell E (1985) *The Healer's Art.* MIT Press, Cambridge, MA.

8   Tolstoy L (1887, reprinted 1995) *The Death of Ivan Ilyich.* Penguin Books, Harmondsworth.

9   Quoted in Heath I (1995) *The Mystery of General Practice.* Nuffield Provincial Hospitals Trust, Guildford.

10 Mann T (1924, reprinted 1960) *The Magic Mountain.* Penguin Books, Harmondsworth.

11 Berger J and Mohr J (1997) *A Fortunate Man.* Vintage Books, New York.

12 Frank A (1997) *The Wounded Storyteller.* University of Chicago Press, Chicago.

13 Barnes C, Mercer G and Shakespeare T (1999) *Exploring Disability: a sociological introduction.* Polity Press, Cambridge.

14 Helman C (1990) *Culture, Health and Illness.* Butterworth-Heinemann, Oxford.

15 Woolf V (1948) *The Moment and Other Essays.* Harcourt Brace Jovanovich, New York.

16 Bauby J (1998) *The Diving-Bell and the Butterfly.* Fourth Estate, London.

17 Elliott C (ed.) (2001) *Slow Cures and Bad Philosophers.* Duke University Press, Durham, NC.

18 Gorovitz S (1982) *Doctors' Dilemmas: moral conflict and medical care.* Macmillan, New York.

19 Hauerwas S (1988) *Suffering Presence – Theological Reflections on Medicine, the Mentally Handicapped and the Church.* T & T Press, Edinburgh.

20 Kafka F (1915, reprinted 1996) *Metamorphosis.* Dover Publications, New York.

21 Brody H (1987) *Stories of Sickness.* Yale University Press, New Haven, CT.

22 Price R (1994) *A Whole New Life.* Atheneum, New York.

Further reading

- Bauby J (1998) *The Diving-Bell and the Butterfly.* Fourth Estate, London.
- Brody H (1987) *Stories of Sickness.* Yale University Press, New Haven, CT.
- Donne J (1624, reprinted 1959) *Devotions Upon Emergent Occasions and Several Steps in My Sickness.* Ann Arbor, University of Michigan Press, MI.
- Gide A (1949, reprinted 1970) *Fruits of the Earth.* Penguin, Harmondsworth.
- Kafka F (1915, reprinted 1996) *Metamorphosis.* Dover Publications, New York.
- Kleinman A (1988) *The Illness Narratives: suffering, healing and the human condition.* Basic Books, New York.
- Sacks O (1986) *A Leg to Stand On.* Pan Books, London.
- Sontag S (1983) *Illness as Metaphor.* Penguin, Harmondsworth.
- Tolstoy L (1887, reprinted 1995) *The Death of Ivan Ilyich.* Penguin Books, Harmondsworth.

CHAPTER 6

Chronic illness and the sociology of disability

When Gregor Samsa awoke from troubled dreams one morning, he found that he had been transformed in his bed into an enormous bug. He lay on his back, which was as hard as armour, and, when he lifted his head a little, he saw his belly – rounded, brown, partitioned by arch-like ridges – on top of which the blanket, ready to slip off altogether, was just barely perched. His numerous legs, pitifully thin in comparison to the rest of his girth, flickered helplessly before his eyes.

Franz Kafka, *The Metamorphosis*[1]

I also learned that the cripple must be careful not to act differently from what people expect him to do. Above all they expect the cripple to be crippled, to be disabled and helpless, to be inferior to themselves, and they will become suspicious and insecure if the cripple falls short of these expectations.

F Carling, *And Yet We Are Human*[2]

The long-term physically impaired are neither sick nor well, neither dead nor fully alive, neither out of society nor wholly in it. They are human beings but their bodies are warped or malfunctioning, leaving their full humanity in doubt. They are not ill, for illness is transitional to either death or recovery. ... The sick person lives in a state of social suspension until he or she gets better. The disabled spend a lifetime in a similar suspended state. They are neither fish nor fowl; they exist in partial isolation from society as undefined, ambiguous people.

R Murphy, *The Body Silent*[3]

One day, for example, I can find it amusing, in my forty-fifth year, to be cleaned up and turned over, to have my bottom wiped and swaddled like a newborn's. I even derive a guilty pleasure from this total lapse into infancy. But the next day, the same procedure seems unbearably sad, and a tear rolls down through the lather a nurse's aide spreads over my cheeks.

Jean-Dominique Bauby, *The Diving-Bell and the Butterfly*[4]

Introduction

In the last chapter we examined reactions to acute illness and the long-term effects that these can have on individuals. It is time now to progress to illnesses that are currently incurable but which not are immediately life-threatening. In Western societies these chronic illnesses dominate the work of healthcare professionals. Included in this group are congenital abnormalities, degenerative diseases that accompany ageing or bodily abuse, arteriosclerosis, the autoimmune illnesses, the allergic conditions, genetic diseases, and those forms of cancer that are treatable but not curable.

Most chronic diseases are multi-factorial, caused by the interplay of genetic predisposition, personal behaviour and environmental triggers. Infections have a major role in the causation of chronic illness in traditional cultures, where lack of money and refrigeration facilities mean that immunisation against preventable illnesses, such as polio, is not feasible. Infection in the industrialised world is still an important factor in some chronic neurological illnesses (e.g. multiple sclerosis) and probably in some rheumatological illnesses, too. Where illness causes inability to perform tasks that most healthy people consider to be normal, the individual suffers from impairment. Not all impairments are caused by illness, of course. Environmental damage and accidents are two other crucial causes of impairment. Many patients with impairments do not feel ill and cannot be helped significantly, or maybe at all, by healthcare professionals. The relationship between impairment and disability will be examined later in this chapter.

Reactions to chronic illness

Doctors, probably more than other healthcare professionals, particularly enjoy curing people. There is nothing a doctor likes better than heroically charging about with defibrillator paddles. No self-respecting actor dies on screen these days without learning how to mimic the joy of 200 joules of electricity coursing through the veins. Failing this, being up to your elbows in blood comes a close second. This should come as no surprise. What can be a greater privilege for a human being than to save the life of another? Can any experience compare to pulling a baby's body out through an incision in a uterus that is pumping blood like a fountain? These opportunities can occur at any time and in any place. Once I successfully resuscitated a woman as my wife and I were strolling into Glyndebourne Opera. As the poor woman was sprawled, by now topless, on the path in the twilight receiving her fifth electric shock courtesy of St John Ambulance, the rest of the audience filed politely by with eyes forward in the tradition of the cultured. This episode proved to be a turning point for this woman, in more ways than one. Once the paramedics finally stopped getting lost in the Sussex countryside, we moved on to watch Mozart's *Don Giovanni*.

The motivation to save the lives of others is not confined to medicine, being shared by countless other occupations and any citizen who donates or works for charity, trains in basic life support or turns out in a lifeboat or mountain/caving rescue team. The problem with saving life for healthcare professionals is that caring for those we cannot cure can be considerably less exciting. Indeed, in preventive care things get positively dull. For example, when a primary care team is working well nothing appears to be happening. People are busy not having strokes or heart attacks, not getting pregnant by mistake, not committing suicide, not complaining or taking legal action, and not getting upset because of delayed or missed diagnoses. This is approximately as exciting as watching paint dry. It is only when a healthcare professional with dubious motivation or poor clinical skills turns up that circumstances change – and that difference, in my experience, is sudden and dramatic.

This lack of excitement can quickly be translated into boredom, and is then easily detected by the chronically ill. There is also our inherent desire to be of help to others, in itself a noble enough goal, but counter-productive if its frustration cannot be tolerated. To have nothing to offer a fellow human being who is suffering, apart from our support and presence, is difficult. It can be tempting to embark on treatments that have no hope of success. These factors may lie at the heart of problems that occur between patients with chronic illness or impairments and their professional attendants.

Personal reactions to chronic illness are far from straightforward. As previously noted in Chapter 3, good health is usually taken for granted and only appreciated once it has been lost. The psychological reaction to chronic illness and impairment has been likened by some to the bereavement reaction, with its phases of shock, denial, anger, guilt, depression and resolution. However, there are important differences between bereavement and chronic illness/impairment. Bereavement is a reaction to a finite and unchangeable event, and as such tends to run a natural course and resolve with time. Living with a chronic inability to undertake normal activities or with chronic pain or fatigue is a continuous recurrent problem. It is only natural to dream of a magic cure, or to hope to wake one morning with function fully restored. Acceptance suggests that the patient has resolved the situation once and for all, and is no longer harbouring feelings of resentment, envy, anger or hope. This is a medical pipe dream. Kleinman shows us the way in his seminal book *The Illness Narratives*:

> The undercurrent of chronic illness is like the volcano: it does not go away. It menaces. It erupts. It is out of control. One damned thing follows another. Confronting crises is only one part of the total picture. The rest is coming to grips with the mundaneness of worries over whether one can negotiate a curb, tolerate flowers without wheezing, make it to the bathroom quickly enough, eat breakfast without vomiting, keep the level of back pain low enough to get through the workday, sleep through the night, make plans for a vacation, or just plain face up to the myriad of difficulties that make life feel burdened, uncomfortable, and all too often desperate.[5]
>
> (pp. 44–5)

The attitude to chronic illness in the community in which we live naturally influences our own thoughts. Historically, illness tended to be viewed as a punishment, or sometimes a trial, from God. In traditional societies, illness may be viewed as the result of malevolent spirits or neighbours. In a culture of materialism, atheism and individualism, illness or impairment is an affront to personal justice or, at the very least, an unnecessary inconvenience for which someone must be held accountable. For those who have yet to deal with the reality of their inevitable decline and death, the illness presents the person with an outrage to their consciousness (or lack of it).

The reaction to illness shown by family, friends and acquaintances can be unpredictable or at times even bizarre. The healthy may fear contamination or personal upset, or lay the blame firmly at the ill person's feet. Woe betides the ill person who has smoked, drunk, overeaten, fornicated, eaten meat, worked hard or otherwise enjoyed him- or herself. The behaviour of family and friends can prove tactless at best, or cruel and insensitive at worst. This behaviour can sorely try the patience of those who are already overburdened with illness. It can also lead to a conviction, which may be well founded, that only those who suffer the same fate can really understand their predicament. This is the central role that self-help groups fill in supporting patients and helping them to adapt to chronic illness.

The healthcare professional needs to listen to the patient's experience and demonstrate empathy in order to successfully enter the world of chronic illness. Artistic expressions of those who have suffered from these illnesses can also help. We need to understand the omnipresent influence that illness can have on the joys of life. Consider, for example, how a chronic condition such as type 1 diabetes interferes with diet, exercise, flexibility, sex life, and so on. How well we will cope personally with chronic illness when it comes is as unpredictable as how well we might survive torture or imprisonment.

Reactions to impairment

To an extent the concept of 'non-disabled' or 'normal' is an illusion and, if such people exist, they are in a minority. It is important that those who are disabled avoid stereotyping those outside their particular inner circle. In Box 6.1 a list of characteristics of the 'normal' is shown. Pressure to conform to these criteria is especially important for members of royal families, American presidents, despots, dictators and any future son-in-law. Those blessed with normality may be discouraged to hear that, according to Bollas, they have an illness that he calls 'normotic':

> A normotic person is someone who is abnormally normal. He is too stable, secure, comfortable and socially extrovert. He is fundamentally disinterested in subjective life and he is inclined to reflect on the thingness of objects, on their material reality, or on 'data' that relate to material phenomena.[6]
>
> (p. 136)

Box 6.1: Characteristics of the 'normal'

- Young, white, male and heterosexual
- Tall, slim, fit and attractive
- Intelligent, well educated, confident and psychologically robust
- Non-smoking, non-addictive personality
- Emotionally and financially successful
- Physically perfect with all senses intact and no bodily blemish
- Fertile, libidinous and well endowed
- Honest, with no criminal record

Some have argued that consumer societies rely on promoting an obsession with achieving normality – it certainly does no harm to the income of plastic surgeons.

The dream of physical perfection has been going strong since Ancient Egyptian times, through Ancient Greece, into the Renaissance and unswervingly into Hollywood. There is certainly a section of the population for whom chronic illness and impairment happen to 'others' and, in general, to 'losers'. Their instinct is that there is no impairment that cannot be removed by sheer force of will and determination. The 'body-as-temple' approach may offer one area in which individuals exert control over an ever-changing world and establish their personal identity. Alternatively, this could be viewed as just another form of narcissism. Worshipping at the altar of self every Sunday can take place either at the gymnasium or the shopping mall. Shilling writes:

> If one feels unable to exert control over an increasingly complex society, at least one can have some effect on the size, shape and appearance of one's body.[7]

> (p. 7)

The problem with regard to this obsession with diet and exercise, labelled 'body fascism' by some, is intolerance of those with illness or impairment. Perhaps this is just another example, learned in our childhoods, of identifying with the 'in crowd'. We deal with our feelings of inferiority by alienating chosen others, ostracising them, or using them as scapegoats for our fears. Our central concern, whatever our ability or disability, is whether or not we are *loveable* – this is the essence of human vulnerability. As infants and children we have all experienced dependency, bodily and emotional incontinence, stupidity and feelings of ugliness or monstrosity (particularly at puberty). We fear pain, dementia, insanity and disfigurement. Old age threatens a return to childhood dependency and must be resisted at all costs. Alienating those with disability allows us the fantasy of being omnipotent, 'undamaged, whole and good'.[8] Fear and discomfort drive us to prejudice, segregation, discrimination, mockery and bullying.

Not all reactions to impairment are negative. Embarrassment and inquisitiveness are natural, but it is a short step from curiosity to voyeurism. History again shows this to be an ancient pastime – examples include the Hunchback of Notre Dame, Cyrano de Bergerac, Beauty and the Beast and the Ugly Duckling, to name but a few. In Hollywood, few disabled people get to portray their fictional counterparts – at the end we can get the feel-good factor of knowing that Al Pacino isn't really blind, it was only pretend. The freak shows of the early twentieth century have been replaced by an insatiable appetite for 'human-interest' journalism and medical documentaries.[8] Siamese twins, a direct affront to the concept of individuality, are particularly media-worthy.

Impairment often generates feelings of sympathy, empathy and compassion. Disabled people generally do not value pity or a patronising attitude. Professionals need to be conversant with the terminology preferred by those with impairments. Treating fellow humans with dignity and avoiding behaviour that dehumanises are crucial, and can be facilitated by understanding that we are all handicapped in one form or another.

Whatever the cause of our prejudice, negative reactions to those with obvious deformity or disability are a potent factor in the disillusionment that many disabled people feel. Responses to impairment are summarised in Box 6.2.

Box 6.2: Reactions to people with impairments

- Pity
- Sympathy
- Empathy
- Compassion
- Caring
- Embarrassment/discomfort
- Avoidance
- Segregation/exclusion/alienation
- Prejudice/discrimination
- Mockery/bullying/stigma
- Patronising/over-solicitous attitude
- Professional dominance/dehumanisation
- Hostility
- Curiosity/voyeurism/narcissism
- Fear
- Extermination/termination

Sociological models of disability

Sociologists have proposed two models of disability, namely the medical (or individual) model and the social model. The medical model of disability was initially described by British sociologists in the 1980s, when they attempted to develop an alternative way of looking at the causes of disability. The medical model was therefore defined by default rather than by intention, and healthcare professionals may struggle to identify with or relate to this proposed model of how they work.

Sociologists are concerned with institutions and with inequalities within society that result from differences in class or status. Sociology aims to influence political and social attitudes, and both organised conflict and personal protest are seen as legitimate means of effecting social change.[9] Disabled sociologists feel that they have helped with 'the collective empowerment of disabled people' and with publicising critical views of healthcare received by disabled people.[10] Most of the sociologists who worked on the social models of disability were physically handicapped themselves, and their central tenet was that disability as a category could only be understood within a framework, which suggested that it was culturally produced and socially structured.[11]

According to disability academics, the traditional approach to disability is an individual one. The theory put forward is that conventional approaches to impairments rest on the assumption that the individual has suffered a personal tragedy and that every effort must be made to restore that person to their former state. Opportunities for the individual to celebrate their difference from 'normals' are missed. Rehabilitation is seen at times as a relentless and cruel obsession of healthcare professionals with restoring function to normal, whatever the cost in personal pain and humiliation to the disabled person. Doctors who concern themselves with disabled people are parasites interested in personal profit, aggrandisement and holding power over their oppressed disabled patients. Doctors do not listen to or have any interest in their disabled patients, and decisions about management are made without deference to the wishes of the patient. Surgeons perform endless unnecessary operations on the impaired in their futile quest to make the disabled person look more 'normal'. Patients with impairments are expected to accept their impairment graciously, but then to strenuously and courageously overcome their difficulties, rather like Daniel Day Lewis in his Oscar-winning role of Christy Brown in the film *My Left Foot*. Those impaired individuals who fail to achieve great things have less courage and are perhaps responsible for their pitiful lives.[8]

There is a problem in trying to defend a model specifically described in order to launch a revolution against it. It may come as no surprise that the political underpinning of the disability movement has been identified by some as 'Neo-Marxist'.[8] On the other hand, the fact that the architects of the social model are themselves disabled gives their views authenticity and weight. Even if they are perceived as a vocal and unrepresentative minority, it would be churlish to discount their views. Moreover, this challenge to the stranglehold that the medical and allied professions have on the welfare of the disabled deserves serious consideration. How well has the traditional medical approach served those with chronic impairments and what are its limitations?

Successes of the medical model

The orthodox medical approach to a patient with an impairment is to make a diagnosis and then proceed with an attempt to cure or ameliorate the condition. Medical science was often then asked to find ways of preventing the condition from occurring at all. Infectious disease was the major cause of disability in developed societies in the past, and in poor countries it is still the most important aetiological factor. Medical science can take some credit for improvements in this area, although improvements in nutrition, housing, water supply and sanitation have been far more influential.

Important infectious illnesses that causes impairments which can be treated or prevented by medical science include smallpox, tuberculosis, poliomyelitis, rubella, measles, pertussis, meningitis, epiglottitis, osteomyelitis, diphtheria, gonorrhoea, syphilis, malaria, river blindness and HIV.

The prevention of rhesus incompatibility and improvements in obstetric care have reduced perinatal causes of disability. Neonatal care has successfully reduced the death rate from prematurity and increased the viability of extreme prematurity, but the rates of impairment in survivors have remained high, albeit in babies who would previously have died. Routine ultrasound scanning and blood testing in pregnancy have reduced the numbers of live births of babies with major disabilities such as microcephaly and severe spina bifida, although only via the unsatisfactory method of fetal termination. Down's syndrome screening arose more by accident than design as a chance finding on a blood test introduced to detect open neural-tube defects. Selective termination for this condition is even more controversial.

Other medical cures of note include the rectification of deficiency states such as hormone, vitamin and dietary deficiencies. Thyroxine to prevent neonatal brain damage, vitamin D to prevent rickets, and iron to prevent anaemia are just three examples. Medical science is castigated for its obsession with cure, but this accusation ignores the legions of treatment that alleviate but do not banish impairments. Most of the treatments currently prescribed in the Western world would come under this heading. This category includes inhaled steroids in asthma, antidepressants and lithium, antipsychotics, anticonvulsants, anti-anginal and heart failure treatments, L-dopa for Parkinson's disease, insulin for diabetes, oral steroids for rheumatic and other autoimmune illnesses, chemotherapy for cancer and rheumatology, allopurinol for gout, drops to prevent glaucoma, laser treatment for diabetic eye disease, and steroid creams for eczema. Condemnation of this type of medication tends to come from those who are not affected by disease. For example, much criticism is levelled at antidepressant prescribing by those who have never suffered from depression. All patients have the option of stopping long-term medication (and most of us will do so if we can), but there are relatively few people with significant impairment in these categories who decide to forgo the benefits of modern treatment. Curiously (or perhaps not), the same does not always apply to the parents of affected children.

Even in situations where regular medication successfully prevents impairment, the response of both healthcare professionals and the public can be half-hearted. Treatment for preventing stroke and heart disease using anti-hypertensives, aspirin and cholesterol-reducing medication is rarely headline news. Patients with family memories of disability or early death from these diseases (as is often the case) are usually more than willing to take regular medication in order to avoid following in the family footsteps.

As was mentioned earlier, the nature of the medical model described by sociologists and academics may not be easily recognisable to the healthcare professional of today. Indeed, the 'medical model' is generally used as a term of abuse by disability studies theorists.[8] Look at the following description of the medical model according to Bilton et al.,[12] written in 1996.

- Disease is an organic condition: non-organic factors associated with the human mind are considered unimportant or even ignored altogether in the search for biological causes for pathological symptoms.
- Disease is a temporary organic state which can be eradicated or cured by medical intervention.
- Disease is something experienced by the sick individual who is then the object of treatment.
- Disease is treated after symptoms appear; the application of medicine is a reactive healing process.
- Disease is treated in a medical environment – a surgery or a hospital – away from the site where the symptoms first appeared.

In a similar vein, Marks writes:

The implications of the medical model are that all illness and disability, including mental 'illness', is caused by biochemical changes, and the fundamental agent shaping human experience is the biological constitution of the body. The logic suggests that if only we could treat all illnesses and impairments, we could eradicate disability.[8]

(p. 59)

Kraemer goes further to explain why doctors are incapable of inaction in the face of incurability:

The tendency of professionals to 'shut their eyes and go stupid not just because it is painful, but because it is unbearable to see damage and not be able to repair it, not be able to put it right.'[13]

(p. 36)

One of the problems of modern medicine stems from its very success in relieving impairment using artificial, animal or human 'spare parts'. The huge industry that follows a major step forward, such as artificial hip replacement, reflects the enormous levels of impairment in an increasingly ageing population. Joint replacement, open heart surgery, organ transplantation, pacemaker insertion, cataract removal, hearing aids and cochlear implants are all personal triumphs for those who regain function previously lost. The problem with this success is that medicine appears to have a cure for every ill, and the process begins to resemble a factory production line.[8] As hospital doctors have their results scrutinised, there is a natural trend towards increasing specialisation. Most of us can look forward to not one but a whole raft of procedures and operations to alleviate the inevitable degenerative diseases of increasing maturity.

Limitations of the medical model

Clearly the scientific medical method has brought great benefits in terms of preventing, curing or ameliorating impairments, but disabled sociologists have rightly pointed out that an overemphasis on this approach leads to serious shortcomings for disabled people, particularly for those with an untreatable or incurable condition. They argue that so much funding goes to the search for cures that the provision for basic assistance for those with impairments is much lower.[8] In addition, some disabled people feel that treatment from the medical professions is half-hearted because the quality of their lives is prejudged as poor. For example, Mailhot wrote the following in 1995:

> Utilitarian thinking, which sees disabled people's lives as being of less value, forms an implicit (although not acknowledged) assumption in medical practice ... and that, as a consequence, many disabled people live in terror that their illnesses will be treated as an opportunity for 'release' from a painful or difficult life.[14]

(p. 39)

People with impairments often feel abused by the rituals and gaze of the healthcare professions, feeling more like a piece of meat or a collection of malfunctioning organs than a fellow human being. As one disabled adult reported in a survey:

> It did not seem anything out of the ordinary. The way the porter looked inside my nightie and lifted it up and touched me seemed, I think, just like what had been done to me a thousand times before by doctors and other people who wanted to look and prod and poke and talk – all as though I did not exist.[15]

(p. 125)

Healthcare professionals may appear arrogant, oppressive or emotionally detached. Referring to nurses in a psychiatric setting, Spillius writes:

> Since nurses cannot get away from the madness physically, they get away from it emotionally; they develop some form of relationship that locates madness in the patient and sanity in themselves, with a barrier to prevent contamination. ... Talking to patients is dangerous because it threatens to puncture the barrier that keeps sanity and madness in their proper places.[16]
>
> (pp. 604–5)

The medical profession has historic associations with eugenics and forced sterilisations. In Nazi Germany, physicians helped in the mass murders of disabled people and continued to do so for over six months after the liberation of concentration camps. No doctor was ever prosecuted for war crimes.[17] No wonder, then, that some disabled people feel apprehensive about euthanasia. In addition, of course, termination of a fetus with an anticipated impairment is allowed on the grounds that a disabled child places an excessive burden on the mother, family or society. To those disabled with a similar impairment this suggests a general hostility towards their disability. The advance of genetic manipulation and selection raises similar concerns. This view has been summarised by Davis, who stated that this line of approach suggests that 'the earlier a handicapped person is killed off, the better for all concerned.'[18]

Sociologists were critical of the medical model because they felt that it ignored the disabled person's personality, feelings and experience. The psychological reaction to impairment usually describes phases of shock, denial, anger, depression and acceptance (based on the bereavement model), and this model is felt to be stereotypical and condescending. Once-and-for-all acceptance of impairment is probably unrealistic, and the favoured stance for a patient of passive acceptance, gratitude and a cheerful exterior is a tall order indeed. In 1982, Zola wrote:

> It would be nice if, at some point, growing up ends and maturity begins, or if one could say that successful adjustment and adaptation to a particular difficulty has been achieved. For most problems, or perhaps most basic life issues, there is no single time for such a resolution to occur. The problems must be faced, evaluated, re-defined, and re-adapted to, again and again and again. And I knew now that this applied to myself. No matter how much I was admired by others or by myself, there was still much more I had to face. 'My Polio' and 'My Accident' were not just my past; they were part of my present and my future.[19]
>
> (p. 84)

Disability sociologists argue that personal tragedy theory fosters inert subjects who are childlike, dependent, and need professionals to speak on their behalf, decide on their benefits and supervise their psychological adjustment and physical rehabilitation.[20]

They also assert that the individual model fails to take account of the social and economic structures that may have caused disability or which make living with a disability much more difficult. The social model argues that disability results not from an individual impairment or malfunctioning body but from a social environment that is oppressive and exclusive. It was argued that this oppression had an institutional base rather than being a product of the prejudice of individuals.[21]

The social model stemmed from the experience of discrimination, isolation and dependency felt by many disabled people. As a manifesto for political and civic protest, it set its aims clearly as eliminating unnecessary barriers to those with impairments and confronting discrimination against people with impairments. It was designed to take account of the effect that disability has on the person and their family, their income and financial support, their education and employment, their housing, transport and the built environment in which they live, work and spend their free time.[20]

New definitions for impairment and disability were drawn up to counter those previously provided by the medical establishment. The World Health Organization defined handicap as 'a disadvantage for a given individual, resulting from an impairment or disability, that limits or prevents the fulfilment of a role (depending on age, sex, social and cultural factors) for that individual'.[22] In contrast, the Union of the Physically Impaired Against Segregation defined disability as 'the disadvantage or restriction of activity caused by a contemporary social organisation which takes no or little account of people who have physical impairments and thus excludes them from the mainstream of social activities'.[23] In a similar vein, Barnes defined disability as 'the loss or limitation of opportunities to take part in the normal life of the community on an equal level with others due to physical or social barriers'.[24]

The crucial difference between these definitions is the responsibility that society is given to remove disabling barriers in order to allow people with impairments a full role in society. In 1992, Vasey wrote:

> The social model is not about showing that every dysfunction in our bodies can be compensated for by a gadget, or good design, so that everybody can work an 8-hour day and play badminton in the evenings. It's a way of demonstrating that everyone – even someone who has no movement, no sensory function and who is going to die tomorrow – has the right to a certain standard of living and to be treated with respect.[25]
>
> (pp. 42–4)

According to the model donated to medicine by disability sociologists, all disability is viewed as a physiological problem, whereas the social model sees disability as a form of sociological oppression, like ageism, sexism or racism. Certainly it is true that not all disability is caused by illness, and the division between ability and disability is a spectrum and not a clear-cut boundary. The problem for governments is that disability and sickness benefits are either paid or not paid, and even if they are structured as tiered benefits there will always have to be winners and losers and someone to judge how people's function measures up to the stated criteria. In addition, there will always be a small minority of people who feign illness for monetary gain. It was with considerable relief in the UK in the 1990s that family doctors were largely relieved of the burden of making these decisions on behalf of their own patients, as clearly there was a conflict of interest here, and a threat to the harmony of the doctor–patient relationship. The involvement of disabled patients on appeal tribunals for those who have been turned down is another welcome step. In addition, the new system allows the family doctor to lobby the authorities on a patient's behalf if decisions seem unjust. Supporting patients with impairments when housing, employment, benefit, education, transport or access needs are not being met is seen by most healthcare professionals as a reasonable part of their role.

Social model theorists have justifiably attacked the use of disablist and offensive descriptions of impairment and handicap, so that terms like 'moron', 'mental defective' and 'mentally handicapped' have been replaced by 'learning difficulty'. In a similar vein, 'blindness' has been replaced by 'visual impairment'. However, even the disability theorists acknowledge that the use of descriptive language is fraught with difficulty and cultural overtones.[20] There is a tendency for the preferred term to gradually accumulate baggage and negative connotations, so there may always be a need to change it periodically.

One of the other criticisms of the medical model made by disability academics concerned its role in the segregation and institutionalisation of people with impairments. Their argument was that labelling people with impairments as disabled, and then putting professionals in charge of assessing their educational and personal needs, inevitably led to their separation from the community and from mainstream education. Prior to industrialisation, the theory goes, those with impairments worked harmoniously on the land with their families, and it was only when people were required to work efficiently with machines that the disabled were alienated from society and the workplace. The disappearance of the roles of 'beggar' and 'village idiot' appears to be a matter for nostalgic regret.

What seems to be far more important is the massive social change that occurs when people no longer work primarily from home, as they do in agrarian societies. Also ignored is the tendency for some parents to disown impaired children because of the stigma and personal shame attached to them in some cultures. There appears to be a relative lack of historical evidence about this issue. Certainly we know that poverty became a large enough issue in the UK to trigger the Poor Law Amendment Act in 1834. Five categories of poor people who needed support were recognised, namely children, the sick, the insane, 'defectives' and the 'aged and infirm'. In Marxist rhetoric, institutions become weapons of social control for the capitalist ruling class, with professionals acting as their lackeys. Medical imperialism drove healthcare professionals to medicalise social phenomena.[11] To some extent this is a 'chicken-and-egg' argument. Were institutions a reflection of a need to help and house the dispossessed and starving, or a form of capitalist conspiracy? Were people with impairments segregated from society because healthcare professionals were parasites looking for a job, or because the general public wanted the stigma and discomfort of impairment hidden from their view? Perhaps there were elements of both. I suspect that the quality of life of humans with impairments has never been better than it is today, but this is not to argue that there is nothing left to do in order to make those of us with impairments feel valued, worthy and equal to others.

The social model of disability has certainly focused attention on crucial issues for people with impairments. It has acted as a rallying point for disabled people to lobby for political change, to raise public awareness of their problems and to press for their social inclusion. Other advantages claimed by the instigators include an increase in the strength and pride of disabled people, an improvement in the autonomy of and choices for those affected and, through self-help groups and disabled arts projects, a reduction in social isolation. The model stresses the importance of occupation on the financial security and social benefits for disabled people and it has supported legislation to act against occupational discrimination. Accessibility of housing, public transport and places of employment is clearly a crucial aspect of this problem, but so is employer attitude. Disabled applicants are six times more likely to receive a negative response to a job application than non-disabled applicants, even though studies in America and the UK report that disabled employees do not have higher absentee rates or a lower-rated job performance, and that workplace adaptations cost much less than employers anticipated.[20] In the UK, government funding is available for employers who need to provide special modifications or equipment.

Enthusiasts for the social model claim that it encourages independence rather than dependence by enabling disabled people to do things for themselves,[11] and it certainly provides a challenge to professional dominance, aloofness and depersonalisation. The rationale for segregation, institutionalisation and education outside the mainstream system has also been confronted – no bad thing when you read of personal experiences of institutional care:

> As we moved from room to room, I could hear the shuffling of feet, the muted voices, the tap-tap-tapping of canes. Here was the safe, segregated world of the sightless – a completely different world, I was assured by the social worker, from the one I had just left… I was expected to join this world. To give up my profession and to earn my living making mops. The Lighthouse would be happy to teach me how to make mops. I was to spend the rest of my life making mops with other blind people, eating with other blind people, dancing with other blind people. I became nauseated with fear, as the picture grew in my mind.[26]
>
> (pp. 37–8)

To a large extent the move away from institutions had occurred well before the social model was formulated. In the 1980s in the UK less than 2% of the estimated 360 000 disabled children lived in institutions.[27] The drive towards care in the community also has its problems, as it is frequently under-funded and may cause enormous stress both for the disabled person and for their family. In circumstances where the family is unwilling or unavailable to provide care, community care can be a lonely existence, particularly for the housebound and the mentally ill. When there is no alternative to institutional care, a trend towards smaller informal units in residential areas has become the norm. Finding staff for these units is difficult, partly because State funding levels often mean low wages, and partly because the work can be both physically and emotionally draining. In 1978, Jones and colleagues wrote:

> To the politician, 'community care' is a useful piece of rhetoric; to the sociologist, it is a stick to beat institutional care with; to the civil servant, it is a cheap alternative to institutional care which can be passed to the local authorities for action – or inaction; to the visionary, it is a dream of the new society in which people really do care; to social services departments, it is a nightmare of heightened public expectations and inadequate resources to meet them.[28]
>
> (p. 114)

The inclusion of children with disabilities in mainstream education is another positive step, and this may help to remove ignorance and stereotyping in the younger generation, as well as offering a broader curriculum and a greater variety of teaching staff. The social model aims to explore the personal experiences of the disabled in terms of sexual and marital relationships, housework, abuse/violence and gender differences. Disabled women may be viewed as both uneconomic to employ and unfit for motherhood. Frequently seen as asexual, they are generally deemed to be unsuitable for, or incapable of, motherhood.[11]

A model of disability for the twenty-first century

Does the medical model of disability have any role in the twenty-first century? It might be fair to say that the model represents an approach to disability that was most prevalent in the nineteenth and first half of the twentieth century. Rather than sweeping it away with the social model, itself very much a product of the 1980s, it might be wise to look at the limitations of the social model before seeking the nirvana of disability theories, which is destined to be labelled the holistic model, whether it likes it or not.

The major drawback of the social model is that it ignores the feelings and sensibilities of the human beings involved. It is natural for those of us with disabilities to feel angry, bitter and envious of the able. We may resent the need for help from others or be unable to accept such help graciously. If the medical model focuses unduly on the impairment, then the social theory concentrates too heavily on the social environment, and neither gives enough consideration to the emotional experience.[29] Oliver Sacks writes honestly of his experience of neurological damage to his left leg after a climbing accident. During his convalescence he watched schoolboys playing rugby:

> I was surprised and appalled at a spasm of hate in myself. I hated their health, their strong young bodies. I hated their careless exuberance and freedom – their freedom from the limitations which I felt so overwhelmingly in myself. I looked at them with virulent envy, with the mean rancour, the poisonous spite, of the invalid, and turned away: I could bear them no longer. Nor could I bear my own feelings, the revealed ugliness of myself.[30]
>
> (p. 136)

The construction of the social model by academics and sociologists with disabilities is both a strength and a weakness. Enthusiasts may be dogmatic and uncompromising. As Goffman noted:

> Representatives are not representative, for representation can hardly come from those who give no attention to their stigma, or who are relatively unlettered.[31]
>
> (p. 40)

> First, in making a profession of their stigma, native leaders are obliged to have dealings with representatives of other categories, and so find themselves breaking out of the closed circle of their own kind. Instead of leaning on their crutch, they get to play golf with it, ceasing, in terms of social participation, to be representative of the people they represent.[31]
>
> (p. 39)

Disabled activists are predominantly white, male, Western, middle-class intellectuals with a static physical disability who use wheelchairs and live independently.[8] The social model remains largely silent about those with learning, emotional, communication and psychiatric difficulties. Apsis claims that 'people with learning difficulties face discrimination in the disability movement' partly, he claims, because those in the movement fear being labelled as 'stupid, thick, mental and mad' by the non-disabled public.[8] The social model puts the onus on the disabled person to 'fight the system' and to be confrontational. It is less relevant to those who have no possibility of living independently, to those with progressive disease, and to those who enjoy a good relationship with healthcare professionals whose help they value and admire.

In the social model there is discrimination against, and stereotyping of, healthcare professionals. All concern, helping, caring, altruism and charitable work for others can be viewed negatively (and often is). The disability movement is prejudiced against and makes assumptions about the human qualities of healthcare professionals. For disability academics to accuse healthcare professionals of being 'parasites' seems curiously ironic. The feelings engendered in the public and the healthcare professions by relating to people with impairments are either ignored or viewed pessimistically. Understanding the emotions of pity, sympathy, empathy and compassion in the role of caring is challenging work, and disabled people need to be involved enthusiastically and sensitively with this. Goffman quotes examples of disabled people who comprehend the issues:

> I think it is not the responsibility of society to understand the cerebral palsied, but rather it is our duty to tolerate society and, in the name of chivalry, forgive and be amused by its folly. I find it a dubious honour, but challenging and entertaining. Putting obviously disturbed or curious people at ease before they have a chance to complicate a situation places the handicapped in a role superior to that of the agitators and adds to the human comedy. But this is something it takes a very long time to learn.[31]
>
> (p. 142)

> If the cripple wants the ice to be broken, he must admit the value of help and allow people to give it to him. Innumerable times I have seen the fear and bewilderment in people's eyes vanish as I have stretched out my hand for help, and I have felt life and warmth stream from the helping hands I have taken. We are not always aware of the help we may give by accepting aid, that in this way we may establish a foothold for contact.[2]
>
> (pp. 67–8)

This is not to say that healthcare professionals cannot strive to improve their understanding of, or communication with, those with impairments. Our psychological reactions to impairments are complex, reminding us of our inevitable decline into vulnerability, dependency and senility (if we get to live that long). There are elements of voyeurism, sadism and narcissism in our reactions, and these can quickly be converted into the more comfortable reactions, of guilt and desire to secure forgiveness.[8] Most of us are unsure how to behave when faced with people with obvious impairments. We may be over-anxious not to patronise, or we may feel simply overwhelmed by their suffering. As children we are taught 'not to stare', and as adults we are unsure whether 'to mention or not to mention.' People with hidden impairments such as impotence, enuresis and mental illness face the same dilemma of when and to whom they disclose.

Healthcare professionals may enjoy working with disabled people due to a number of worthy and legitimate motives. Helping those less fortunate than themselves can remind the able-bodied to appreciate their own good fortune. Some of the most courageous and inspiring humans we meet in our work have coped with dreadful adversity. Sacks writes of his life as a neurologist prior to his accident:

> The patients I work with are chronically ill. They have, they know they have, little or no hope of recovery. Some of them show a transcendent humour and gallantry, an unspoilt love and affirmation of life. But others are bitter, virulent, envenomed – great haters, great spiters, murderous, demonic. It is not the sickness but the person that shows here, his collapse or corruption with the cruelties of life. If we have youth, beauty, blessed gifts, strength, if we find fame, fortune, favour, fulfilment, it is easy to be nice, to turn a warm heart to the world. But let us be disfavoured, disfigured, incapacitated, injured; let us fall from health and strength, from fortune and favour; let us find ourselves ill, miserable and without clear hope of recovery – then our mettle, our moral character, will be tried to the limit.[30]
>
> (pp. 137–8)

The more the professional listens to the impaired person, the more impressed they are likely to be. The ability to remain cheerful and just to keep going against massive odds can be both astonishing and humbling. Kleinman writes:

> Few of us are heroes in the grand sense; but in a small, quiet way and in a moral rather than a military sense, there are real heroes among the chronically ill.[5]
>
> (pp. 144–5)

Irrespective of models, there are some grounds for optimism about the future for disabled people. As life expectancy improves, more and more impairment in the population will become the norm. In view of pension shortfalls, the days of early retirement look numbered, and both society and employers will have to come to terms with flexibility and accessibility. The growth in the proportion of impaired people will give this section of society both commercial and political clout. Information and other technology will increasingly facilitate employment from home for those who are housebound. Society, with or without protest movements, is becoming increasingly pluralist and aware of the need for personal dignity, autonomy and respect. Post-modernity emphasises the existence of multiple realities, discontinuity and difference, while also challenging the notion of traditional authority and hierarchies of knowledge.[20] Sociology will continue to have a role in these processes – it does not mean replacing 'error' with 'unquestionable truth' but its intention is to critically scrutinise beliefs and practices that would otherwise be maintained without examination.[32]

References

1   Kafka K (1915, translated and reprinted 1996) *The Metamorphosis.* Dover Publications, New York.
2   Carling F (1962) *And Yet We Are Human.* Chatto & Windus, London.
3   Murphy R (1987) *The Body Silent.* Dent, London.
4   Bauby J (1997) *The Diving-Bell and the Butterfly.* Fourth Estate, London.
5   Kleinman A (1988) *The Illness Narratives.* Basic Books, New York.
6   Bollas C (1987) *The Shadow of the Object: psychoanalysis of the unthought known.* Free Association Books, London.
7   Shilling C (1993) *The Body and Social Theory.* Sage, London.
8   Marks D (1999) *Disability.* Routledge, London.
9   Turner B (1987) *Medical Power and Social Knowledge.* Sage, London.
10 Oliver M (1998) Theories of disability in health practice and research. *BMJ.* 317: 1446–9.
11 Oliver M (1990) *The Politics of Disablement.* Macmillan Education, Basingstoke.
12 Bilton T, Bonnet L *et al.* (1996) *Introductory Sociology.* Macmillan, London.
13 Kraemer S (1994) The body goes mad. In: A Erskine and D Judd (eds) *The Imaginative Body.* Jason Aronson, Northvale, NJ.
14 Mailhot A (1995) Quoted in Marks D: Any Choice You Want: As Long As It's Death. *The Disability Rag and Resource.* January/February.
15 Kennedy M (1996) Sexual abuse and disabled children. In: J Morris (ed.) *Encounters with Strangers.* Women's Press, London.
16 Bott Spillius E (1990) Asylum and society. In: E Trist and H Murray (eds) *The Social Engagement of Social Science. Volume 1.* University of Pennsylvania Press, Philadelphia.
17 Gallagher H (1985) *By Trust Betrayed: patients and physicians in the Third Reich.* Henry Hold, London.
18 Davis A (1987) Women with disabilities: abortion or liberation. *Disabil, Handicap Soc.* **2**: 287.
19 Zola I (1982) Social and cultural disincentives to independent living. *Arch Phys Med Rehabil.* **63**: 84.
20 Barnes C, Mercer G and Shakespeare S (1999) *Exploring Disability : a sociological introduction.* Polity Press, Cambridge.
21 Oliver M (1998) Theories of disability in health practice and research. *BMJ.* 317: 1446–9.
22 World Health Organization (1980) *International Classification of Impairments, Disabilities and Handicaps.* World Health Organization, Geneva.

23 Union of the Physically Impaired Against Segregation (UPIAS) (1976) *Fundamental Principles of Disability*. UPIAS, London.

24 Barnes C (1994) *Disabled People in Britain and Discrimination: a case for anti-discrimination legislation*. Hurst and Company, London.

25 Vasey S (1992) A response to Liz Crow. *Coalition*. **September**: 42–4.

26 Keitlen T (1962) *Farewell to Fear*. Avon, New York.

27 Smyth M and Robus N (1989) *OPCS Surveys of Disability in Great Britain. Report 5 –the financial circumstances of disabled children living in private households*. HMSO, London.

28 Jones K, Brown J and Bradshaw J (1978) *Issues in Social Policy*. Routledge and Kegan Paul, London.

29 McDermot J (1986) *Streams of Experience: reflections on the history and philosophy of American culture*. University of Massachusetts Press, Amherst, MA.

30 Sacks O (1986) *A Leg to Stand On*. Picador, London.

31 Goffman E (1968) *Stigma: notes on the management of spoiled identity*. Pelican, Harmondsworth.

32 Bauman Z (1990) *Thinking Sociologically*. Blackwell, Oxford.

Further reading

- Barnes C, Mercer G and Shakespeare T (1999) *Exploring Disability: a sociological introduction*. Polity Press, Cambridge.
- Bauby J (1998) *The Diving-Bell and the Butterfly*. Fourth Estate, London.
- Goffman E (1968) *Stigma: notes on the management of spoiled identity*. Pelican, Harmondsworth.
- Kafka F (1915, translated and reprinted 1996) *The Metamorphosis and Other Stories*. Dover, New York.
- Marks D (1999) *Disability: controversial debates and psychological perspectives*. Routledge, London.
- Oliver M (1990) *The Politics of Disablement*. Macmillan, Basingstoke.
- Sacks O (1986) *A Leg to Stand On*. Pan Books, London.

CHAPTER 7

Mental illness and the poetry of despair

Poetry demands a man with a special gift for it, or else one with a touch of madness in him.

Aristotle, *Poetics*[1]

For a wounded spirit who can bear?… Imagine what thou canst, fear, sorrow, furies, grief, pain, terror … dismal, ghastly, tedious … it is not sufficient, it comes far short, no tongue can tell, no heart conceive it. 'Tis the epitome of hell.

Robert Burton, *The Anatomy of Melancholy*[2]

If in the midst of life we are in death, so in sanity we are surrounded by madness.

Ludwig Wittgenstein, *Remarks on the Foundations of Mathematics*[3]

Introduction

The experience of mental illness is hard to describe to those who have not been personally affected. The problem of empathising with those who are ill is difficult whatever the illness, but in the case of mental illness it is particularly hard because disorder of the mind often interferes with the processes of consciousness and cognition. For example, the person with depression may think, take decisions and speak with considerable difficulty. In people with disturbance of perception and communication, as in schizophrenia, it can become almost impossible to reach out and share their world. Even if communication is possible, other mental illnesses, such as dementia, can rob the sufferer of memory and understanding. It is this quality of mental illness, whereby it interferes with what most of us treasure as the heart of being human, that strikes dread in the heart. Most of us fear pain, physical suffering and death, but the spectre of losing our reason is, for many, the most terrifying prospect of all. In addition, the effect of mental illness on the patient's family can be devastating.

How can the humanities help us to gain a better understanding of the suffering of those with mental illness? Can they shed any light for those without first-hand experience? Fortunately, the answers to these questions are positive. Mental illness is not an essential ingredient for artistic achievement, but those who have suffered mental illness leave a considerable creative inheritance. This is not to suggest that mental illness necessarily aids creativity. However, it is the artist's lot to illuminate life experiences for the benefit of others. In addition, creativity may facilitate healing.

In this chapter I have concentrated primarily on the poetry of mental illness, particularly depression, which is the commonest and most readily treatable form of mental illness. For the reasons discussed above, creativity in schizophrenia and dementia is seriously impaired by the nature of these disorders, but there are notable exceptions. The painter William Utermohlen has left us a haunting series of self-portraits that document his perceptive and creative decline as Alzheimer's disease wreaked relentless havoc upon him.[4] Poetry is only one way into the world of mental illness. The music of Schumann, Tchaikovsky and Rachmaninov, or the paintings of van Gogh, Munch and Picasso are equally valid routes.

Mental illness and creativity

There is a high incidence of mental illness among artists, and this raises interesting questions about possible links between mental disorders and creativity. Anthony Storr believes that the main criterion which marks out creative individuals is their ability to link the inner world of the subconscious to the outer world with which we are more familiar. In *The Dynamics of Creation*, he argues:

> Man carries with him throughout his life a discontent, varying in degree, but always present, as a consequence of the intrinsic frustrations of his infancy. This drives him to seek symbolic satisfactions: ways of mastering the external world on the one hand, and ways of integrating and coming to terms with his internal world on the other. It is by means of his creativity, both in art and science, that man has survived and achieved so much. His prolonged and unsatisfactory infancy is itself adaptive, since it leaves him with a 'divine discontent' which spurs him on to creative achievement.[5]
>
> (p. 224)

He believes that this is the reason why schizophrenia generally impairs creativity:

> It is in schizophrenia that the inability to make any link between inner and outer worlds is seen in its full malignancy. The schizophrenic becomes 'mad' when he substitutes his inner world for external reality, and it becomes obvious that ordinary people can neither share nor understand his way of looking at things.[5]
>
> (p. 245)

Storr believes that creative people are more open, not only to their own deepest and darkest feelings and emotions, but also to impressions and new ideas from the outside world. Discovering and displaying profound thought and emotion helps to define their unique identity. Demonstrating such candour requires honesty and courage, and Storr believes that many artists develop a persona for the public to protect their sensitive inner core. Their creative work, he believes, is their real personality. Storr quotes the composer Aaron Copland:

The serious composer who thinks about his art will sooner or later have occasion to ask himself: why is it so important to my own psyche that I compose music? What makes it seem so absolutely necessary, so that every other daily activity, by comparison, is of lesser significance? And why is the creative impulse never satisfied; why must one always begin anew? To the first question – the need to create – the answer is always the same – self-expression; the basic need to make evident one's deepest feelings about life. But why is the job never done? Why must one always begin again? The reason for the compulsion to renewed creativity, it seems to me, is that each added work brings with it an element of self-discovery. I must create in order to know myself ...[6]

(pp. 40–1)

The division between one's inner and outer worlds creates discontent, and imagination is one means of trying to bridge this gap. Illness, unhappiness or undue isolation in childhood may foster a lively imagination, but also makes mood disorders more likely. Those with acute sensitivity to the needs and feelings of others may be easily wounded by the vagaries of life and human nature. Imaginative effort, says Storr, may not make mankind whole, but 'they constitute his deepest consolations and his greatest glories'.[5]

The artistic contribution of those suffering from manic-depressive illness is particularly large. Some of the characteristics of mania, such as original thinking, heightened sensitivity and increased productivity, can be useful creative tools, although a person in the throes of mania is usually unable to complete artistic work of value because of their restlessness and flight of ideas. Hypomania is associated with increased fluency, confidence and frequency of thoughts. Mania and creativity both function well with little sleep, and both are characterised by emotional intensity and extreme personal conviction. Depression, of course, is associated with completely the opposite and is unlikely to stimulate creativity, except perhaps during the recovery phase. The treatment of manic-depressive illness may prevent much suffering but can also interfere with the creative drive.

Arnold Ludwig studied 1004 deceased men and women who lived during the twentieth century and gained prominence in the arts, the sciences and other social activities. About one-third of eminent poets, musical performers and fiction writers suffered from serious psychological symptoms of some kind as teenagers, a rate that ballooned to about 75% when they reached adulthood. More than 50% of writers, painters and composers experienced periods of serious depression, at least twice the rate observed in eminent persons in other fields. Mania appeared most often in actors, poets, architects and non-fiction writers, with lifetime rates ranging from 11% to 17%, compared with a mere 1% of the general population.[7]

In his book *Solitude*, Anthony Storr argues that creativity helps to protect the individual against the effects of depression:

The creative process can be a way of protecting the individual against being overwhelmed by depression, a means of regaining a sense of mastery in those who have lost it, and, to a varying extent, a way of repairing the self damaged by bereavement or by the loss of confidence in human relationships which accompanies depression from whatever cause.[6]

(p. 143)

Mental illness and the poets

Kay Redfield Jamison has found that poets have a particularly high rate of serious mood disorder, with 50% being hospitalised or receiving antidepressants, electro-convulsive therapy (ECT) or lithium. She found their suicide rate to be six times higher than normal.[9] When Robert Burton wrote *The Anatomy of Melancholy* in 1621 he claimed that 'All poets are mad, a company of bitter satirists, detractors, or else parasitical applauders.' Clearly he exaggerated the incidence, but he did have a point.[10] Indeed, some poets have been reluctant to receive treatment for mood disorders in case they lose their creative drive. Rainer Maria Rilke is reputed to have concluded his first and only session of psychotherapy with the statement 'If my devils leave me, I am afraid my angels will take flight as well.'

I suspect that some people do not decide to become poets, but rather that poetry imposes itself on some people. Pablo Neruda writes:

> And it was at that age ... Poetry arrived
> in search of me. I don't know, I don't know where
> it came from, from winter or a river.[11]
>
> (p. 13)

Poems appear mysteriously, sometimes whole, but more usually in pieces that need to be put together with care and love. The life of the poet is revelatory at times, but rarely easy. William Carlos Williams wrote:

> We are blind and live our lives out in blindness. Poets are damned but they are not blind, they see with the eyes of angels.[12]

Poets are poets whether they like it or not. As with constipated patients or pregnant mothers, there comes a time for pushing. Pablo Neruda writes:

> I do not want to be the inheritor of so many misfortunes.
> I do not want to continue as a root and as a tomb,
> as a solitary tunnel, as a cellar full of corpses,
> stiff with cold, dying with pain.[11]
>
> (p. 19)

A few poets, such as Sylvia Plath and Anne Sexton, decided that enough was enough and committed suicide, but most have not done so. William Wordsworth wrote in *Resolution and Independence* about Chatterton's death:

> By our own spirits we are deified:
> We Poets in our youth begin in gladness;
> But thereof come in the end despondency and madness.[13]
>
> (p. 117)

Dylan Thomas describes the poet's task as follows:

> I hold a beast, an angel and a madman in me, and my enquiry is as to their working, and my problem is their subjugation and victory, downthrow and upheaval, and my effort is their self-expression.[14]
>
> (p. 56)

Poems can be expressions of joy, love or transcendence. This being so, why do poetry and mental illness have such a strong link? Perhaps the link relates to the healing power of creativity referred to earlier. John Berger argues:

> Poems, regardless of any outcome, cross the battlefields, tending the wounded, listening to the wild monologues of the triumphant or the fearful. They bring a kind of peace. Not by anaesthesia or easy reassurance, but by recognition and the promise that what has been experienced cannot disappear as if it had never been. Yet the promise is not of a monument. The promise is that language has acknowledged, has given shelter, to the experience which demanded, which cried out.[15]
>
> (p. 21)

Mental illness and the poems

Distinguished poets who have suffered from mood disorders include Blake, Byron, Clare, Dickinson, Neruda, Sexton, Tennyson, Plath and Roethke, to name but a few. There are at least two good anthologies of poetry that can be recommended which illustrate the poetry of mental distress and salute the courage required to overcome it. These are *Beyond Bedlam*, edited by Ken Smith and Matthew Sweeney,[16] and *We Have Come Through*, edited by Peter Forbes.[17] Most of the poems I have used are contained in one or other of these two collections. For reasons of brevity I have usually quoted extracts rather than complete poems, but hopefully the reader may feel inspired to search out the works in their entirety.

Depression is a difficult illness to describe. I suspect that matters are not helped in the English language by the fact that the word is in everyday use as a term for transient unhappiness. In many ways the term 'nervous breakdown' has more to commend it. The public and healthcare professionals do not pretend to understand what a nervous breakdown entails, unless they have suffered one themselves. Breakdown also has the resonance of a drastic and calamitous event – which depression is. The problem, of course, is that medicine cannot stoop to the level of the common man by using the same terminology. Burton uses the term 'Hell on Earth', and this captures the essence and flavour of depressive illness.

The descent to hell

Depression often starts with feelings of anxiety, extreme tiredness or inability to cope with the demands of life. It appears gradually and, except in its mild form, moves inexorably onward. Appeals for help from healthcare professionals can come late from those who have usually coped well with adversity, and with life in general. There is stigma attached to mental illness in most cultures. In China, for example, a family history of mental illness is a serious impediment to marriage. Depression erodes self-confidence, and as the disease progresses it causes self-loathing, feelings of unworthiness and a sense of great personal failure. Thinking slows down and decision making becomes seriously impaired. Perception of the world and one's future change to unremitting gloom and despondency. The suffering of others, particularly that inflicted by cruelty, war or persecution, is felt acutely. Laughter can be faked, but is not felt. Joy is unknown. Sleep is disturbed and all dreams are nightmares. Sleep and holidays produce no benefit. There is no respite. Feelings of love begin to freeze as the person becomes more and more cocooned in convictions of personal shamefulness. Life problems become insurmountable and conviction grows that life is meaningless and not worth living. Depression of any severity is usually accompanied by suicidal thoughts, however vague they may be.

(Excerpts from) *In Tongues of Men*

I looked through the glass darkly;
It was a poor reflection,
We were puzzled
And the harder we looked,
The darker our soul became.

Our pupils were wide with disease;
Life was a stinking sewer,
We were sorrowful
And the lower we sank,
The worse our excuses seemed.

I read through an arcane book;
Let little children suffer,
We tortured them,
And the more we made them dance in pain,
The faster the piper's tune.

I stared into murky waters;
When the prince of darkness came,
We were entwined
I cut out his heart and half of mine,
Because our faces looked the same.

Peter Barritt

John Clare is a good example of poetry choosing a person. As the son of a farm labourer, his attendance at school was erratic, and he left at the age of 11 years. His enormous poetic output (some 10 000 pages) was heavily edited, partly because of spelling and grammatical problems. His wife and family spent much of their life impoverished, even close to starvation, as a consequence of his poetic affliction. Fame as a 'poetic peasant' beckoned in London for a while, but then dwindled, leaving him with a sense of bitterness as well as a sexually transmitted disease. Insanity followed, and he spent the last 27 years of his life in an asylum. The following poem, *I Am*, was written in Northampton Asylum and is quoted in its entirety:

I Am
I am – yet what I am, none cares or knows;
My friends forsake me like a memory lost:
I am the self-consumer of my woes –
They rise and vanish in oblivions host,
Like shadows in love's frenzied stifled throes
And yet I am, and live – like vapours tost

> Into the nothingness of scorn and noise,
> Into the living sea of waking dreams,
> Where there is neither sense of life or joys,
> But the vast shipwreck of my life's esteems;
> Even the dearest that I love the best
> Are strange – nay, rather, stranger than the rest.
>
> I long for scenes where man hath never trod
> A place where woman never smiled or wept
> There to abide with my Creator God,
> And sleep as I in childhood sweetly slept,
> Untroubling and untroubled where I lie,
> The grass below, above, the vaulted sky.[18]

(pp. 221–2)

The feeling of tiredness and tearfulness is clear in the following extract from Pablo Neruda's poem *Walking Around*:

> It happens that I am tired of being a man.
> It happens that I go into the tailor's shops and the movies
> all shrivelled up, impenetrable, like a felt swan
> navigating on a water of origin and ash.
>
> The smell of barber shops makes me sob out loud.
> I want nothing but the repose either of stones or of wool,
> I want to see no more establishments, no more gardens,
> nor merchandise, nor glasses, nor elevators.
>
> It happens that I am tired of my feet and my nails
> and my hair and my shadow.
> It happens that I am tired of being a man.[19]

There is a feeling of wanting to hide, to withdraw from the world, to climb into a dark warm hole, away from cares and responsibilities. Stevie Smith looks for a soft grey wing in the poem *I Wish*:

> Oh I wish that there were some wing, some wing,
> Under which I could hide my head,
> A soft grey wing, a beautiful thing,
> Oh I wish that there were such a wing,
>
> And then I should suddenly be quite sure
> As I never was before,
> And fly far away, and be gay instead
> Of being hesitating and filled with dread,
> Oh I wish I could find a wing.[20]

Sylvia Plath also seems to wish for rest and escape in the poem *I Am Vertical*:

> It is more natural to me, lying down.
> Then the sky and I are in open conversation,

And I shall be useful when I lie down finally:
Then the trees shall touch me for once, and the flowers have time
for me.[21]

(p. 162)

The sense of being in a cocoon comes through in Stevie Smith's poem *Every Lovely Limb's a Desolation*:

> I feel a mortal isolation
> Wrap each lovely limb in desolation,
> Sight, hearing, all
> Suffer a fall.
>
> I see the pretty fields and streams, I hear
> Beasts calling and birds singing, oh not clear
> But as a prisoner
> Who in a train doth pass
> And through the glass
> Peer;
> Ah me, so far away is joy, so near.[20]

In depression there is a sense of suffocation, a drowning in sorrow and, as in a nightmare, there is nothing that can be done about it. Sufferers describe a vicious cycle or a spiralling down to the depths. Emily Dickinson likened her breakdown to falling:

> I felt a Funeral, in my Brain,
> And Mourners to and fro
> Kept treading – treading – till it seemed
> That sense was breaking through –
>
> And when they were all seated,
> A Service, like a Drum –
> Kept beating – beating – till I thought
> My Mind was going numb –
>
> And then I heard them lift a Box
> And creak across my Soul
> With those same Boots of Lead, again,
> Then Space – began to toll,
>
> As if the Heavens were a Bell,
> And Being, but an Ear,
> And I, and Silence, some strange Race
> Wrecked, solitary, here –
>
> And then a Plank in Reason, broke,
> And I dropped down, and down –
> And hit a World, at every plunge,
> And finished knowing – then –[22]

Reversing the slide downhill in moderate and severe depression is impossible both for the patient and for their loved ones. Wendy Cope describes the frustration of the inability to reach out in her poem *Depression*:

> You lie, snail-like, on your stomach –
> I dare not speak or touch,
> Knowing too well the ways of our kind –
> The retreat, the narrowing spiral.
>
> We are both convinced it is impossible
> To close the distance.
> I can no more cross this room
> Than Zeno's arrow.[23]

For the sufferer, even God seems unable or unwilling to help. Patrick Kavanagh suffered mood disturbances primarily because of drinking problems:

> From a confessional
> The voice of Father Mat's absolving
> Rises and falls like a briar in the breeze.
> As the sins pour in the old priest is thinking
> His fields of fresh grass, his horses, his cows,
> His earth into the fires of Purgatory.
> It cools his mind.
> 'They confess to the fields,' he mused,
> 'They confess to the fields and the air and the sky,'
> And forgiveness was the soft grass of his meadow by the river;
> His thoughts were walking through it now.
>
> His human lips talked on:
> 'My son,
> Only the poor in spirit shall wear the crown;
> Those down
> Can creep in the low door
> On to Heaven's floor.'[24]

(p. 81)

The time in hell

The depths of depression are a life in limbo. All pretence at coping is lost, and time at home or in hospital is needed for the responsibilities of life to be temporarily lifted. The comic and poet Spike Milligan calls for three qualities in those who look after the mentally ill, namely love, understanding and tolerance, of which he believes the first is the most crucial. His poem *Manic Depression* was written while he was an inpatient in Woodside Hospital:

> The pain is too much
> A thousand grim winters
>   grow in my head.
> In my ears
>   the sound of the
>   coming dead

> All seasons, all same
>> all living
>> all pain
> No opiate to lock still
>> my senses.
> Only left, the body locked tenser.[25]

Life becomes a matter of living day by day, praying for a miracle that is promised but seems implausible. Resignation is called for in the poem *Only So Much*:

> There is a maze without a map,
> An eddy without joy,
> A whirlpool spinning drunk with gloom ...
> I made a visit there.
>
> This is the place
> Where no light shines,
> Where laughter's swallowed whole,
> Where only so much loving
> Can lift your aching soul.
>
> Peter Barritt

The sense of resignation to fate comes through in John Clare's sonnet *I Am*:

> I feel I am, I only know I am
> And plod upon the earth as dull and void
> Earth's prison chilled my body with its dram
> Of dullness, and my soaring thoughts destroyed.
> I fled to solitudes from passions dream
> Bur strife pursued – I only know I am.
> I was a being created in the race
> Of men disdaining bounds of place and time –
> A spirit that could travel o'er the space
> Of earth and heaven – like a thought sublime,
> Tracing creation, like my maker, free –
> A soul unshackled like eternity,
> Spurning earth's vain and soul-debasing thrall
> But now I only know I am – that's all.[18]

The place of safety may open the sufferer's eyes to a new world. Listen to Dylan Thomas in *Love in the Asylum*:

> A stranger has come
> To share my room in the house not right in the head,
>> A girl mad as birds
>
> Bolting the night of the door with her arm her plume.
>> Strait in the mazed bed
> She deludes the heaven-proof house with entering clouds

> Yet she deludes with walking the nightmarish room,
>> At large as the dead,
> Or rides the imagined oceans of the male wards.[26]

(p. 56)

Coming to terms with the emotional hurricane of depression requires reflection. Here is an extract from *The Passing Cloud* by Stevie Smith. She was writing from the Royal Bethlehem Hospital in London (known colloquially in the seventeenth century as Bedlam), a hospital that has been caring for the mentally ill since 1377 and which, from the seventeenth to the nineteenth centuries, displayed them for public entertainment:

> I thought as I lay on my bed one night, I am only a passing cloud
> And I wiped the tear from my sorrowful eye and merrily cried aloud
> Oh the love of the Lord is a fearful thing and the love of the Lord is
>> mine
> And what do I care for the sins of men and the tears of our guilty
>> time
> I will sail my cloud in the bright blue sky, in the bright blue sky I sail
> And I look at the sea so merrily swung in the path of the Arctic
>> whale.[20]

I suspect that electroconvulsive therapy (ECT) will become obsolete as antidepressant drugs continue to improve, but the concept of inducing convulsions by applying electricity to the brain adds to the weirdness of mental illness, seeming more at home in a Frankenstein movie than on the ward. In Ken Kesey's book *One Flew Over the Cuckoo's Nest,* ECT is used as a punishment for acts of token rebellion by the inmates, and this only added to the folklore surrounding the treatment. Kesey worked as an orderly on a psychiatric ward when he was writing this book, and his perceptions of this time were heavily influenced by LSD. Nonetheless, the book is an excellent portrayal of the abuse of power by people on one side of a divide treating people on the other side.[28] This dynamic can be witnessed in healthcare, prisons and most institutions, whatever their purpose. Ivor Gurney was both a poet and a musical composer. He suffered from manic-depressive illness and was declared insane in 1922 and admitted to the London Mental Hospital, where he died 15 years later aged 47 years. I assume that he received ECT, although the treatment was only starting to be used in the 1930s. Here is an extract from his poem *To God*:

> Why have you made life so intolerable
> And set me between four walls, where I am able
> Not to escape meals without prayer, for that is possible
> Only by annoying an attendant. And tonight a sensual
> Hell has been put on me, so that all has deserted me
> And I am merely crying and trembling in heart
> For death, and cannot get it. And gone out is part
> Of sanity. And there is dreadful hell within me.
> And nothing helps. Forced meals there have been and
>> electricity

And weakening of sanity by influence
That's dreadful to endure.[29]

The public understands the severity of depression that necessitates ECT – gossip about its use is newsworthy. Here is an extract from *The Volunteer* by Jo Pestel:

My father's had electricity shot through him
and nobody must know.

Will he be blackened like lightning trees
lying sideways in the wetlands?
My huge horse-chestnut father
who'd made my special saddle on his bike
when I was little

'It was voluntary'
My mother whispered of sums
mumbled all night that never added up
of days hunched over the table
his hands ringed in two black tunnels
for his eyes to look through
and not see
'I was at my wits' end'.

So this patient voluntary man crept home
with two rough circles at his temples
where they'd jump-started him.

'It's shingles,' my mother explained
as she hurried past the neighbours.[16]

(p. 115)

Recovery

Poets, of course, never miss an opportunity to break into verse. Even their medication may be celebrated. In an extract from *The Hand of God*, Harry Smart writes:

The hand of God comes to me with a bottle
and the label on the bottle says take two,
Nitrazepam, Temazepam, and sleep.
And who would not be grateful for it,
who profess no need? Only a fool.
I take the medicine God has handed out
and, magically, I sense it start to work.[16]

(p. 98)

The gift of sleep without nightmares is a priceless treasure in depression, and hypnotics have a valuable role to play in the early stages of treatment. The trip to hell is never forgotten, but recovery can be savoured. Elizabeth Jennings writes of her recovery in the following extract from *Into the Hour*:

> I have come into the hour of a white healing.
> Grief's surgery is over and I wear
> The scar of my remorse and of my feeling.
>
> I have come into a sudden sunlit hour
> When ghosts are scared to corners. I have come
> Into the time when grief begins to flower
>
> Into a new love.[31]

Recovery also brings a return of the spirit – the ability to question treatment dogmas. I shall end with an extract from Sophie Hannah's poem *Homeopathy*:

> I did not feel my interests would be served
> by spreading peace where it was not deserved.
> What about standards, justice, right and wrong?
> She said our meeting had gone on too long
>
> and that the remedy that she'd prescribed
> right from the start, if properly imbibed,
>
> erodes those thoughts that play a harmful role
> leaving what's beneficial to the whole
> person (in this case, me). If this is true
> then since I did just what she told me to –
>
> taking my medicine, the right amount
> at the right time – surely she can't discount
>
> the feelings that remain. She should concede
> that these must be exactly what I need
>
> and that my grudge, impassive and immense,
> is good for me, in a holistic sense.
>
> I proved my point like a triumphant kid.
> She laughed a lot. I gave her sixty quid.[17]

(pp. 122–3)

References

1 Aristotle (350BC) *Poetics*. 1455a35.
2 Burton R (1621) *The Anatomy of Melancholy*. Quoted in Kleinman A (1988) *The Illness Narratives*. Basic Books, New York.
3 Wittgenstein L (1956) *Remarks on the Foundations of Mathematics*. Quoted in Elliott C (ed.) (2001) *Slow Cures and Bad Philosophers*. Duke University Press, Durham, NC.

4   Crutch S, Isaacs R and Rossor M (2001) Some workmen can blame their tools: artistic change in an individual with Alzheimer's disease. *Lancet.* 357: 2129–33.

5   Storr A (1993) *The Dynamics of Creation.* Ballantine Books, New York.

6   Copland A (1952) *Music and Imagination.* Oxford University Press, Oxford.

7   Ludwig A (1995) *The Price of Greatness.* Guilford Press, London.

8   Storr A (1997) *Solitude.* Harper Collins, London.

9   Jamison K (1996) *Touched with Fire: manic-depressive illness and the artistic temperament.* Free Press, Old Tappan, NJ.

10 Burton R (1621, reprinted 2002) *The Essential Anatomy of Melancholy.* Dover Publications, New York.

11 Neruda P (1995) *Love Poems.* Harvill Press, London.

12 Williams WC (1955) Introduction to Ginsberg A (1956) *Howl and Other Poems.* City Light Books, San Francisco, CA.

13 Wordsworth W (1989) *William Wordsworth: an anthology.* Jarrold Colour Publications, Norwich.

14 Fitzgibbon C (1965) *The Life of Dylan Thomas.* Little Brown, Boston, MA.

15 Berger J (1991) *And Our Faces, My Heart, Brief as Photos.* Vintage Books, New York.

16 Smith K and Sweeney M (eds) (1997) *Beyond Bedlam.* Anvil Press Poetry, London.

17 Forbes P (ed.) (2003) *We Have Come Through.* Bloodaxe Books, Newcastle upon Tyne.

18 Robinson E and Summerfield G (eds) (1966) *Clare: selected poems and prose.* Oxford Unversity Press, Oxford.

19 Neruda P (1975) Walking around. In: N Taru (ed.) *Selected Poems.* Jonathan Cape, London.

20 Smith S (1985) *Collected Poems.* Penguin Books, Harmondsworth.

21 Plath S (1981) *Collected Poems.* Faber & Faber, London.

22 Frankl R (ed.) (1998) *The Poems of Emily Dickinson.* Harvard University Press, Cambridge, MA.

23 Cope W (1980) *Across the City.* Priapus Press, Berkhamsted, Hampshire.

24 Kavanagh P (1996) *Selected Poems.* Penguin Books, Harmondsworth.

25 Milligan S (2002) *The Essential Spike Milligan.* Fourth Estate, London.

26 Davies W (ed.) (1997) *Dylan Thomas Selected Poems.* Everyman's Poetry, London.

27 Sexton A (1991) *Selected Poems.* Virago, London.

28 Kesey K (1976) *One Flew Over the Cuckoo's Nest.* Penguin Books, Harmondsworth.

29 Kavanagh P (ed.) (1982) *Selected Poems of Ivor Gurney.* Oxford University Press, Oxford.

30 Sexton A (1981) *The Complete Poems of Anne Sexton.* Houghton Mifflin, Boston, MA.

31 Jennings E (2002) *New Collected Poems.* Carcanet Press, Manchester.

Further reading

* Forbes P (ed.) (2003) *We Have Come Through.* Bloodaxe Books, Newcastle upon Tyne.
* Kesey K (1976) *One Flew Over the Cuckoo's Nest.* Penguin Books, Harmondsworth.
* Smith K and Sweeney M (eds) (1997) *Beyond Bedlam.* Anvil Press Poetry, London.
* Storr A (1993) *The Dynamics of Creation.* Ballantine Books, New York.
* Storr A (1997) *Solitude.* HarperCollins, London.

CHAPTER 8

Narratives of abuse

What folly it is that daughters are always supposed to be
In love with papa. It wasn't the case with me
I couldn't take to him at all
But he took to me
What a sad fate to befall
A child of three.

Stevie Smith, Papa Love Baby[1]

Where do I run up against a wall when I look into my own heart? What
is the limit?

Thomas Moore, Care of the Soul[2]

It begins in the time before remembering, when despair felt like a heavy
stone inside of me.

Louise Wisechild, The Obsidian Mirror[3]

... my soul was murdered, my body was raped and whipped, my hopes
were dashed, my dreams were turned into nightmares, my ambitions
were castrated, my intelligence was mocked, and my love of family,
children, friends, and country never had a chance to start.

John Wood, quoted in Trying to Get Some Dignity[4]

When obsidian is polished, it is reflective; a glossy black mirror of
volcanic glass. Looking at myself in an obsidian mirror, I see my face
circled with black. After several minutes of looking into the obsidian,
my eyes turn inward, peering inside myself, meeting the blackness within
me.

Louise Wisechild, The Obsidian Mirror[5]

Introduction

In this chapter attention is focused on one of many important aspects of clinical
work that fail to fit the traditional medical paradigm of disease and cure. Abuse is
one example of human behaviour that brings us face to face with the dark side of
human nature, what Carl Jung called 'The Shadow'. All the cruelty that human
beings demonstrate towards other beings is shadow. Our shadow is unconscious
and includes all that we loathe, deny and repress. Greed, cruelty, murderous thoughts,
intent to abuse or rape, sadism, prejudice and action that we consciously consider
ethically or morally wrong are in our shadow.

Jung believed that the mechanism for exploring our shadow is primarily via its projection on to other people, things and places. We reveal our shadow by revulsion, intolerance of others, creation of scapegoats and persecution of selected groups. The hounding of paedophiles in today's society is a classic example, and the Nazi persecution of Jews is another. By picking on others we reassure ourselves that such impulses occur in 'them' and not 'us'. Until we acknowledge our own dark side, we cannot begin to identify with the evil inside each one of us. Examining personal prejudice and hatred becomes fertile ground for self-discovery, and this is where intimate and small-group learning becomes so important. Particular patients or groups of patients who irritate us are usually resonating with our shadows. The more familiar we become with our shadow, the less intolerant we become of others.

I have chosen abuse as an example because it is a common human problem that has a large impact on health services. Abuse causes great human suffering and hardship. It is an area of people's lives that can prove difficult, but not impossible, for healthcare professionals to identify with and to help.

Definitions and incidence of childhood abuse

Maltreatment of children is taken to include physical, sexual and emotional abuse and neglect. There is no watertight definition of abuse because cultural and historical factors are so strong. Forty years ago it was routine for head teachers to cane the naked bottoms of young children and for teachers to hit children around the head with blackboard cleaners or gym shoes. It appears that personal humiliation in public is still alive and well in the teaching institutions of the healthcare professions. Relying on individuals to decide whether they have been abused or not can be unreliable, as children who have only known cruelty and neglect may be unaware that in other families the situation is very different. In the UK in the year 2000 the National Society for the Prevention of Cruelty to Children (NSPCC) studied 2869 young people aged 18–24 years who had been randomly selected and who were then asked to complete a confidential computerised questionnaire about their childhood experiences.

Experience in childhood lies on a spectrum, so there is no definitive cut-off point between adequate and abusive or neglectful parenting. One is left to establish a consensus of reasonable parenting for a particular culture at a particular time. In the NSPCC survey, over nine out of ten participants agreed with the statement that they had had a 'warm and loving family background', and the same proportion described their relationship with their mothers as 'very close' or 'fairly close', with their relationship with their fathers coming close behind (seven out of ten). Around 90% felt that they had been given considerable freedom to develop their own values and beliefs. Discipline primarily involved being 'grounded' or 'sent to their rooms', with 75% receiving mild and infrequent physical discipline, mainly involving slapping of legs, arms, hands or bottoms. One-third of respondents lived in households with a 'lot of stress' due to financial or other worries. One-fifth of the sample had experienced parental separation, and a similar proportion regularly had to shoulder adult responsibilities at an early age because of parents who were ill, disabled, had substance misuse problems or needed emotional support through divorce or bereavement. It was interesting to examine the attitudes of the sample to reasonable parenting, as those in the study were clearly the parents of today.

Occasional use of a slap with an open hand was supported, but more than six out of ten respondents thought it was never justified to refuse to speak to a child, or to threaten them with beatings. More than seven out of ten participants said that it was never justified to make a child miss a meal, or to embarrass or humiliate a child. Using implements to hit a child or hitting them with a closed fist were unacceptable to almost the whole sample.[5]

Bullying and discrimination are the most common forms of harmful aggression in childhood, with 43% of respondents affected and most of this behaviour occurring at school. Violent physical abuse was defined as being hit with implements, or being punched, kicked, knocked down, shaken, deliberately burned or scalded, throttled or threatened with a knife or gun. Approximately 25% of the sample had experienced at least one of these forms of abuse. Most of the violent treatment (78%) happened at home, most often inflicted by the child's mother (49%) or father (40%). Of those who had suffered violent treatment, approximately one in five individuals experienced it regularly. This form of abuse is significantly more common in lower social groups. Overall, around 7% of the sample was assessed by observers as having been seriously physically abused. A similar proportion was estimated to have suffered serious physical neglect, which included frequently going hungry, having dirty school clothes, looking after themselves because their parents were absent or incapacitated by alcohol and/or drugs, being deserted or abandoned, or living in homes with dangerous physical conditions.

Emotional or psychological abuse or neglect is even more difficult to define or measure. The central feature of childhood abuse is often a desire to dominate and control the child using physical, sexual or emotional abuse (or all three), and this is often accompanied by deliberate isolation of the victim from relationships that could offer alternative sources of support and comfort. In the survey, one in ten respondents were made to miss meals, were locked in rooms or cupboards, were regularly sworn at or were told by one or both parents that they wished the child was dead or had never been born.

The number of respondents who had experienced sexual activity with relatives against their wishes or with a person 5 or more years older was rather less. Around 3% reported touching or fondling and 3% witnessed relatives exposing themselves. Oral or penetrative sexual acts or attempts, or forced engagement in voyeurism/pornography was reported by 1%. Sexual acts performed by known age peers (schoolfriends, boyfriends, girlfriends, etc.) were much more common. Abuse by known people who were not relatives occurred in 11% of respondents, and abuse by strangers or someone they had just met affected 4%. In total, 6% of the total sample considered that they had been sexually abused.

This study provides a useful insight into the prevalence and variety of child maltreatment in the UK around 10–20 years ago. Considering the difficulty of being a good parent, it is encouraging to find such a high proportion of children feeling loved. The incidence of bullying highlights the importance of tackling this problem at a school level. Similarly, the commonest form of sexual abuse took place within the child's peer group, and this also indicates the importance of dealing with the problem within that setting. Overall, around 13% of respondents assessed themselves as having been abused and were also considered by the researchers to have been seriously maltreated. Severe abuse and physical abuse were more common in lower social groups, but occurred in all groups. Although most sexual abusers were male, women were as likely as men to be involved in physical and emotional maltreatment. Very few respondents were physically, sexually or emotionally abused by step-parents, very few were sexually abused by strangers or in public places, and there were no examples of sexual abuse by care workers or youth workers.[5] Although there is no room for complacency here, the numbers involved look manageable, at least in a prosperous society.

The experience of childhood abuse

There is nothing more important for a society to confront than the maltreatment of its children. There is increasing openness in today's society to admitting and facing up to the existence of abuse, and there are promising developments in its prevention, detection and treatment. The significance of childhood abuse in clinical practice is the catastrophic effect that it has on the child's development. Severe abuse has been compared, with good reason, to life in a concentration camp, and those who have lived through this cruelty have generally opted for the term 'adult survivors of childhood abuse'. The term 'survivor' is apt, as unfortunately many children do not survive. Some are murdered or permanently maimed by their abusers, some commit suicide or die of narcotic overdoses, some die of AIDS as a result of prostitution, and some simply disappear into the murky world of the homeless. What is the nature of the experience of abuse and why does it cause such devastation to the soul?

Before we move on to consider this question, I am aware that for a significant proportion of readers this topic may awaken painful memories. In these circumstances it may be sensible to skip this chapter and move on to the next one, or to enlist help from someone you can trust. Childhood abuse is such a traumatic experience that it is buried in the subconscious, often for decades and sometimes for life. There is a right time for each person to deal with these events, and this must never be rushed or forced upon someone before they are ready. Helpline numbers are readily available on the Internet or in phonebooks.

Family life is a central conundrum of human existence. Thomas Moore believes that it reflects 'the nature of the world, which runs on both virtue and evil. ... Usually it presents the full range of human potential, including evil, hatred, violence, sexual confusion, and insanity.'[2] Each family possesses its own shadow, and complete denial of serious abuse is usual – presumably it is buried in the family subconscious. It is as if we cannot face up to the cruelty in our hearts. Here is Alexa Donath:

> When words and violence are used against a child, it's a type of rape – rape of the body, mind and soul.
>
> My mother slapped me with her hands, gouged me with her nails, wrenched my arms, pushed me, and used whatever was handy: high-heeled shoes, a hanger. It all hurt, but the words hurt the most. Words that hurt are powerful and ongoing. They kill the good feelings you have about yourself.[4]
>
> (p. 89)

Often abusive families strive to be seen as happy and successful by outsiders. They may be the pillars of the local community or church. Jobs with automatic power, such as the professions, appeal to those who relish control over others. Within the family, secrecy is crucial and outsiders are not to be trusted or encouraged. Valerie Butler recalls her youth:

> For me, as a child, religion was a monster in the sky that was ready to zap
> you. We were told to kneel and pray when we did something wrong. Or,
> if they wanted to know the truth about something, they would make us
> line up and get the Bible out. You would put your hand on the Bible and
> swear that you didn't do it. We would tremble in our boots fearing that
> we were going to hell.[4]
>
> (p. 291)

In general, abused children are aware that their life is one of misery and sadness, and most long for proper parents and a normal family – for care, love and attention. This longing often persists through life:

> You're still holding on to the fantasy that they love you, the hope that
> underneath it all, your mother loves you. You can't face it that she didn't
> love you.[4]
>
> (p. 314)

Celia Golden describes her childhood as 'a state of imprisonment in which my captor had total control over my existence and unlimited access to my body'. She likens her experience to the victims of the Holocaust.[4] Unlike an adult hostage or political prisoner, the child has no comprehension of what is being done, or why. Grown-ups are powerful, strong and intimidating. The abused are robbed of their childhood and many experience death of their spirit – all pleasure in life is taken from them. Alice Brand Bartlett compared her growing up in her extremely abusive family to brainwashing or terrorism. The final stage is when children are coerced into becoming perpetrators of abuse themselves. If they perform horrendous acts themselves, or at least believe that they have, they may no longer feel able to accept any goodness themselves.[4] Those from loving homes may struggle to comprehend the extreme and lasting damage incurred:

> My friend was made to feel like he was the most wonderful person in the
> world. He has no conception of what it means, as a child forming your-
> self, to grow up thinking that you're a piece of shit.[4]
>
> (p. 5)

> The emotional essence of incest is to feel oneself becoming spoiled to the
> core and powerless to stop it. I don't know how you spent your child-
> hood, but I spent my childhood feeling guilty, dirty, and ashamed.[4]
>
> (p. 69)

Some abusive parents demonstrate love as well as hate, and this can cause great confusion in a young child's mind. Young children tend to blame themselves for bad things that happen, and self-hate is a common emotion among the abused. Self-esteem is low or non-existent, particularly when emotional abuse occurs. Children who experience abuse from more than one person are even more likely to feel that something bad about them is at the root of their suffering, generating feelings of complete worthlessness. Louise Hill recalls conversations with her mother:

> 'What's wrong with you? Something wrong with you? Don't you have
> any friends? Do I have to pay people to be your friends? Go out in the

sunshine, go outside, go out in the light, go out in the light. It's a beautiful day, there's sun outside, sitting in here, what's wrong with you?' And what was I doing in the house that she would say this? I was reading a book, probably, or making up some creative game. So being alone was very bad.[4]

(p. 253)

One of the most moving accounts of survival of severe childhood abuse comes from Louise Wisechild. In *The Obsidian Mirror* she describes the humiliation of sexual abuse by her Uncle Kevin:

My body is confused. Thick, strange feelings come from between my legs. But Kevin feels horrible. He feels hating. He feels old. This is dying. It seems like he will crush my body underneath his weight. I cannot breathe. I cannot move. Every time he bears down on me he calls me a name. No one has ever called me these names before. But I know what they mean. They mean I'm bad. 'Bitch. Cunt. Whore.' My body stops feeling. I become vacant.[3]

(pp. 101–2)

As an adult survivor she struggles with one occasion of inadvertent orgasm with the hateful uncle. On another occasion he pushes her head down the toilet and forces her to eat his faeces. She writes about her difficulty in coping with sex in an adult loving relationship:

I can't masturbate any more let alone make love. Being aroused is terrifying. I throw up instead of climaxing. I hate my body for feeling sexual at all. I don't want to feel sexual ever.[3]

(p. 159)

There is a profound depth of shame, grief and rage. There is both personal shame and shame of the family. Betrayal or complicity among siblings may make matters even worse, destroying any remaining vestiges of trust. Anger must be suppressed. Here is Anne O'Neil, one of the 20 male and female survivors whose accounts make up *Trying to Get Some Dignity*:

I can tell you how it was with mother. She required first, admitting the offence she suspected you'd committed; second, apologising; third, taking the punishment, the beating; fourth, thanking for the beating – 'Thank you, dear mother, for loving me enough to discipline me'; fifth, not showing any residual physical manifestation whatsoever of what you had just experienced. No crying, nothing. You have to cry during the beating, and then afterwards you may not cry at all or show any lingering response such as sobbing or shortness of breath. Rigorously applied, this practice leads to what Schreiber calls 'soul murder.'[4]

(p. 79)

Sometimes controlling anger is the only means of effective protest. Here is Skye Smith:

I was called ugly all the time. By everybody. You're bad, you're ugly. That was their word for misbehaving – 'Don't be ugly. You're being ugly.' I was so stubborn. I think stubbornness was my attempt to hold on to myself and who I was. I remember from earliest memory on: I never cried when they beat me. Never. And that enraged them – We're not getting to her.[4]

(p. 303)

The comparison to holocausts, prison camps and brainwashing is explained by Richard Rhodes:

What happened to you happened to Jews in the Nazi camps, happened to the disappeared in Argentina, happens to small children all over this country in every social milieu, and the patterns are identical. The pattern of abuse involves taking away your privacy, humiliating you, depriving you physically and psychologically, and inflicting physical violence.[4]

(p. 327)

Terror and fear are a universal feature of abuse. Many survivors doubted that they would come out alive. There is fear of further abuse and of threats that have been used. Children are frequently told that they will go to prison, to hell or to a mad-house. Parents may threaten to tell friends, teachers and the church. Threats include destroying favourite possessions or harming pets. One abuser in my practice trod on a pet goldfish in front of the child in retaliation. There may be fear of pregnancy or faecal incontinence. Disclosing abuse outside the family risks total rejection from within.

Some physical and sexual abuse stops when children become old enough and strong enough to resist it. However, it is hard to protect against emotional abuse at any age. Despite a more open approach within society to the reality of abuse, it is still disheartening that we know of more adult survivors than of children being abused. Children find it difficult to understand and accept what is happening to them, and they may lack the vocabulary to describe it. They worry, with justification, that disclosure may not be believed. The child often has nowhere else to go and may realise that the family will be split as a result of their revelations. Presents may be given for maintaining secrecy.

Feelings engendered by abuse are summarised in Box 8.1.

Box 8.1: Feelings engendered by abuse

Hate
Guilt
Shame
Humiliation
Anger
Fear and terror
Secrecy
Betrayal
Disgust

Presentations of childhood abuse

In childhood the behaviour that results from abuse is probably best detected by schoolteachers. Problems with inappropriate sexual, physical or emotional behaviour may be encountered. There is often a decline in schoolwork, and children may appear lonely, unhappy and intense. Anxiety and fears are common. Attempts to leave home may be made at a very young age.

As children develop into teenagers, self-abuse becomes more apparent. Superficial cutting of wrists seems to be particularly frequent, and should always alert the professional:

Sally of the Alley
This
is the way of the world,
this is life in the alley
Sally.

Sally
with the dead fox
round her neck,
picking at the eyes
prodding with dirty nails
at a mouth long dead.

Sally
with the devil tattoo
on young flesh,
with lank hair
curtains, over satin
Satan eyes.

Sally
who lives in the graveyard
and talks with the recent dead,
the white girl, the silent one
with her pure and slender head.

Sally
with the knife
and the scars to prove it,
never enough blood to show,
never near enough.

Sally
with four drunken fathers
and semi-professional mums,
the sky a roof
the stars her lights
on a long nightmare run.

Sally
we stand forlorn
I to help, you to dodge

this,
the way of the world.

Embrace, Sally,
embrace your sullen fate!
your cup is heavy,
drink your fill of
the poison of the world.

Peter Barritt

Overdoses and suicidal attempts are usual. In one of the families I was involved with, a woman who had been abused set fire to herself and jumped off a block of flats. Depression is typical, and attempts to leave home via early relationships with unsuitable partners are frequently unsuccessful. Promiscuity or prostitution may lead to early pregnancy. Many girls plan pregnancies at a very early age, hoping perhaps for something to love and someone to love them back. Drug and alcohol abuse are ubiquitous, and this may lead on to criminal activity. Gang culture may offer a sense of family, and violence can provide excitement or an outlet for sadomasochism.[4]

When we examined patients in our practice who had experienced multiple terminations we recognised most of them as adult survivors of childhood abuse. Eating disorders may be another manifestation of abuse, offering control of self and delaying sexual development:

Bulimia
Let fall in lushness, ruby lips
heave in suffocating sips,
swallow milk in velvet fold,
bury meat in scarlet mould.

Peel back flesh from these thin thighs,
lift your lonely furrow sighs,
wash out slime and stomach bile,
squeeze a tear from forlorn smile.

Petals sink in heavy scent, hold
the stolen childhood soul,
suck, don't bite, Dad's ripened fruit,
let Mother thrash your birthday suit.

Let fall in lushness, ruby lips
clang the cymbal on your hips,
of men and angels, silent tongues,
have no love, sound the gongs.

Peter Barritt

In adult life, recurrent and persistent depression is usual. Relationships with parents may be distant or non-existent. Problems with intimacy, sexuality and relationships are frequent. Barbara Hamilton explains:

Sex, guilt and numbness were always intertwined. I didn't know that what I really hungered for was being loved, not making love.[4]

(p. 255)

Relationship breakdown or early divorce may result from psychosexual and relationship difficulties. Adult survivors describe feelings of uncontrollable anger or aggressiveness. Anxiety is often experienced, and may surface when children are born or when they reach the age when the parent's own abuse commenced. Low self-esteem tends to cause difficulty in accepting praise:

> When you're trying to get compliments or when you're hoping that somebody will say something nice – or if they do say something nice – you put it down, you won't accept it. It sucks, really. Because you're trying to make them praise you more.[4]
>
> (p. 248)

Survivors tend to feel unworthy of praise, love, success or happiness. They often develop a defensive shell, which Louise Wisechild calls her mask:

> I call feeling away from my eyes, they stay flat on my face, allowing nothing to sink inside. A smile staples the corners of my mouth in place. My jaw waits, tense, ready to push my words back down my throat. When I wear this mask I can pretend that nothing happened. I can pretend that my body doesn't exist and my soul is out of reach.[3]
>
> (p. 138)

Abuse commonly leads to addictions of one kind or another, such as drug addiction, alcoholism, workaholism or addiction to success. Spendaholics purchase endless goods, resulting in momentary joy and long-term guilt. Taking care of others or trying to please all of the people all of the time are frequent character traits. Some are just addicted to endless activity, like Karen Seal, who admits 'I'll do anything but sit quietly and just feel feelings. I told my analyst that when I think about myself and all my achievements I just feel like icing on a turd.'[4] David Ray explains:

> ... you can't suffer a success because you feel worthless.
>   You can't tolerate failure because you're looking to the outside to confirm that you're worth something, because you don't really believe it inside.[4]
>
> (p. 253)

Behaviour towards healthcare professionals frequently makes the professional feel angry, powerless or 'impotent'. Abused women usually find physical examination difficult, and may refuse cervical cytology for this reason. Years of abuse can make people sullen, and inexperienced professionals may take this personally. Here is Roddy Doyle writing as a battered wife in *The Woman Who Walked Into Doors*:

> –   Put this woman to bed the minute you get her home, Mister Spencer, and bring her a cup of tea.
> –   Yes, doctor.
> The two of them, looking after me. Laughing at me. The woman who walked into doors. They didn't have to wink at each other because they didn't have to.

They were all the same; they didn't want to know. They'd never ask. Here's a prescription; now fuck off. The young ones were the worst, the young ones in Casualty. So busy, so important.
–   It's people like you that waste my time.
I should have boxed her ears. A kid in a white coat, playing. Shouting at the nurses. A fuckin' little child with no manners. And I took it from her.
–   Sorry, doctor.
–   Next.[6]

(p. 190)

Denial and disclosure

The experience of abuse is too traumatic to remain in conscious memory. Children learn to distance themselves from what is happening. Anne O'Neil describes this:

> … I knew I couldn't think about it. There's a profound separation, a split, when you can't allow yourself to know what you know.[4]
>
> (p. 153)

This shrinking into oneself is also described by Louise Wisechild:

> I grow smaller and smaller. I send my consciousness into the size of a small dot. I hide in a tiny place that is deep inside of my soul. In that hiding place I take up no room at all, I don't even breathe.[3]
>
> (p. 24)

Once in the secret place it can be hard to break out of it. Disclosure may take decades or for ever. As Wisechild observes, survivors do not *want* to recall the events that are buried in their subconscious. Instead, the journey starts because survivors feel 'crazy or lost or dead or ashamed.' She continues:

> Breaking out of secrecy necessitates communication: telling our stories, articulating that which once seemed too much, too hard, too lonely.
>
> For me, knowing about the incest of my childhood was profoundly important for my healing. It made sense of my pain, my fear, my beliefs about my self and my relationship with my family. The body sensations, emotions, flashbacks and mental pictures of this sexual abuse were the vivid record of my history.[3]

It is impossible to heal if you do not know your wounds. As Alice Brand Bartlett points out, 'the main purpose of remembering is to make sure that the rest of your life isn't spent repeating the past.'[4] To an extent, too, remembering honours the child that was – 'the one who had the strength and the faith to wake up every day in a house where she didn't have a prayer.'[4]

When patients disclose abuse it is important to remember that you may be the first person on the planet to hear this. Often disclosure is made to partners, teachers or friends. When the healthcare professional is chosen, the manner in which they receive the news is absolutely crucial. The moment is described by Celia Golden:

> I expected my therapist to vomit on the spot and throw me out of her office – as though I were the perpetrator. If she had raised one eyebrow indicating shock, repulsion, or disbelief, she would never have seen me again.[4]

(p. 282)

In general, survivors are looking for someone trustworthy who will listen to and believe their story. They want support but not sympathy; they require a companion for their feelings. They do not need to have their abuse ranked in severity, or minimised. Acknowledging the difficulty of disclosing abuse, and providing follow-up and support, are important. If referral to others with more experience may be needed, make sure that this is not perceived by the patient as abandonment. Also offer to continue providing support yourself. The patient should be in complete control of what they disclose and when they choose to do this. Non-verbal communication will transmit our emotions if we feel accepting and warm, not fearful or disgusted. When the time is right, I believe it can be helpful to let the patient know if you have previous professional experience of successfully helping people through this difficult process. Confidentiality needs to be discussed, but not promised in advance, if the patient is under 16 years of age. At the time of first disclosure, physical contact or being in close proximity to the patient is generally inappropriate.[7] Hearing accounts of those who have been abused can be extremely upsetting, but this needs to be dealt with at another time and in another place (such as a professional small group or mentoring session).

The recollection of memories of abuse and the decision to disclose the abuse is a time of extreme danger. Healthcare professionals can be of great help at this time, particularly if they are available regularly and at short notice. Often survivors of severe abuse develop clinical depression, and prescription of antidepressants that are safe in overdose may be required. One-to-one counselling and group therapy by those experienced in helping survivors can be helpful. Continuity of care is crucial, as healing from abuse generally takes years rather than months.

Healing from abuse

The capacity to create a loving home for others when one's childhood has been blighted by severe abuse seems to me to be one of the supreme achievements of the human spirit. It is truly a state of grace. People have rightly been honoured for surviving prolonged imprisonment for their religious or political faith and subsequently showing a spirit of reconciliation, but adults can make sense of such suffering, and to some extent the path has been personally chosen. There is a strength and courage about survivors of childhood abuse that is both inspiring and humbling. It is very important in these circumstances that the nature and goals of healing are set by the survivors and not by their professional helpers. The job of the professional is to believe, to support and to continue to be available over a long period of time, but not to set the agenda.

Many survivors do not triumph over adversity in the same way, and our compassion here is even more crucial. We consult with those who are hooked into destructive addictions, with those who cannot move on from victimhood and with those who are abusing others. It is perfectly reasonable for adult survivors to criticise others who fail to deal with their own abuse and in turn abuse their own children. Such criticism is less helpful coming from healthcare professionals who have not lived in this alien world. How do we know what an experience like sodomy by a father from the age of three is like, or how difficult or impossible it is to confront that particular shadow? Our condemnation of abusers may serve to reassure ourselves, but it is unlikely to be helpful in the consultation. The effects of abuse are felt everywhere in healthcare – in mental illness, addictions, sexually transmitted disease, requests for terminations, inexplicable physical symptoms, attempted suicide, trauma due to violence, 'difficult' patients, disturbed children and anxious or phobic parents. Try to be open rather than judgemental when these problems present themselves. Make time to listen to these patients' stories.

There is a question here about why some triumph over abuse, while others appear not to do so. Sometimes love comes from one parent and not the other, although complicity in abuse or failure to protect the child is always an issue. Mothers have often been abused themselves, and turning a blind eye maintains financial security. Mothers may be jealous of attention paid to their children, however negative that attention may be. There is much to do with narcissism and a desire to dominate and completely control the lives of children in abusive relationships:

> Parenting is a terrible assault on a parent's narcissism. Here's this child who's supposed to be your gift to the world and the perfect extension of you – but faultless, of course. And you're the only one who has produced this perfect child; everybody else's child is less perfect than your perfect child. Then the little kid has the audacity to begin to develop their own sense of self.[4]
>
> (p. 85)

Some abusers are paedophiles whose intention is not necessarily to cause pain. Some are sadists. Some abuse primarily when they are angry or intoxicated. Celia Golden believes that it is more common for women who sexually abuse their children to be sadistic than it is for men. She believes that women are often very angry when they sexually abuse, and she points out that women have always had the greatest opportunity to abuse children.[4] When love from parents is absent, love between siblings may provide strength. Many survivors remember relationships outside the family, sometimes only experienced briefly, that have fortified their spirit. As adults, loving relationships with partners and friends are often the most important healing influence. Once disclosure has been made, total ostracism by the rest of the family is common. Family denial leads to the accuser being made the scapegoat.

Disclosure and healing can cause dramatic personal change, and this can take its toll on relationships. Partners may have been chosen for their safety or low sex drive, and once sexuality has been regained, these partners may be unable to cope. Survivors may wish to regain a youth that was stolen from them, and this can result in teenage behaviour that destroys the old relationship. Those who were previously sullen and withdrawn can be transformed into vivacious and outgoing personalities.

Creativity can be a catalyst for healing. Richard Rhodes, who co-authored *Trying to Get Some Dignity,* talks of his therapist encouraging him to channel anger in a positive direction:

> ... the rage was part of the person I had become and his sense [Richard's therapist] that it simply needed direction toward the real work of the world.[4]
>
> (p. 300)

Another survivor, Andrea Ashworth, wrote of her traumatic childhood in *Once in a House on Fire.* In the book she describes the importance of writing poetry in her life:

> A poem was a box for your soul. That was the point. It was the place where you could save bits of yourself, and shake out your darkest feelings, without worrying that people would think you were strange. While I was writing, I would forget myself and everyone else; poetry made me feel part of something noble and beautiful and bigger than me.[8]
>
> (p. 245)

While some create, others find meaning in religion or worthwhile work. Those with the courage to commit their abuse to print offer us a window into their painful childhood world.

Anger against perpetrators drives some to directly confront their abusers. Louise Wisechild's experience of doing this echoes that of patients whom I have known in my career. Complete denial seems to be the rule. Perhaps the crime is too great to admit to. I have never known the guilty confess. Letting go of anger can be therapeutic. Here is Louise Wisechild again:

> My fists fly in the air, my feet stomp against the dirt. 'I could kill him. Damn, damn, damn, how dare you! How dare you do that to me!' I tear rocks from the ground and throw them. I decimate his penis in every way imaginable. I am a mindless tornado of anger.[3]
>
> (p. 65)

Forgiving the crime should not be part of the therapist's goal. The crime is usually too great, and the perpetrator has not generally admitted guilt or apologised. Here is Barbara Hamilton:

> He never said he was sorry. He never asked my forgiveness. He never acknowledged his responsibility. I feel absolutely no need to forgive.[4]
>
> (p. 319)

Sometimes the abused seek justice and official recognition of the crimes committed by taking the perpetrators to court. In our area of the UK the police and courts handle this with great sensitivity. One of my patients successfully pursued a prosecution against her father for abuse some 20 years earlier. In the end, however, imprisonment of her father seemed to bring little comfort to the patient. This is not to say that we should not support those who feel this is the right way for them to go.

If forgiveness seems unreasonable, then perhaps acceptance of what has happened and the impetus to move on from the past is more realistic. Here Roddy Doyle's character Paula Spencer looks back on life with her violent husband 'Charlo':

> Every day. I think about it every minute. Why did he do it? No real answers come back, no big Aha. He loved me and he beat me. I loved him and I took it. It's as simple as that, and as stupid and complicated. It's terrible. It's like knowing someone you love is dead but not having the body to prove it. He loved me. I know it. But if he loved me, why did he hit me? Why did he hit me so hard and so often? The questions are never answered. They always torment me. And his love becomes a cruel thing, like a smile on a Nazi's face. You don't hit the people you love. You might, once or twice – it's only human. But not the way he did it, again and again. You don't pull fingers back till they snap. You don't wake them in the morning with a kick in the stomach. You don't hold their face over the chip pan and threaten to dump their head in boiling fat. You don't beat them in front of their children. That's not love.[6]
>
> (pp. 192–3)

Sometimes a ritual such as writing to the abuser and burning the letter once it has been written can draw a line under the past. Here is Louise Wisechild performing a ritual to acknowledge her losses and affirm her healing:

> I gather dead leaves and heavy rocks. I place my collection on the wet grass and walk clockwise around it. I walk in a circle around the incest. Circling the memory of remembering what I had forgotten. I walk for the time without memory, the time I felt dead and dirty.
>
> I walk for the tears and for the anger that shook my body hard and left me soft in its releasing. My feet mark the times I met my despair and feared that the misery was bottomless. I walk the lies I believed as a child.[3]
>
> (p. 246)

Here, too, is the final irony. Child abuse will never disappear because most children will never tell. Louise Wisechild explains:

> Years of wanting to tell clash with years of terrified silence. 'I hurt all the time ...'[3]
>
> (p. 91)

> It always seemed like I had something I wanted to tell someone. But I couldn't remember what it was. It was a secret.
>
> Anyone could tell on a child. Children could tell on each other. But children couldn't tell on adults.[3]
>
> (p. 87)

References

1   Smith S (1978) *Selected Poems.* Penguin Books, Harmondsworth.
2   Moore T (1992) *Care of the Soul.* Judy Piatkus Ltd, London.
3   Wisechild L (1988) *The Obsidian Mirror.* Seal Press, New York.
4   Rhodes G and Rhodes R (1996) *Trying to Get Some Dignity.* William Morrow & Co., New York.
5   National Society for the Prevention of Cruelty to Children (NSPCC) (2000) *Child Maltreatment in the UK: a study of the prevalence of abuse and neglect.* NSPCC, London. www.nspcc.org.uk
6   Doyle R (1998) *The Woman Who Walked Into Doors.* Vintage, London.
7   Jones H (2003) Personal communication.
8   Ashworth A (1998) *Once in a House on Fire.* Picador, London.

Further reading

• Doyle R (1998) *The Woman Who Walked Into Doors.* Vintage, London.
• National Society for the Prevention of Cruelty to Children (NSPCC) (2000) *Child Maltreatment in the UK: a study of the prevalence of abuse and neglect.* NSPCC, London. www.nspcc.org.uk
• Rhodes G and Rhodes R (1996) *Trying to Get Some Dignity.* William Morrow & Co., New York.
• Wisechild L (1988) *The Obsidian Mirror.* Seal Press, New York.

CHAPTER 9

Dances with death

What has happened will happen again, and what has been done will be done again; there is nothing new under the sun.

Ecclesiastes 1:9[1]

The flowers they were roses
and such sweet fragrance gave
that all my friends were lovers
and we danced upon her grave.

Leonard Cohen, from *Ballad*[2]

I saw that everyone was condemned to death, and quite soon at that. I saw the people, the little egos, existed like blown leaves floating meaninglessly on an ocean of death, and this ocean of death was the great universe itself in all its beauty and order.

Jacob Needleman, *The Way of the Physician*[3]

The patient suffers, the family threatens, the colleagues frown, the nurse laughs, Death grins, and the young doctor dances a crazy jig amidst the tumult, while once he dreamt he would glide along the floor with Death in a perfectly controlled tango.

Bert Keizer, *Dancing with Mister D*[4]

Introduction

Much of the behaviour of a secular Western society is attributed to the modern inability to acknowledge death. The implication appears to be that previous generations had an ability to accept death in a way that we have now lost. In this chapter I hope to show that our relationship with death has always been an uneasy one. The fear of death is fear of the unknown. In an atheistic society, death represents annihilation, the end of being. This dread of obliteration might represent love of life, or merely clinging to the familiar. Within a religious framework, death may presage divine judgement and punishment for earthly sins. Faith in an afterlife does not insulate individuals from panic when death approaches, as those who have provided terminal care for the clergy may testify. Only the most devout have absolute certainty in better things to come, and such faith can have explosive consequences. That is not to denigrate the underlying principle among world religions that encourages a virtuous and thoughtful existence by reminding us that life is short and death is near. As we saw in Chapter 4, preparation for death is a crucial part of most Eastern religions and the manner of dying is fundamental to successful reincarnation.

Dwelling on personal mortality is neither amusing nor enjoyable, and it comes as no surprise that most people prefer not to do it. Our ephemeral existence generally becomes reality only when serious illness occurs. Even when death is imminent, not all patients want a cosy heart-to-heart with their favourite healthcare professional. A substantial proportion of patients have no desire to discuss death, preferring to maintain a dignified denial that may accompany them to their grave. Heroic medical measures may be called for. If the patient refuses to accept the invitation, it is up to their family and the professionals to take death by the hand for the last dance.

The speaker in Ecclesiastes reminds us that there is nothing new under the sun. In the ancient Hindu sacred verse *Mahabarata*, Arjuna speaks with a lake that is actually Brahman, or his father. Arjuna is set riddles to solve:

> Lake: 'What is the greatest wonder?'
> Arjuna: 'Every day Death strikes everywhere, yet we live as though
>   we were immortal. That is the greatest wonder.'[4]
>
> (p. 82)

Should rumination on mortality be encouraged? For the fit and healthy, perhaps, and for the healthcare professional, definitely. As Anthony Storr comments:

> Man is the only creature who can see his own death coming; and, when
> it does, it concentrates his mind wonderfully.[5]
>
> (p. 169)

Stanley Hauerwas argues that in Western society there are few things on which we can agree, but 'almost everyone agrees that death is a very unfortunate aspect of the human condition which should be avoided at all costs.'[6] Death divides love, and this can be a painful reality. In rural Greece, bereaved women mourn for a period of five years. During this time, they wear black, visit the grave of the deceased daily, and begin by conducting conversations with the departed.[5] In this sense, it is life that is the problem, not death.[3]

Why should we come to terms with mortality? The process seems to encourage maturity and spiritual growth. We are less prone to tilt at windmills or to live our lives in a way that we subsequently regret. Bert Keizer writes:

> Terborgh offers his classification of people: those who know about Death,
> and worry about it with a laugh, a tear, a poem or a symphony; the
> confessed mortals, say. And those who write 'death' with a small d.[4]
>
> (p. 275)

Here is Mozart (aged 31 years) writing what turned out to be his last letter to his father in 1787, a month before his father's death and four years prior to his own:

> As death, strictly speaking, is the goal of our lives, I have been for some
> years past been making myself so familiar with this truest and best friend
> of man that its aspect has not only ceased to appal me, but I find it very
> soothing and comforting! And I thank my God that he has vouchsafed
> me the happiness of an opportunity (you will understand me) to recognise

it as the key to our true bliss. I never lie down to sleep without reflecting that (young as I am) I may perhaps not see another day – yet none of those who know me can say I am morose or melancholy in society – and I thank my Creator every day for this happiness and wish that all my fellow men might share it.[7]

(p. 1065)

Dancing with death

The concept of stripping naked with a group of like-minded friends, dancing merrily and loudly on top of the freshly dug grave of the dear departed, and then fornicating in public is an enduring image. No wonder it has stimulated artists for 600 years and continues to do so. This is the *Danse Macabre* or *Dance of Death*. In a more restrained manner this fine Pagan dancing tradition lives on in England among Morris dancers. (This may explain their unexpected appearance on the patio outside the ward of our local hospice when I was holding the hand of a dying friend some years ago.) The Dance of Death might be viewed as an adult version of that perennial children's favourite, 'I'm the King of the Castle, and you're the Dirty Rascal'.

Ivan Illich gives an excellent summary of the history of the Dance of Death in his book *Medical Nemesis*. He writes that dancing with death was an occasion for 'affirming the joy of being alive and was the source of many erotic songs and poems'. The *Danse Macabre* was not exactly what Christianity according to St Paul wished to encourage, and from the fourth century onwards the church spent the best part of a thousand years trying to suppress it, without much success.[8] Dancing mania was common in the thirteenth century, and dancers would sometimes die 'on the job' due to lack of sleep, drink or food. The standard treatment was to play soothing music to try to slow down the action. The cause of dance mania is unclear. Some believe that it may have been due to poisoning by ergot or magic mushrooms, while others feel that hysteria in the face of the Black Death was to blame. In Italy, dancers believed that tarantula spiders had bitten them.

During the late fifteenth century the Dance of Death became less frenzied and more institutionalised. The two most frequent types of death dance were those depicted in mural paintings in churches or cemeteries and those published as books illustrated with woodcuts.[9] The first painting of the Dance of Death appeared in 1424 on the walls of the Cemetery of the Innocents in Paris. People from different stations of life each dance with a corpse that is a mirror image of themselves. They dance through life carrying their death with them as they go. This was at the time time when mirrors had first been in common use. As the fifteenth century progressed, Death was transformed from a mirror-image to a separate being, cutting people down in their prime. In 1491, Caxton published a do-it-yourself guide to dying like a gentleman, called *The Art and Craft to Knowe ye Well to Dye*. This became a best-seller and stayed in print for 200 years. Illich writes:

> It was a 'how to' book in the modern sense, a complete guide to the business of dying, a method to be learned while one was in good health and to be kept at one's fingertips for use in that inescapable hour.[8]

(p. 130)

In the sixteenth century, Death became a major figure in morality plays, and in 1538 it featured in Hans Holbein's picture book *The Danse Macabre*. In Holbein's book the Dance of Death becomes an illustrated poem in which accusations of abuse of power are levelled at different social orders, and where those who do abuse power are reminded that death will call them to account. In an English version of the Dance of Death, different occupations were ranked in order of importance, with the Pope at number 1 and the hermit at number 36. Physicians might be interested to know that they featured at number 23, just above the amorous squire but below the usurer and poor man.[10] Death has shed clothes and flesh, and each person now dances with their skeleton.

As the sixteenth century progressed, the rise of individuality took place and death became a personal and individual experience. In the seventeenth century there was a growing interest in ghosts and souls, and fear of death started to replace the more traditional fear of divine judgement. In English churches, the Dance of Death became a standard decoration in the entrance porch. During this period a dignified death was valued, and both the patient and their loved ones had specific roles. Doors were kept open for death to arrive, and noise was avoided so that he was not scared away.[8] John Donne (1572–1631) wrote a Holy Sonnet encouraging readers not to fear death:

> Death be not proud, though some have called thee
> Mighty and dreadful, for thou art not so;
> For those whom thou think'st thou dost overthrow
> Die not, poor death, nor yet canst thou kill me.
> From rest and sleep, which but thy pictures be,
> Much pleasure, then from thee much more must flow;
> And soonest our best men with thee do go,
> Rest of their bones, and souls' delivery.
> Thou art slave to Fate, chance, kings, and desperate men,
> And dost with poison, war, and sickness dwell,
> And poppy or charms can make us sleep as well,
> And better than thy stroke; why swell'st thou then?
> One short sleep past, we wake eternally,
> And death shall be no more, Death thou shalt die.[11]

Donne's poem illustrates a change in thinking towards viewing death as a natural event rather than the act of some evil agent. The corpse also assumes a new identity, no longer being sacred as in the Middle Ages, but essentially viewed as dead meat left by the soul and spirit. The corpse becomes inanimate, and this frees the physician to regularly perform post-mortem dissection as a means of learning more about the body. At the same time, Francis Bacon (1561–1626) was the first person to speak about prolongation of life being a task for the physician, giving medicine three major roles:

> First, the preservation of health, second, the cure of disease, and third, the prolongation of life ... the third part of medicine, regarding the prolongation of life: this is a new part, and deficient, although the most noble of all.[8]

(p. 135)

As the eighteenth century progressed, the Industrial Revolution led to improved living and working conditions for the more affluent. This allowed them to continue working despite age or infirmity in sedentary jobs, which had become more widespread, and to afford the services of a personal physician. According to Illich, this was the start of the medicalisation of death:

> The ageing accountant wanted a doctor who would drive away death; when the end approached, he wanted to be formally 'given up' by his doctor and be served his last repast with the special bottle reserved for the occasion. The role of the valetudinarian was thereby created and, with it, the economic power of the contemporary physician.
>
> Health became the privilege of waiting for timely death, no matter what medical service was needed for this purpose. In an earlier epoch, death had carried the hourglass. In woodcuts, both skeleton and onlooker grin when the victim refuses death. Now the middle class seized the clock and employed doctors to tell death when to strike.[8]
>
> (pp. 138–9)

As industrialisation progressed in the nineteenth century, the germ theory and classification of diseases took hold. The doctor as hero was shown in paintings battling with disease at the bedside of the young and beautiful, wrestling with and triumphing over death. Illich believes that the myth of medicine's powerful hold over death started here. Keizer believes that the myth is still alive and well:

> We all seem to labour under that false assumption of the doctor's power to snatch the patient away from the abyss of Death. As if, with our scalpel, we could out-slash Death with his scythe.[4]
>
> (p. 5)

Death became a medical affair. In England, the coroner had been in existence since the twelfth century, but in 1836 he was allowed to pay for medical witnesses to appear and clarify causes of death. In the UK the legislation for medical certification of death was passed in the nineteenth century and currently stands unaltered. From this point onwards, no one was allowed to die without a doctor's permission. Those who break this rule are subjected to a post-mortem examination and sometimes to a coroner's inquest as well. People no longer die in their own time – they die when the doctor arrives to confirm that they have.

During the twentieth century, medical technology mushroomed. The development of artificial respiration machines proved life-saving in severe cases of paralytic poliomyelitis, but raised the dilemma of being able to maintain life when death has become inevitable. This further reinforced the God-like nature of the healthcare professional, who was now able to bring about death by switching off the life-support machine. In 1947, the first human heart was brought out of ventricular fibrillation using electric shock treatment. The occasional success of this treatment brought about what some see as the modern version of the Dance of Death, namely the cardiac arrest. Suddenly the healthcare professional was charging about both in hospital and in the wider world jumping on unsuspecting citizens who had just tried to breathe their last. Still, as Larry Churchill points out, even when the patient does not benefit, the teamwork and exercise makes the healthcare professional feel better. He argues that resuscitation fulfils a ritualistic role, giving us something to do and showing the public that everything possible is being done:

> Resuscitation attempts are the medical and hospital equivalent of Catholicism's last rites. The sin is to die without receiving them.
>
> Resuscitation attempts – never mind their success – give those who participate in them power over death.
>
> Resuscitation, when it succeeds, shows that we have conquered death, at least 'for a little while'. When it fails, it provides the reassuring demonstration that although our patient is dead, we are alive.[12]
>
> (pp. 41–3)

Churchill's writing brings back memories of days as a house physician on a crash team where the only customers likely to benefit (i.e. those having heart attacks) were looked after elsewhere. The lovely but slightly eccentric ward sister on one of the general medical wards was a devout Irish Catholic with a heart as big as a lion's. She had notices placed above each bed on her ward, written personally in red paint, which read 'In case of cardiac arrest call Father Murphy on 733451'. In Stoke-on-Trent Royal Infirmary no poor soul was allowed to die without flapping white coats and a brief acquaintance with the National Grid. On occasion, Father Murphy didn't make it in time.

Resuscitation techniques and defibrillators are major advances that save many lives, and encouraging the public to learn about and practise using them makes absolute sense. Problems only arise when resuscitation is embarked upon in situations that are patently hopeless or inappropriate. Fortunately, there has been considerable progress in this area, too. Paramedics in our part of the world have been encouraged to avoid attempts to resuscitate when they judge it unlikely to serve a useful purpose, and they are also allowed to certify death. Personal experience to date shows that they approach this new responsibility with their customary decisiveness and common sense.

Churchill takes issue with hospice models of 'a good death' where mechanically supported, painful and prolonged death is avoided. He argues that a resigned low-technology approach may not meet the wishes of the dying or their relatives.[12] This approach may smack of cost cutting or 'not bothering' – for those fully conversant with the medical technology of soap opera and documentary. In American TV dramas, the very least one can expect is to have one's sternum split open and internal paddles to be used on the warm but lifeless heart.

We have briefly examined some of the historical developments in public attitudes to death, and the way in which the healthcare industry gradually took over the process of dying. My argument is that coming to terms with death is uncomfortable, and the prospect of dying is usually frightening and emotionally painful, and always has been. Here is Ruth Picardie writing about life with breast cancer a year before her death in 1998:

> But whichever bit of my failing anatomy collapses first, I'm pretty upset. What hurts most is losing the future. I won't be there to clap when my beloved babies learn to write their names; I won't see them learn to swim, or go to school, or play the piano; I won't be able to read them *Pippi Longstocking*, or kiss their innocent knees when they fall off their bikes.

Meanwhile, it's bloody tough living in limbo, not knowing exactly how long I've got left. Do I get a 4-month or a 12-month prescription prepayment certificate? Do I bother stocking up on Sisley day facial scrub, when I've got a whole tube of La Prairie night cleanser left?

And looking back, I don't have many regrets.

And the future will get on just fine without me. OK, so Matt never waters the garden, which means the wisteria is hardly likely to make the next century. ... Otherwise, I think life will continue just fine. It's just that I'll miss it so.[13]

(pp. 58–9)

Illich believes that the medical profession wheedled their way into the natural process of dying for reasons of prestige and monetary gain. Healthcare professionals might argue that patients and relatives appreciate their help and confidence at a time of suffering and distress.

Approaches to the dance

The curious thing about death, of course, is how peaceful it usually is. William Osler found time to study it:

I have careful records of about five hundred death-beds.... Ninety suffered bodily pain or distress of one kind or another, eleven showed mental apprehension, two positive terror, one expressed spiritual exaltation, one bitter remorse. The great majority gave no sign one way or another; like their birth, their death was a sleep and a forgetting.[14]

(p. 19)

One can almost hear the old chap leaning over and whispering 'Any mental apprehension, my dear?'. As Keizer points out, it can be difficult to know when you are dying:

Usually people die unknowingly. Come to think of it, can you die knowingly? Putting it awkwardly, we are died as we are delivered. Nobody delivers himself on to this planet as nobody dies himself off it. So dying is hard to define. The most satisfactory idea is that of a struggle near the exit after which you are let through.[4]

(p. 17)

Susan Sontag seems more downbeat. She probably subscribes to the Golden Age of dying, when religion was a comfort and people welcomed death with open arms as part of their natural inheritance:

For those who live neither with religious consolations about death nor with a sense of death (or of anything else) as natural, death is the obscene mystery, the ultimate affront, the thing that cannot be controlled. It can only be denied.[15]

(p. 59)

Michael Ignatieff also feels that atheism poses great problems for the dying:

> We are still coming to terms with what it means to die outside the fold of religious consolation.[16]
>
> (p. 101)

This is, I believe, an oversimplification of religious thought. There are few belief systems that promise eternal happiness in the afterlife irrespective of personal conduct on earth. It must surely be a minority of us who face divine judgement with complete equanimity. Denial may be too strong a word to summarise the Western approach to death. Perhaps it is no more than a desire to think of something more pleasant. Fighting against death is a dubious concept at the best of times, perhaps of more use to relatives and onlookers. Here is Dylan Thomas urging his father on:

> And you, my father, there on the sad height,
> Curse, bless me now with your fierce tears, I pray.
> Do not go gentle into that good night.
> Rage, rage against the dying of the light.[17]
>
> (p. 94)

Larry Churchill has reflected on Wittgenstein's work and produced three major stereotypes of the differing approaches to death. At the one end of the spectrum are the *Fearful Minimalists*, who want to exit life with the minimum fuss and expense possible. He allows that some are motivated by noble aspirations, such as preserving their grandchildren's inheritance or sparing their family the pain and inconvenience of looking after them. He believes that they are usually driven by fear of a fate worse than death – a prolonged, expensive, technologically maintained existence cared for by people who are afraid of litigation or in the grip of religious dogma, surrounded by a guilt- or denial-ridden family. He acknowledges that their best bet is a set of robust legal documents (living wills, advance directives, etc.) and a preparedness to risk premature death in order to avoid a 'lingering, expensive, painful or vegetative one.'

At the other end of his spectrum are the *Hopeful Vitalists*, who are ardent fans of the medical model. They believe in regular medical breakthroughs, cures around the corner, winning wars against cancer and heart disease and being on the brink of reversing the ageing process. Churchill feels that these people are genuinely hopeful rather than just optimistic, because they 'hold their views not because of, but in spite of, evidence to the contrary.' Any degree or quality of life is worth the candle, and no expense should be spared. Churchill writes:

> If one must die, the ethical imperative is not to die too soon. So what some would regard as inappropriately aggressive, painful and burdensome care, these people want. There are more of us in this category than one might think. The findings of Danis and her co-investigators confirm that a majority of patients want intensive care and maximal treatment to preserve life, even for just a few days. Lots of patients never give up hope of recovery until the very end, if at all. And even if a patient wants to forgo maximal efforts at survival, the family may not.[12]
>
> (p. 39)

Churchill's final group, who occupy the middle ground, he calls the *Anxious Agnostics*. This group is not sure of the best policy, fearing both under- and over-treatment:

> Anxious Agnostics simply want to die at an appropriate time, without too much expense and too much pain and with minimal family burdens, but they also do not want to go before they really have to, when they will be 'ready.'
>
> And for that signal of readiness they depend fundamentally on their families, their friends, clergy, and especially their physicians. They look to all these persons to confirm their sense that this is a good time to stop, or that it is not.[12]
>
> (p. 40)

In essence, Churchill believes that the model of *a good death*, as defined by the hospice movement, is simplistic. Each patient has deep-seated beliefs about how they should die, and these need to be understood and genuinely valued when decisions are being made. Here is another excerpt from a poem by Dylan Thomas:

> And death shall have no dominion.
> Dead men naked they shall be one
> With the man in the wind and the west moon;
> When their bones are picked clean and the clean bones gone,
> They shall have stars at elbow and foot;
> Though they go mad they shall be sane,
> Though they sink through the sea they shall rise again;
> Though lovers be lost love shall not;
> And death shall have no dominion.[17]
>
> (p. 9)

The good death

The concept of a good death therefore needs to be based on the beliefs and values of each individual patient. Edicts such as 'All patients should be told the truth' and 'No patient should die in pain' need to be challenged, and each death should be treated on its own merits. During my professional lifetime, the prescribed wisdom about what to tell patients with fatal disease has swung from telling complete lies to telling complete truth. Both of these extremes have the ability to produce unnecessary emotional distress. Healthcare professionals are often surprised by patients failing to retain bad news. Renate Rubinstein wrote a bestseller about her experiences of multiple sclerosis, called *Take It and Leave It*. Here she explains how forgetting acts to protect us:

> The unconscious, the existence of which is so often contested, is there. I have experienced it myself. Like a heavenly mother it protects you against hard blows; even the rudest modern purveyors of total truth can't break through it. My unconscious self protected me. Illusions cannot be taken away by 'them', at least not immediately, and not for good, they belong to the psychic nature of the beast to whom truth is of no concern.[18]

Like telling the truth, pain relief needs to be considered on an individual basis. Complete pain relief may cause loss of conscious ability. Floating out of existence on the wings of morphine may suit some, but not all.

The concept of a 'good' or 'natural' death is relatively recent, as Illich reminds us. Sontag sounds sceptical about the whole idea:

> All this lying to and by cancer patients is a measure of how much harder it has become in advanced industrial societies to come to terms with death. As death is now an offensively meaningless event, so that disease widely considered a synonym for death is experienced as something to hide. The policy of equivocating about the nature of their disease with cancer patients reflects the conviction that dying people are best spared the news that they are dying, and that the good death is the sudden one, best of all if it happens while we're unconscious or asleep.[15]
>
> (p. 12)

I suspect that a good death is like a magpie, hard to describe but 'you know one when you see one.' One sunny autumn morning I was called to see a retired international banker and well-known local bon viveur. To 'pop in for an early cocktail' was generally acknowledged to be unwise unless you had no plans for the rest of the day. His wife (a raven-haired beauty by the look of her photo on his desk) had died some years earlier but he had several women whom he took out to lunch on a regular basis and according to a strict rota, swearing each one to strict secrecy in case the others found out. I discovered him at approximately 11am reclining on a favourite wicker armchair with sun streaming in through the conservatory roof, panama hat pulled down over his face, cigar gently smouldering in an ashtray, newspaper on his lap, an enormous brandy in a glass by his side. Now *that* is my idea of a good death.

Hauerwas confirms that in today's society most of us want to die quickly, painlessly and without being a burden on those we love. Dying without warning is a popular choice, particularly in our sleep. However, as Hauerwas points out, attitudes are heavily influenced by the times and the culture in which we live. Death without confessing one's sins in medieval times would lead to eternal damnation. Illnesses that allowed a lingering death, or at least one that enabled proper spiritual preparation, were preferred.[6] However, even today a sudden unexpected death gives no opportunity to express those feelings one always intended to share but did not have the opportunity or the courage to convey.

In general, modern society finds the death of children the most difficult to bear. The older we get the more likely we are to come to terms with our mortality. Many very elderly patients talk openly about their desire to die. Most of their friends and family have already succumbed, and some appear tired of life, some are ready for new adventures and many are keen to rejoin loved ones. Alisdair MacIntyre talks of 'the right time to die':

> If I have work to do in the world, the time will come when it is done, and when that time comes it is right to die…. Each of us is permitted to occupy a certain space in time, a certain role in history; without that particular place and role our lives would be without significance. To recognise that it is our particularity and finitude that give our lives

significance can save us from being consumed by that terrible and destructive desire to remain young that preys on so many Americans.[6]

(p. 122)

We have used the Dance of Death to examine Western attitudes towards dying through the ages. The contention is that human beings find death frightening and emotionally painful, and probably always have done. The metaphor of the dance is not intended to encourage a flippant or facetious approach to such a critical and important event, but to bring the issue to life.

Professional response

Caring for the dying takes its toll on the healthcare professional. Facilitating an uneventful and dignified death is a rewarding part of our work, but sufferings and tragedies stay with us. As my senior partner once remarked, after 20 years in a practice you lose a friend every month or two. To drive past homes in the practice area is to remember ghosts and recall distant memories. The death of a patient may stay with us throughout our career and beyond. Here is a poem written 25 years ago when I was a junior doctor in paediatrics:

> Was it sin delivered
> Through the gaping wound?
> Was it greed ripped
> From an anxious mother's womb?
>
> What is the secret
> In its tiny pearly palm?
> Why does it lie clasping
> The acrid orchid bloom?
>
> What was the rasping whisper
> In the purple person's tune?
> Where was the suckling shroud
> On the drunken magnate's loom?
>
> The babe has felt thy sting
> Oh Lord
> But where,
> Oh shallow grave,
> Where was thy victory?[19]

Similarly, Alfred Tauber in his book *Confessions of a Medicine Man* remembers an incident from 23 years earlier:

Mr DiVilo walked into the waiting room carrying Tony, draped in his arms exactly like Michelangelo's *Pieta*. The body was grey, and serenely beautiful. A black lock of hair over his forehead. The eyes closed. The father handed me his child, whom I took to an examining room and placed on a table. I was alone with him, and waves of emotion charged through me as I peered at his lifeless body. I was numb. I did not cry. I did not go to the funeral. I never spoke with Mr. DiVilo again. I ran away.[20]

(p. ix)

Bert Keizer, who worked in a nursing home for the elderly and terminally ill, wrote about his experiences in *Dancing with Mister D.* It is a funny and thought-provoking book, but there is an undercurrent of a good doctor feeling overwhelmed by the task of caring for so many dying patients. Here he is at the funeral of a favourite patient:

> Some have the cheek to come up to me, as her doctor, and with an angry toss of the head demand an explanation. As politely as I can manage I give them my whispered answer that it was possibly a case of idiopathic paroxysmal calcium fluxus resulting in intra-cardiac anarchy.
> 'Yes, and in plain English?' one insists.
> 'Oh, it's quite rare, not a disease that has its place in common parlance.'[4]

(p. 90)

I suggested earlier that healthcare professionals should be encouraged to consider their own mortality. Indeed I suspect that the public would be amazed if, with our close acquaintance with death, we had not already done so. However, this is not the way of things, and all healthcare professionals can ignore and deny death if they try hard enough. Doctors may end up continuing aggressive medical treatment past the time when it is humane to do so, or ignoring the human being and concentrating instead on symptom relief and pathology. Nurses may appear distant or curiously uncaring towards the dying. Medical students find black humour a useful technique for keeping reality at bay and letting off emotional steam. A feeling of 'them' and 'us' is protective, as only 'they' get ill or die. All of these techniques protect the healthcare professional from close identification with those who suffer, and reduce the likelihood of treating patients with the kindness and consideration that we all hope to receive when our time comes. Much work has already been done in this area. In some medical schools where post-mortem dissection is still part of the learning experience, students are encouraged to meet the dead person's family and to attend the funeral service once dissection is complete.

The post-mortem examination is another difficult area. The system of coroners, post-mortems and death certification is intended to protect patients from harm either from incompetent/criminal doctors or from others who might wish them ill. In fact, the system in England failed to detect or prevent at least 215 murders by Dr Harold Shipman over a period of 20 years before he was finally put on remand in 1998 and subsequently convicted. The other rationale behind post-mortem examination is to improve the accuracy of statistics concerning causes of death. Sometimes the post-mortem can give comfort to both relatives and healthcare professionals, confirming that nothing has been missed or that nothing further could have been done to prevent death. It can also allow us to learn if mistakes have been made. It was helpful to learn that nothing could have helped my mother when she died suddenly, but the marks of post-mortem are an abiding memory of a personal farewell in the chapel of rest. Family doctors know the distress that post-mortems cause to relatives, so we gladly pluck a diagnosis out of the ether when necessary, particularly in the case of the very elderly who have earned a good rest without further disturbance. Keizer considers post-mortems to be 'a transgression, like examining somebody's belongings in a thoroughly disgusting manner after he's dropped dead.'[4] Humanity is called for, and sometimes it is virtuous to bend the rules a little.

Most healthcare professionals find caring for dying children most distressing of all. This issue is examined in detail by Stanley Hauerwas in *God, Medicine and Suffering.* The dynamics here are very complicated, with both parents and staff often feeling unable to help the dying child. Being truthful (open awareness) and denying the truth (mutual pretence) can both be problematic. The children have no future, they attend hospital and not school, and they are keen to spare their parents' suffering. Myra Bluebond-Langner is an anthropologist who spent time studying and talking to children with leukaemia, and wrote of her experiences in *The Private Worlds of Dying Children.* In general she found that mutual pretence was often the best option. Here is her advice:

> That person should listen to what the children say, taking their cues from them, answering only what they ask, and on their terms. Remember, children will honor whatever rules are set up.
>
> The issue then is not whether to tell, but what to tell, in a way that respects the children and all of their many, often conflicting needs.[21]
>
> (p. 235)

Personally I believe this to be good advice whatever age the patient may be. Following this advice minimises the chance of the patient feeling emotionally deserted by those around him or her. Our conduct becomes personally tailored to suit the patient's wishes. We become a witness and a companion. Here is advice from Nicholas Wolterstorff, who writes in *Lament For a Son* about life after his 25-year-old son died in a climbing accident:

> Death is awful, demonic. If you think your task as comforter is to tell me that really, all things considered, it's not so bad, you do not sit with me in my grief but place yourself off in the distance away from me. Over there, you are of no help. What I need to hear from you is that you recognise how painful it is. I need to hear from you that you are with me in my desperation. To comfort me, you have to come close. Come sit beside me on my mourning bench.[22]
>
> (p. 34)

The closer we approach the death of others, the more likely we are to face up to our own.

References

1 *Revised English Bible.* Ecclesiastes 1:9.
2 Cohen L (1969) *Poems 1956–1968.* Jonathan Cape, London.
3 Needleman J (1992) *The Way of the Physician.* Penguin Books, Harmondsworth.
4 Keizer B (1996) *Dancing with Mister D.* Transworld Publishers, London.

5   Storr A (1997) *Solitude.* HarperCollins, London.
6   Hauerwas S (1990) *Naming the Silences: God, medicine and the problem of suffering.* WB Eermans, Grand Rapids, MI.
7   Mozart W (1787). Quoted in *BMJ.* **319**: 1065.
8   Illich I (1975) *Medical Nemesis.* Calder & Boyars, London.
9   Mackenbach J (1995) Social inequality and death as illustrated in late-medieval death dances. *Am J Pub Health.* **85**: 1285–92.
10 Mackenbach J (1996) Dances of death, occupational mortality statistics, and social critique. *BMJ.* **313**: 1587–91.
11 Donne J (1950) *Donne: selected verse.* Penguin Books, Harmondsworth.
12 Churchill L (2001) Patient multiplicity, medical rituals, and good dying. In: C Elliott (ed.) *Slow Cures and Bad Philosophers.* Duke University Press, Durham, NC.
13 Picardie R (1998) *Before I Say Goodbye.* Penguin Books, Harmondsworth.
14 Osler W (1905) A study of death. *Bibl Osleriana.* **969**: 19.
15 Sontag S (1983) *Illness as Metaphor.* Penguin Books, Harmondsworth.
16 Ignatieff M (1994) *The Needs of Strangers.* Vintage, London.
17 Thomas D (1997) *Dylan Thomas.* Everyman's Poetry, London.
18 Rubinstein R (1985) *Take It and Leave It.* Marion Boyars, London.
19 Barritt P (1979) *Through the Glass Darkly.* Outposts Publications, Walton-on-Thames.
20 Tauber A (1999) *Confessions of a Medicine Man.* MIT Press, Cambridge, MA.
21 Bluebond-Langner M (1978) *The Private Worlds of Dying Children.* Princeton University Press, Princeton, NJ.
22 Wolterstorff N (1987) *Lament for a Son.* Eerdmans, Grand Rapids, MI.

Further reading

* Bluebond-Langner M (1978) *The Private Worlds of Dying Children.* Princeton University Press, Princeton, NJ.
* Danis M *et al.* (1996) A prospective study of the impact of patient preferences on life-sustaining treatment and hospital costs. *Crit Care Med.* **24**: 1811–17.
* Elliott C (ed.) (2001) *Slow Cures and Bad Philosophers.* Duke University Press, Durham, NC.
* Hauerwas S (1990) *Naming the Silences: God, medicine and the problem of suffering.* WB Eermans, Grand Rapids, MI.
* Illich I (1975) *Medical Nemesis.* Calder & Boyars, London.
* Keizer B (1996) *Dancing with Mister D.* Transworld Publishers, London.
* Needleman J (1992) *The Way of the Physician.* Penguin Books, Harmonsworth.
* Picardie R (1998) *Before I Say Goodbye.* Penguin Books, Harmondsworth.

PART THREE

Healing: the soul of healthcare

CHAPTER 10

The history of healing

> 'One of the hardest but most fascinating of all intellectual problems is
> how not to patronise the past,' someone wrote. The problem is unknown
> among doctors: they look on their colleagues from the past as a bunch of
> poor sods trying to kill a bacterium with a wooden club.
>
> Bert Keizer, *Dancing with Mister D*[1]

Definitions of healing

The *Concise Oxford Dictionary* defines healing as to 'become sound or healthy again;
to cause a wound, disease or person to heal, be cured or be made sound again; to put
right; or to alleviate sorrow'. The healer is defined as a person who heals others or
as a thing that heals or assists in healing.[2] Healing, like most other words, has a
variety of meanings depending on the context in which it is used. In addition, the
belief system of the individual, the social and cultural milieu in which he finds
himself and the period of history in which he lives all influence the significance of
the word. My understanding of healing is of an object, a process or an act of a person
who facilitates recovery from illness, injury or suffering.

Healing has a long historical and religious background and we need to explore
this dimension if we are to honour the concept. The rise of science and atheistic
humanism has challenged the relevance and authority of religious perspectives on
illness and recovery. Those of us who are involved in healing would do well to study
our historical and spiritual inheritance, whether or not we personally subscribe to
an organised religion. Understanding the feelings of distress and loss that illness
and disability engender in the afflicted is also important if we are to help those who
suffer.

Historical perspectives

It seems reasonable to assume that healers and healing may be as old as humanity
itself. It is argued that man is the only species on earth that understands the concept
of illness and is aware of the inevitability of death. That stern critic of the medical
profession, Ivan Illich, writes in his classic text *Medical Nemesis*:

> Mankind is the one living species whose members are aware of being
> frail, partly broken, and headed for total breakdown, i.e. death. The
> clearer this consciousness, the greater the need for dealing symbolically
> with the inevitable. The well-being of men and women increases with

their ability to assume personal responsibility for pain, impairment, and their attitude towards death.[3]

(p. 87)

Although it is increasingly recognised that animals use certain plants, insects and minerals to remain healthy, it is generally believed that this behaviour is instinctive and fostered by Darwinian evolution and selection. That is not to say that the process whereby the earliest human beings tested plants and other substances was radically different. Indeed the method used by the pharmaceutical industry to discover new drugs today is largely based on trial and error, the major difference being that chemicals are randomly tested on animals for the benefit of humans. Perhaps speech and cognition are the main factors that have allowed humans to change therapeutics from a lottery into a discipline.

Physical evidence of the use of herbs to heal dates back 60 000 years to a burial site in a cave in northern Iraq. Analysis of soil surrounding human bones revealed the pollen of eight different plants, seven of which are still used throughout the herbal world.[4] All cultures have traditional healers with a long history of the use of plants among their armamentaria. Drugs still used in Western medicine that are derived from plants include digoxin, aspirin, colchicine, vincristine and ergot.

The first written evidence of herbal healing dates back to 2000 BC, both on clay tablets from Mesopotamia and on papyrus from Egypt. The Ebers Papyrus written around 1500 BC contains 876 prescriptions made from over 500 different substances.[5] Many scholars now believe that the first celebrated healer was Imhotep, who was a magician, architect, poet and healer to King Zoser of the third Egyptian dynasty in 2900 BC. His name means 'he who comes in peace', and many see him as the father of mental and spiritual healing. Imhotep's cult and fame passed from Egypt into Persia and Greece, where temples were erected to him under the name Asklepios, the god of healing, regarded as the son of Apollo. People with a need for healing slept in or near the temples, and the gods and goddesses brought about cures or prescribed treatments in their dreams. Priest–physicians whispered in the ears of the sick as they slept. The symbol of the god was a snake, and harmless yellow snakes were kept around the temple and trained to lick the wounds of patients and thus heal them.[6]

At this point in history it is impossible to separate magic, religion and the use of plants, animals and minerals in the healing process. Magic rituals and incantations, bathing or drinking sacred waters and animal sacrifice were all part of healing activities. Arguably these processes are still an inherent part of healing today, certainly among traditional healers. Visiting prehistoric sites of healing in the UK, for example, reveals that there are clearly people who still make offerings for the sick at holy wells and leave pieces of material ('clouties') hanging on nearby bushes to free themselves of affliction.

The propensity for humans to ingest foreign materials in order to encourage healing has not always met with approval. Galen, for example, writes thus:

> All who drink of this remedy recover in a short time, except those whom it does not help, who all die. Therefore, it is obvious that it only fails in incurable cases.[7]

(p. 492)

Wendell Holmes is even more forthright in his condemnation:

> The disgrace of medicine has been that colossal system of self-deception, in obedience to which mines have been emptied of their cankering minerals, the vegetable kingdom robbed of all its noxious growths, the entrails of animals taxed for their impurities, the poison-bags of reptiles drained of their venom, and all the inconceivable abominations thus obtained thrust down the throats of human beings suffering from some fault of organisation, nourishment or vital stimulation.[8]
>
> (p. 265)

In this excerpt Wendell Holmes may be overstating the case against healers, as clearly there is a great appetite for potions that aim to heal. Solzhenitsyn illustrates the point well in his novel *Cancer Ward*:

> Whether they admitted as much or denied it, they all without exception in the depths of their hearts believed that there was a doctor, or a herbalist, or some old witch of a woman somewhere, whom you only had to find and get that medicine … to be saved. … It just wasn't possible that their lives were already doomed. However much we laugh at miracles when we are strong, healthy and prosperous, if life becomes so hedged and cramped that only a miracle can save us, then we clutch at this unique, exceptional miracle and believe in it![9]
>
> (p. 156)

The use of surgical techniques has also been discovered to reach back to antiquity. Cranial trephining, the surgical opening of the skull by means of primitive tools, appears to have started about 7000 years ago. The motives for trephining in the Neolithic period are conjectural, and may have included religious or therapeutic reasons. Only a small percentage of discovered skulls are trephined, but the practice was widespread. It was performed on both the living and the dead and frequently there is evidence of skull fracture, leading to speculation that it may have been performed for the relief of headaches caused by raised intracranial pressure.[10] Not only is trephining used in modern neurosurgery, but do-it-yourself enthusiasts are still prepared to undergo the procedure and now have their own website at www.trepan.com.

Religious perspectives

In Chapter 4 we discussed how religion may have arisen from man's desire to make sense of illness and suffering. Certainly religious sites and ceremonies have been inextricably linked to attempts to heal. Stone Age monuments have been used throughout the ages for healing, and probably still are. Circular stones such as the Men-an-Tol near Penzance in Cornwall in the UK have long traditions of fertility and healing associated with them. Ian Cooke writes:

> Traditional rituals at the Men-an-Tol involved passing babies and children naked through the holed stone three times and then 'drawn on the

grass three times against the sun', while adults were expected to pass through the stone nine times to achieve the desired benefits of healing or fertility, and it was generally appreciated that such rituals would only be effective at particular times of the lunar month.[11]

(p. 5)

The dawn of human religious experience is generally considered to have occurred during the Neanderthal period, with the discovery of graves decorated with animal horns and tools for use in the afterlife. Prehistoric mural art found in caves in Western Europe shows human figures dressed in animal masks. The belief that humans and animals had souls has been termed Animism, after the Latin word *anima*, meaning 'soul'.[12]

Much traditional healing in developing countries is still based on the precepts of Animism. The shaman, the medicine man and the witch doctor have much in common with their ancient ancestors. In The *Elements of Shamanism*, Nevill Drury writes:

> It may be that the shaman is a healer, able to conquer the spirits of disease, a sorcerer, skilled in harnessing spirits as allies for magical purposes, or a type of psychic detective able to recover lost possessions. At other times the shaman may seem to be somewhat priest-like – an intermediary between the gods of Creation and the more familiar realm of everyday domestic affairs. But whatever the specific role, the shaman, universally, is one who commands awe and respect, for the shaman can journey to other worlds and return with revelations from the gods.[12]

(p. 1)

The shaman employs a number of ways of journeying to meet the gods, which include fasting, drumming, sensory deprivation, meditation, chanting and taking hallucinogenic substances. The discipline involves entering an altered mental state, and this has given rise to comparisons with both schizophrenia and epilepsy, both of which are considered to be manifestations of the spirit world in traditional societies. Illness is often considered to be caused by injured spirits or by divine forces for transgressions of defined taboos. On return, the shaman hears mass confessions from those who have committed misdeeds and the gods then return lost souls, cure illnesses and generally put the world right.[12]

Some traditional healers are called to their vocation because of family links, but many are chosen. In Nepal, young boys are in danger of being captured by 'small people' who then take them away for an extended period of time and teach them the arts of healing. These boys must be unmarked, and for this reason many parents pierce the ears of their sons in order to prevent their abduction. Sometimes the call to healing comes after some great misfortune or serious illness. As children, healers are often perceived to be nervous and withdrawn from their peers. Shamanism occurs in most parts of the world, including northern Europe, North and South America, Australia, Asia and the Far East. Recently it has been proposed that cave paintings may have been created by traditional healers who entered the caves for the purpose of prolonged sensory deprivation.

The Abrahamic religions, namely Judaism, Christianity and Islam, tend to view illness as a creation of God, and historically have had mixed views about man's attempts to alter its course. The historical religious perspective has often been that illness is a divine retribution for previously committed sin, but it is difficult to know if this is primarily a human interpretation of the scriptures by the 'worried well' or the 'smug and righteous'. Most of the references concerning healing in the Old Testament merely reflect that, if healing occurs, it is a function of God's power being used through a human intermediary, usually a prophet. Illness, like all other aspects of the universe, is created by God. Prophets are, of course, central to both Judaism and Islam. In the book of Genesis, Abraham himself is described healing:

> Then Abraham interceded with God, and he healed Abimelech, his wife,
> and his slave-girls, so that they could have children.[13]

The prophet Muhammad was happy to take medicines when he was ill. Prayer is an acknowledged healing process in Islam, as in most other religions. Although Allah is credited with creating illness, he is also believed to have made the cure for each illness available to man. Illness is seen as another challenge or difficulty that human beings must deal with during their brief period of mortal trial on earth prior to the day of judgement when their actions will be taken into account.

Other Jewish literature of the time includes the so-called *Apocrypha*, including the Book of Sirach (or Ecclesiasticus), and there is certainly no conflict seen here between God and man when it comes to the healing of physicians:

> Honour a physician with the honour due unto him for the uses which ye may
> have of him: for the Lord hath created him.
> For of the most High cometh healing, and he shall receive honour of the king.
> The skill of the physician shall lift up his head: and in the sight of great men
> he shall be in admiration.
> The Lord hath created medicines out of the earth, and he that is wise will not
> abhor them.[14]

In the Western world it is undoubtedly the life and teachings of Jesus that have had most religious influence on our understanding of healing. Most of the healings of Jesus as described in the New Testament would classify as miracles (i.e. extraordinary events that can only be explained by supernatural influence).[2] The long period between the life of Jesus and the writing of the gospels calls into doubt their historical accuracy. Certainly no self-respecting prophet, let alone a son of God, would venture abroad without the ability to perform miraculous healings. Even kings were blessed with the healing touch. Until the eighteenth century, the King of England laid hands on those whom physicians had been unable to cure. Epileptics who failed to respond to the regal touch were sometimes executed.[3]

The miracles, if they occurred, would certainly have increased the street credibility of a young Jewish radical of low social rank. This is perhaps a classic example of the use of healing to gain fame and power. Pattison underlines this in *Alive and Kicking*:

> There is no quicker or more concrete way of God showing that he has put
> his power at your disposal than by being able to heal people.[15]

(p. 84)

Jesus taught that belief in God was the way to eternal salvation, and the miracles would have been a potent illustration of this for the general public. In the gospel according to Luke, Jesus refutes the idea that only sinners suffered illness or misfortune.[16] The choice of illness and disabilities that Jesus healed is interesting, and includes leprosy, menorrhagia, epilepsy, blindness, deafness, paralysis and death. Many of these afflictions were associated with considerable social stigma or outright social alienation. Jesus certainly concentrated his compassion on those least fortunate in society, and this has proved a lasting legacy to those who follow him.

Belief and faith in the healer were an important aspect of the healing by Jesus. The manner of healing was varied, and included the laying on of hands, the rubbing of his saliva on to affected body parts and the casting out of unclean spirits. Reference is made on a number of occasions to the feelings of love and compassion that were awoken within Jesus by the plight of human beings. When he healed someone from the dead it was to be Lazarus, a friend of Jesus and brother of Mary and Martha:

> Jesus, again deeply moved, went to the tomb. It was a cave, with a stone placed against it. Jesus said, 'Take away the stone.' Martha, the dead man's sister, said to him, 'Sir, by now there will be a stench; he has been there for four days.' Jesus said, 'Did I not tell you that if you have faith you will see the glory of God?'. Then they removed the stone.
>
> Jesus looked upwards and said, 'Father, I thank you for hearing me. I know that you always hear me, but I have spoken for the sake of the people standing round, that they may believe it was you who sent me.'[17]

Jesus did not monopolise healing, and indeed he actively encouraged his disciples to venture forth and heal the sick:

> Calling the Twelve together he gave them power and authority to overcome all demons and cure diseases, and sent them out to proclaim the kingdom of God and to heal the sick.[18]

When questioned by a lawyer about the means of inheriting eternal life, Jesus told the parable of the Good Samaritan. This parable may prove to be a more useful guide to the earthbound with regard to an everyday form of compassion and healing. The Samaritan poured wine and oil on the man's wounds – wine because it was believed to be antiseptic, and oil because it was believed to assist healing.[6]

The role of the church in healing was influenced by the Epistle of James, the brother of Jesus, who wrote:

> Is one of you ill? Let him send for the elders of the church to pray over him and anoint him with oil in the name of the Lord; the prayer offered in faith will heal the sick man, the Lord will restore him to health, and if he has committed sins they will be forgiven. Therefore confess your sins to one another, and pray for one another, that you may be healed.[19]

The monotheistic perspective on healing therefore has much to do with the fact that recovery from illness and suffering is possible for those with faith in God, particularly if they repent of their sins. Human beings who heal or perform miraculous cures do so as agents of God. The arrival of cures for illness that permeated through the early science of Greece was to greatly unsettle this theory. Herbs and minerals were increasingly shown to be effective *irrespective of the beliefs of the patient*, and this set the tone for a conflict between the church and the medical profession that is still alive and well today.

Healing in religious and traditional practice involves the use of cosmic forces to alleviate suffering and illness. The healer is usually acknowledged as having special or God-given talents, and is often motivated by love and compassion for others. The healed generally require faith in the healer or the force of which the healer is an intermediary. These forms of healing still represent the backbone of medical care in many parts of the world.

Scientific perspectives

The seeds of scientific thinking were sown in the time of Imhotep, and were developed further by the ancient Greeks. In *Greek Medicine*, James Longrigg writes:

> Philosophy, then, came to exercise a powerful influence upon the development of medicine and from this connection medicine derived certain important benefits. It now became incorporated within self-consistent and tightly integrated systems. Rational modes of explanation, based upon formal, deductive reasoning and sustained by logical argument, were now adopted to account for health and sickness. Man himself was considered to be part and parcel of an ordered world whose laws were discoverable, a product of his environment, made of the same substances and subject to the same laws of cause and effect that operate within the cosmos at large.[20]
>
> (p. 39)

Hippocrates was a champion of the rational approach to illness. Writing on epilepsy, which was known as the 'sacred disease', he states:

> I believe that this disease is not more divine than any other disease; it has the same nature as other diseases and a similar cause. It is also no less curable than other diseases unless by long lapse of time it is so ingrained that it is more powerful than the drugs that are applied. Like other diseases it is hereditary. ... The brain is the cause of this condition as it is of other most serious diseases.
>
> In my opinion those who first attributed a sacred character to this disease were the sort of people we nowadays call witch-doctors, faith-healers, charlatans and quacks. These people also pretend to be very pious and to have superior knowledge. Shielding themselves by citing the divine as an excuse for their own perplexity in not knowing what beneficial treatment to apply, they held this condition to be sacred so that their ignorance might not be manifest.[20]
>
> (p. 21)

The scientific vision of specific cures for specific diseases has become such a successful human enterprise, particularly over the past millennium, that healing is in danger of becoming an irrelevance. Indeed the nature of the human being who is suffering or ill could be considered almost immaterial. This is perhaps the background to the complaint that medicine, particularly in hospitals, has turned into a production line for bodies, with minds (let alone souls) being merely an irritating distraction. Of course there is nothing new in this idea. In his dialogue *Charmides,* the great philosopher Plato writes:

> 'For this,' he said, 'is the great error of our day in the treatment of the human body, that physicians separate the soul from the body.'[21]

On the other hand, it is interesting to study the history of conditions such as duodenal ulcer, which have traditionally been ascribed to poor diet, excess stress or 'psychosomatic causes'. Many patients today are still suffering from severe illness that has resulted from stomach operations for duodenal ulcer. The therapeutic advance that has enabled us to cure duodenal ulcer with a week of antibiotics and acid suppressants has made surgery for this condition obsolete.

Science tends to measure the measurable, and concepts such as healing and the soul are unlikely to be acknowledged if they cannot be counted or seen under a microscope. In scientific circles, healing is perhaps restricted to the bodily processes that mop up after the surgeon has finished cutting. Here is TS Eliot in *East Coker*, one of his *Four Quartets*:

> The wounded surgeon plies the steel
> That questions the distempered part;
> Beneath the bleeding hands we feel
> The sharp compassion of the healer's art
> Resolving the enigma of the fever chart.[22]
>
> (p. 29)

If all illnesses could be cured, all suffering banished and life on earth could become eternal, there would be no need to retain the concept of healing at all. However, even if this unlikely event were to occur, there would still be a fundamental problem with the Western biomedical approach. The biomedical model works well enough for the physical bodily ailments, but the influence of mind and soul has no real place in the scheme of things. This is perhaps best illustrated by that most infuriating of phenomena for the scientific zealot – the placebo effect. That dummy injections, procedures and tablets produce benefit in 30–50% of all illnesses is a fact of life which should make any self-respecting scientist weep. Perhaps it would matter less if it were only the suggestible patient who responded in this way, but the placebo effect is no respecter of intelligence, belief system or professorial status.

It is important not to detract from the tremendous achievements of science in lessening the burden of suffering to which humans are subject. Nonetheless, the reality of medicine today is that many conditions can be treated but not cured. Arthur Frank has used the term 'remission society' to describe all of those who are effectively well but who could never be considered cured:

> Members of the remission society include those who have had almost any cancer, those living in cardiac recovery programmes, diabetics, those whose allergies and environmental sensitivities require dietary and other

self-monitoring, those with prostheses and mechanical body regulators, the chronically ill, the disabled, those 'recovering' from abuses and addictions, and for all these people, the families that share the worries and daily triumph of staying well.[23]

(p. 8)

Chronic illness is increasing in incidence as our lives become longer and more medical conditions respond to treatment. Even in the spectacular successes of science, such as the eradication of smallpox, the triumph is often marred by the menace of military and political expediency.

It could be argued that science had achieved almost religious status in the latter half of the twentieth century, with exponents believing that ultimately science would unravel all the mysteries of the multiverse, and that medicine might eventually cure all ills. Clearly this has not struck a universal chord, as the complementary healing industries have never enjoyed such popular appeal. Homeopathy, for example, which is as yet unable to prove that its remedies are anything other than tap water, and with no scientific study ever exceeding placebo rates, is enjoying a spectacular and profitable boom in business. Of course, this being said, one would not want to denigrate the highly respectable figures that placebos can achieve.

Indeed Kleinman, writing in his book *The Illness Narratives*, develops an argument first made by Spiro that doctors might well be judged on their personal placebo rates. They claim that the placebo effect is caused by the non-specific effect of the doctor–patient relationship, and that it is in fact the essence of effective clinical care. Indeed Kleinman urges clinicians to work assiduously to cultivate the placebo effect in routine clinical care:

> It is of the utmost importance that physicians achieve the highest possible placebo effect rates. To do this, doctors must establish relationships that resonate empathy and genuine concern for the well-being of their patients, relationships the patient and family come to believe in as of practical help and symbolic significance.[24]

(p. 245)

This may be overstating the case somewhat, as the placebo effect occurs when patients treat themselves and in many other situations when the doctor–patient relationship is not involved. Nonetheless, it can be argued that the more effective the remedy, the less need there is to worry about professional charisma and good bedside manner. There has certainly has been an emphasis in Western medicine on cure, and this has led in the past to a relative neglect of those who are incurable or dying.

In *The Lost Art of Healing*, Lown quotes a passage written by a patient who was dying of prostate cancer:

> I wouldn't demand a lot of my doctor's time. I just wish he would brood on my situation for perhaps five minutes, that he would give me his whole mind just once, be bonded with me for a brief space, survey my soul as well as my flesh to get at my illness, for each man is ill in his own way.[25]

(p. xv)

The rise in the appeal of science during the twentieth century was accompanied in the Western world by a decline in religious belief. These two trends may have been unrelated, but there is a train of thought that if heaven exists, the Hubble telescope would have found it. We have seen earlier that religion can help to give meaning to suffering and death, with Jesus in particular helping to make suffering a pious activity. In *The Nature of Suffering*, Cassell postulates that the cult of self was also born at this time:

> The decline of the spiritual includes two simultaneous changes: an enlarged belief in a self as a legitimate entity apart from God, and a decline in the power of belief.[26]

> (p. 33)

Robbed of the promise of an afterlife, the individual needs to capitalise on this life, as clearly this is 'as good as it gets'. With death approaching as a fall into oblivion, is it any wonder that eternal youth and eternal life are so appealing? Suffering becomes a pointless activity that should be terminated as quickly as possible or, even better, prevented altogether. Those afflicted with imperfect health or appearance have a right to corrective action, or failing that, some financial compensation. Expressing it more eloquently, Kleinman writes:

> In the fragmented, pluralistic modern world, anxiety increasingly is free floating and requires personal processes of creating idiosyncratic meaning to supplant the shared moral and religious significance that guided our ancestors on how to suffer. Lacking generally agreed upon authorisation for how to interpret misfortune, there is a definite tendency in the contemporary world to medicalise such problems and therewith to turn to the cultural authority of the healthcare professions and science for an answer to our predicaments.[24]

> (p. 28)

Medical science plays its part in fostering the myth of perfect health, where healing would become an irrelevance. Alistair Campbell develops this theme in *Moderated Love*:

> Medical knowledge reveals the inadequacies of societies; it alters lifestyles through spreading awareness of health-risk factors; above all, it raises expectations for health and happiness to previously unimagined heights. (For example, dramatic and widely publicised advances in transplant surgery or in human genetics change the whole climate of expectation, to a point where mastery of life and death is sought as of right.)[27]

> (p. 30)

Healing in the modern world

We have seen that healing is probably as old as humanity itself. The healing tradition is inextricably linked with religious thought and social customs. Traditional healing is still the major force in developing countries, and in Asia as well as Africa many governments have decided that training traditional healers may be the most cost-effective and sensible way of providing primary healthcare. In developed countries non-medical healers are enjoying a boom in popularity.

The common thread in healing is the aim of facilitating recovery from illness or suffering. Healing may occur within a person without the need for any outside agency. Therapeutic writing or art might be straightforward examples of this. Healing in religious terms has, particularly in Christianity, often involved dramatic cures due to divine intervention. We have also seen that the idea that illness and suffering are a punishment for sin is certainly present in some religions, but that a considerable amount of scripture does not support this view.

We have also investigated the idea that the growth of rationality and scientific endeavour has brought spectacular successes in curing and preventing serious illness. The associated decline in religious faith may have contributed to the Western obsession with youth, perfect health and appearance, and a reluctance to come to terms with ageing, suffering or death. However, we have also acknowledged that most patients are not cured of illness or suffering, and that the concept of healing can still have a vital role in the healthcare professions.

In traditional and religious healing, the charisma and mystery of the healer are an important factor in success. In *Alive and Kicking,* Stephen Pattison expresses the view that medicine fosters a similar approach:

> An air of mystery and mystique surrounds religious and medical healing. Healers in both traditions would deny any fostering of illusion in their clients. It seems, however, that they often use the impression of superior knowledge of the unknown and special techniques to arouse the expectations of their clients and to achieve compliance and good results. Technical vocabularies, special settings for healing encounters and assurance on the part of the healer are vital accompaniments to cure.[15]
>
> (p. 61)

Some healers are chosen because of recognised gifts, while others may feel a calling because of some profound personal experience. The impetus for healing may be love and compassion for fellow human beings, but wealth, fame and power may also ensue. The healed may need to have confidence in and respect and admiration (or even love) for the healer. The relationship between the sufferer and the healer can be crucial to success. In *The Nature of Suffering,* Cassell writes about the doctor–patient relationship:

> Through the relationship it is possible, given the awareness of the necessity, the acceptance of the moral responsibility, the understanding of the problem and mastery of the skills, to heal the sick, to make whole the cured, to bring the chronically ill back within the fold, to relieve suffering, and to lift the burdens of illness.[26]
>
> (p. 69)

Indeed, in his book *The Healer's Art,* Cassell expands the concept to embrace the interplay in the therapeutic encounter:

> Important to our consideration of the topic is that the bonding, connectedness, or transference of the sick to the healer is not unidirectional. Both the doctor and the sick person become exquisitely sensitive to each other. ... Indeed that openness of the flow of feeling back and forth enables the physician to use his own feeling in the presence of the patient for therapeutic purposes.[28]
>
> (p. 138)

This theme is developed further by McWhinney:

> To heal the patient, something else is needed: the capacity to understand the patient's inner world – the values she lives by; her thoughts, feelings, and fears; her perception of the injury and its effect on her life. The physicians also need enough self-knowledge to identify their own anger with the patient as a cue to an understanding of her feelings.[29]
>
> (p. 71)

Healthcare professionals need to learn an understanding and tolerance not only of their patients' religious beliefs, but also of their health and illness beliefs. Understanding the long historical roots of seemingly puzzling approaches to illness may be helpful. This has been well summarised by Pattison:

> There is nothing theoretical about being ill or caring for a sick person. It is a severely practical business. This does not mean, however, that it is not important to undertake the task of trying to understand different perspectives on illness. Illness is a mystery which eludes all of our attempts at comprehension and control. When it is presented or dealt with in a simple or one-sided way by healers of any kind, secular or religious, we can be fairly sure that it is being misrepresented.[15]
>
> (p. 45)

Religion and medicine share a common interest in the concept of healing. As noted before, relationships between the two disciplines have not always been harmonious. The church has not always helped its cause by opposing new medical discoveries. Again Pattison elucidates this further:

> The list of medical practices which the churches have objected to on theological grounds, reads like a catalogue of lost causes. Christians have objected to inoculation (unnatural), contraception (defeats the creative purpose of God), anaesthetics, blood transfusions and quarantine measures against epidemic diseases like cholera (all of which were held to be unnatural or frustrations of God's purposes).[15]
>
> (p. 91)

Science, and medicine, have perhaps become more modest about their achievements in recent years, and more tolerant about accepting phenomena that occur but cannot be explained. In an address to the Society of Health and Human Values in 1981, Professor Vastyan said:

'Healing' and 'holy' have a common Old English root in our language. That common etymology well describes the older origin. From cover to cover, healing – holy healing – is the central concern of the Bible: the Jewish Bible, the Christian Bible. There we find a common insistence that healing springs from spiritual insight and spiritual action; that healing – all healing – is a holy task; that all healing has a holy source; that only the wounded can heal; that healing does not follow a path of upward mobility and autonomy and competition and minimum risk, but rather has a path of downward pilgrimage and sharing and community and maximum risk; that all who are touched in any way by the Holy are called to be healers; and that all who are healers, do the work of the Holy.[29]

(p. 99)

I can do no better than finish with the last sentence of Kleinman's *Illness Narratives*:

Against the commercialised self-images of our age, which corrode altruism and convert decency into merely a professional gesture, the experience of the healer can be a quest for a kind of human wisdom, a model of forbearance and of courage, a form of goodness, a lesson in the essentials of humanity.[24]

(p. 267)

References

1   Keizer B (1996) *Dancing with Mister D.* Transworld, London.
2   Thompson D (1995) *The Concise Oxford Dictionary.* Oxford University Press, Oxford.
3   Illich I (1975) *Medical Nemesis.* Calder & Boyars, London.
4   Solecki R (1975) A Neanderthal flower burial of northern Iraq. *Science.* 190: 880.
5   Ackerknecht E (1973) *Therapeutics: from the primitives to the twentieth century.* Hafner Press, New York.
6   Weatherhead L (1951) *Psychology, Religion and Healing.* Hodder & Stoughton, London.
7   Strauss M (ed.) (1968) *Familiar Medical Quotations.* Little, Brown, Boston, MA.
8   Wendell Holmes O (1987) In: *Medical Essays by Oliver Wendell Holmes.* Classics of Medicine Library, Birmingham.
9   Solzhenitsyn A (1971) *Cancer Ward.* Penguin Books, Harmondsworth.
10 Alt K *et al.* (1997) Evidence for Stone Age cranial surgery. *Nature.* 387: 364.
11 Cooke I (1993) *Antiquities of West Cornwall.* Men-an-Tol Studio, Penzance.
12 Drury N (1989) *The Elements of Shamanism.* Element Books, Shaftesbury.
13 *The Revised English Bible.* Genesis 20:17–18.
14 *King James Bible. Apocrypha.* The Book of Sirach 38:1–4.
15 Pattison S (1989) *Alive and Kicking.* SCM Press, London.
16 *The Revised English Bible.* Luke 13:1–5.

17   *The Revised English Bible.* John 11:38–42.

18   *The Revised English Bible.* Luke 9:1–2.

19   *The Revised English Bible.* James 5:14–16.

20   Longrigg J (1998) *Greek Medicine.* Gerald Duckworth, London.

21   Plato (1934) *The Four Socratic Dialogues of Plato.* Translated by Benjamin Jowett. Clarendon Press, Oxford.

22   Eliot TS (1940) East Coker. In: *The Four Quartets.* Faber and Faber, London.

23   Frank A (1995) *The Wounded Storyteller.* University of Chicago Press, Chicago.

24   Kleinman A (1998) *The Illness Narratives.* Basic Books, New York.

25   Lown B (1996) *The Lost Art of Healing.* Ballantine Books, New York.

26   Cassell E (1991) *The Nature of Suffering.* Oxford University Press, Oxford.

27   Campbell A (1984) *Moderated Love.* SPCK, London.

28   Cassell E (1976) *The Healer's Art.* MIT Press, Cambridge, MA.

29   McWhinney IA (1989) *A Textbook of Family Medicine.* Oxford University Press, Oxford.

Further reading

- Campbell A (1984) *Moderated Love.* SPCK, London.
- Cassell E (1976) *The Healer's Art.* MIT Press, Cambridge, MA.
- Kleinman A (1998) *The Illness Narratives.* Basic Books, New York.
- Pattison S (1989) *Alive and Kicking.* SCM Press, London.
- Weatherhead L (1951) *Psychology, Religion and Healing.* Hodder & Stoughton, London.

CHAPTER 11

The dynamics of healing

Do not believe that he who seeks to comfort you lives untroubled among the simple and quiet words that sometimes do you good. His life has much difficulty and sadness and remains far behind yours. Were it otherwise he would never have been able to find those words.

Rainer Maria Rilke, *Letters to a Young Poet*[1]

If he showed fear – frank fear – I should respect that, too. I should respect whatever he said so long as it was frank and showed respect for me, for my dignity as a man.

Oliver Sacks, *A Leg to Stand On*[2]

They supported your process rather than imposing themselves upon you. They encouraged you to trust your self. That is the task of a healer.

Louise Wisechild, *The Obsidian Mirror*[3]

The central tasks of a physician's life are understanding illness and understanding people. Since one cannot fully understand an illness without also understanding the person who is ill, these two tasks are indivisible.

Ian McWhinney, *A Textbook of Family Medicine*[4]

The doctor never looked at me. He studied parts of me but he never saw all of me. He never looked at my eyes.

Roddy Doyle, *The Woman Who Walked Into Doors*[5]

'It's not what you give them, it's how you look while giving it.' And De Graaff knows better than anyone just how he has to look. His solid foundations in biochemistry ascend to a steely blue certainty glittering in his eyes. The guy oozes a diabolical placebo.

Bert Keizer, *Dancing with Mister D*[6]

Introduction

Healing was defined in the last chapter as an object, a process or an act of a person who facilitates recovery from illness, injury or suffering. This chapter will examine some of the personal dynamics that facilitate healing in the interaction between patient and healthcare professional. Most healing takes place away from the influence of healthcare. The body's natural tendency to repair itself, the passage of time and the ministrations of family and friends are often all that is required to recover from infections, minor injuries or significant life events. Those who have benefited from love and attention in childhood are more likely to rely on inner resources and to be in stable relationships with supportive family networks. However, those from dysfunctional or abusive backgrounds have less to fall back on.

In Chapter 3, the importance of good nutrition, a safe water supply and effective sanitation in preserving or regaining health was discussed. The deadly nature of measles in children in the developing world is a good example of this. It is likely that reducing health inequalities by improving social and economic justice within societies not only prevents illness but also bolsters recovery from it.

Individuals may discover their own routes to healing. Creativity is one such road, and religious faith is another. Those who respect the natural powers of recovery may put their trust in allowing nature to take its course. Others who have faith in remedies whose effectiveness has not been proven to exceed placebo rates (e.g. vitamins, tonics and homeopathic remedies) support a booming manufacturing industry.

In this chapter, attention will be focused on the transaction between those who require healing and those who are paid to provide it. What ingredients are needed for healing to take place? Is the ability to heal innate, or can it be learned? What is the nature of the power that healers possess, and what effect does healing have on those who provide it? Curiously, the proposal that healthcare professionals heal may be met with embarrassment or disbelief by those involved. Healing tends to be associated with holy spittle and fits poorly within the scientific framework, except as something that the body does when the surgeon or nurse has finished with it. The placebo effect has much to do with healing, but as we saw earlier, this remains an area of medical discomfort.

My central argument here is that all healthcare professionals are healers, whether they like it or not. The healing task is to promote recovery or, when this is not possible, to relieve suffering and facilitate acceptance that recovery may not occur. Once the task of healing has been acknowledged, time taken to consider how to develop the skill and use it in the patient's best interest is time well spent.

Healing power

Howard Brody has proposed a classification of the components of the healing power of physicians that, I believe, can usefully be applied to all healthcare professionals. In *The Healer's Power* he talks of three components to the healing power of physicians, namely Aesculapian, charismatic and social power.

Aesculapian power is derived from the knowledge of medical facts and theories and the practical skills that relate to putting them into practice. This is the major aspect of healthcare that is taught in health professional education, and it includes the practical manipulation of instruments, technology and parts of the body, as well as some knowledge of the psychology of illness. Aesculapian power is impersonal, in that it is independent of social class and status and is transferable from one professional to the next.

Charismatic power is based on personal merits, and may be acquired by admiration of role models who demonstrate qualities to which we aspire. Such qualities might include giving the patient full attention, seeming unhurried, treating colleagues and patients with respect or making others feel special. Brody writes that 'the origins of the term *charisma* suggest that the source of power of this type is divine grace or gift.' For the atheist healer, secular grace may prove equally effective.

The third component of healing as defined by Brody is social power. This arises from social status and is cultural in origin.[7] Society has expectations of its healers, and in return offers status and prestige. Nurses as angels of mercy or doctors as heroes are examples of popular stereotypes. When medicine had little effective Aesculapian power, the use of charismatic and social power was of paramount importance. Voltaire recognised this when he wrote that the art of medicine consisted of amusing the patient while nature cured the disease.[8] The charismatic and social power to heal remains particularly important in those situations where illness cannot be diagnosed or cured, but Brody goes further when he writes that 'the power to cure without the power to relieve suffering and pain is not worth having'.[7] As Aesculapian power has increased within orthodox healthcare professions, the contribution of charismatic and social components has been largely ignored.

The personal appearance, manner of speech, non-verbal communication and conduct of healthcare professionals have much to do with charismatic and social power. The adjectives that are associated with charisma include magnetic, compelling, alluring, appealing, attractive, charming, fascinating, captivating and enigmatic. A slovenly, bad-mouthed, scruffy healthcare professional with no social graces, sensitivity or compassion might get by on Aesculapian power alone, but inspiring patient confidence is improbable, and healing abilities are likely to be stunted. When medical mistakes or misfortune occur in these circumstances, patients may appear unforgiving. If the healthcare professional is neither liked nor respected, patients may refuse to get better.

Of course, sometimes social and charismatic power can be well developed to cover up woeful or malicious Aesculapian power. One of my patients spent many years under the care of the English family doctor and mass murderer, Dr Harold Shipman, and found him to be a charming and dedicated man for whom 'nothing was too much trouble'. In a Welsh mining valley many years ago the local doctor was discovered to be an ex-priest with no medical training. He was instantly dismissed, but the local population got together a petition to try to reinstate him, saying 'he was the best doctor they'd ever had.' I worked briefly with an orthopaedic surgeon who radiated optimism and charm, and who sported a monocle and a home-grown fresh orchid in his buttonhole every morning, but whose operative results seemed strikingly dire – too much time in the greenhouse, perhaps.

The exercise of power, as Niccolo Machiavelli pointed out, is a difficult business. With trust comes suspicion, with admiration comes condemnation, and with gratitude comes resentment. With power comes responsibility. When healthcare professionals use their power for sadistic gratification, it is a shameful sight. Such abuse of power is part of all of us and lives firmly in our shadow. Our power needs to be used with skill and 'for the purpose of a right and good healing action on the patient's behalf.'[9] Right and good use of healing power relates to professional virtue, and we shall return to this topic in Chapter 15.

There is much talk within the medical profession about a decline in public respect for doctors. Perhaps some of this is wishful thinking, a harking back to a non-existent Golden Age. The medical and nursing professions throughout history, rather like royalty, have always had their ups and downs. If a Golden Age ever existed, perhaps it was in the first half of the twentieth century, when science was held in reverence and awe and Aesculapian power appeared to be limitless. Advances in dissemination of medical information, particularly over the Internet, have demystified the knowledge of the healthcare professional. As social democracy gathers momentum there may be a loss of the social power of healthcare professionals. Experience suggests that there is still plenty of awe and respect available for good healers, but those who dismiss charismatic and social power as irrelevant may miss out.

Healthcare without sensitivity and compassion makes the illness experience a dismal affair. Fortunately, there is now a renewed interest in the importance of both art and science in the care of those who are ill or suffering. A new balance is being struck, and this does not entail loosening a firm grip on Aesculapian power so much as appreciating the need to cultivate the social and charismatic aspects of work as a healthcare professional. Indeed, keeping up to date with the exploding knowledge and skills base is fundamental to survival in a society where patients can quickly become more knowledgeable about their condition than their medical attendants. This is an area where evidence-based medicine, guidelines and protocols can be of great assistance to us.

There is more control over the exercise of healing power in society today than in previous generations. Much of this has to do with advances in information technology and management. It has become easier to examine performance, particularly the Aesculapian component of healing. Although competent healthcare professionals have nothing to fear from their standards being monitored, this end of the spectrum tends to become unnecessarily apprehensive and paranoid when society institutes quality control. The usual objections are that measures of quality either reduce professional freedom or measure nothing worthwhile. Certainly if the freedom to perform poorly or dishonourably is being eroded, this is no bad thing. An example of this is provided by the league tables that have been introduced in the UK since the Shipman murders. Each family doctor is given a personal mortality rate once a year, adjusted for socio-economic factors (such as social deprivation, the proportion of elderly patients in their practice or provision of care for those in residential or nursing homes). There is debate about how meaningful these statistics are, but I for one was relieved not to feature at the head of the league. The idea that charismatic and social aspects of healing cannot be assessed is, I believe, incorrect. If we wish to know whether patients were made to feel welcome, were treated with dignity and respect, had their suffering acknowledged and were treated with sensitivity and compassion, then we merely have to ask. Perhaps healthcare professionals resent loss of control or being answerable to those whose care provides their livelihood.

Brody brings to attention another aspect of medical power, namely 'the power to deplete the public coffers in the name of healing.'[7] We saw in Chapter 3 that promoting health in a society has nothing much to do with healthcare. There is not a country on earth that can afford all of the technological wizardry and medical enthusiasm on offer, and there probably never will be. Healthcare professionals who resent public debate about the sensible and equitable use of available resources are living in 'cloud-cuckoo-land'. Cost containment of healthcare is an essential mandate for politicians.

The charismatic power of the healer has much to do with humane personal qualities. The American Board of Internal Medicine has drawn up an interesting summary of essential humanistic qualities, listing integrity, respect and compassion as the crucial characteristics. They defined integrity as a personal commitment to be honest and trustworthy in evaluating and demonstrating one's own skills and abilities. Respect was defined as a personal commitment to honour the choices and rights of others with regard to themselves and their medical care. Compassion was described as an appreciation that suffering and illness engender special needs for comfort and help, without evoking excessive emotional involvement that could undermine professional responsibility for the patient. Proposals were made that doctors who lacked these virtues would not be granted board certification.[7]

Healing relationships

Having talked at some length about the personal characteristics that contribute to healing power, it is time to move on to examine how the relationship between the healthcare professional and the patient can facilitate healing. The previous chapters on suffering, the experience of illness (both physical and mental) and the fear associated with death and dying should help us to understand this.

Helping others to heal is a complex task that is emotionally draining but professionally rewarding. Attempting to understand others is inextricably bound up with understanding ourselves. This is where the analogy of glass, pools and mirrors reappears. When patients come to us for help in making sense of illness, they need us to reflect their despair, but they also need to see through our dark glass to sense fellow humanity. When we confront the suffering of others, we see our own mortality and suffering before us. A successful encounter leads to growth and self-knowledge in both sufferer and healer. Here is Eric Cassell writing in *The Nature of Suffering*:

> It has been one of the most basic errors of the modern era in medicine to believe that patients cured of their diseases – cancer removed, coronary arteries opened, infection resolved, walking again, talking again – are also healed, are whole again. Through the relationship it is possible, given the awareness of the necessity, the acceptance of the moral responsibility, the understanding of the problem and the mastery of the skills, to heal the sick, to make whole the cured, to bring the chronically ill back within the fold, to relieve suffering, and to lift the burdens of illness.[10]
>
> (p. 69)

Closeness in therapeutic relationships

The relationship between the healthcare professional and the patient needs to be close but not too close. The difficulty of providing healthcare for loved ones and family is evidence enough to demonstrate that deep affection for others is a bar to rational and sensible decision making. Alastair Campbell highlights the importance of understanding the difference between a professional relationship and a personal friendship in his book *Moderated Love*:

> We might say that a *critical distance* is required between the helper and the person helped – too great a distance prevents the helper from

responding to the other's need: too little distance disables the helper from seeing the problem objectively and offering support from outside the situation.[11]

(p. 81)

The relationship between helper and sufferer can be anything but ideal, but it cannot be renounced:

> The relationship exists even if or when the doctor is burned out, nasty, callous, mean, cruel, and ignorant – and even when the doctor does not believe in the relationship. The doctor–patient relationship can be employed, exploited, badly used, or sabotaged, but it cannot be disowned; it is there whether a doctor wants it to be or not.[10]

(p. 68)

The healthcare professional who appears remote when confronted with suffering can be the hardest to tolerate. Henri Nouwen addresses much of his book, *The Wounded Healer*, to the clergy, but the underlying principles apply equally to healthcare professionals:

> If there is any posture that disturbs a suffering man or woman, it is aloofness. The tragedy of Christian ministry is that many who are in great need, many who seek an attentive ear, a word of support, a forgiving embrace, a firm hand, a tender smile, or even a stuttering confession of inability to do more, often find their ministers distant men who do not want to burn their fingers.[12]

(p. 71)

Distance and defensiveness often reveal a person who has lost the courage to remain vulnerable, usually through past experience of emotional pain when defences were down. Emotional abuse in childhood, for example, necessitates the erection of personal defences in order to protect the integrity of the personality. There is safety in defence and in being aloof, but such sanctuary can be lonely and sterile. The more that suffering is understood and shared, the closer the bond between professional and patient and the stronger the trust engendered. There is an issue of commitment here, too – a commitment to genuinely care for the suffering of others. This is the essence of compassionate healthcare. Here is Nouwen again:

> ... no one can help anyone without becoming involved, without entering with his whole person into the painful situation, without taking the risk of becoming hurt, wounded or even destroyed in the process.
> Who can save a child from a burning house without taking the risk of being hurt by the flames? Who can listen to a story of loneliness and despair without taking the risk of experiencing similar pains in his own heart and even losing his precious peace of mind? In short, 'Who can take away suffering without entering it?'[12]

(p. 72)

Without this openness to the suffering of others, healthcare professionals are in danger of abusing their healing powers. They may bully patients or junior staff, often by humiliating them in front of others. Medical procedures may be conducted with sadistic brute force. A 'them and us' mentality protects the professional from sharing suffering, and black humour rounds off the entertainment. Healthcare professionals can adopt a siege mentality, seeing patients as the enemy sent in hordes to persecute them with unnecessary problems. In these circumstances healthcare professionals spend most of their working life feeling sorry for themselves and bemoaning their fate.

Witness and recognition

Why is the ability and willingness to enter wholeheartedly into the suffering of the patient so important? In Chapter 5 we identified a sense of isolation, puzzlement and alienation in the early stages of illness. The healthcare professional recognises, identifies and names the illness and, in this process, helps to define, limit and depersonalise it.[13] Once defined, the illness can be confronted and dealt with. In *A Fortunate Man*, John Berger puts forward the idea that even when the doctor cannot treat or cure the patient, the role of empathic witness is equally important:

> He does more than treat them when they are ill; he is the objective witness of their lives.[13]

> (p. 109)

There are responsibilities that come with objective witnessing, and these include a pledge not to abandon the patient and a commitment to do one's best. In *The Illness Narratives*, Arthur Kleinman writes that empathic witnessing is 'a moral act, not a technical procedure.'[14] The healthcare professional needs to acknowledge the unique suffering of each individual but also to link the person back to the rest of the world. The healer acts as a bridge from the world of the ill to the world of the well.

Fraternity and love

The nature of the relationship between the suffering and the healer is hard to quantify. Those of us who have benefited from such a relationship while suffering will recall a magical quality. Jacob Needleman writes of such an experience in *The Way of the Physician*:

> … your concern to help was a completely different level of feeling and love. You were not out to 'please' anyone. You were not concerned with 'the relationship to the patient', as they put it nowadays. And I, as a patient, felt that and it gave me more strength and more trust in you than you can possibly imagine.[15]

> (p. 15)

The relationship represents a form of love, probably *agape*, the Greek word for brotherly love. This is the central theme in Alistair Campbell's book *Moderated Love*:

... the greatest problem for the professional helper is the demand for *agape* – the love which risks self in order to enhance value. *Agape* requires that no help, however well intentioned, should stamp out one's own or another's individuality. Genuine help must see each person, including the helper, afresh, as a new and separate being, for whom no real parallel exists in prior experience – the unique encountering the unique.[11]

(pp. 82–3)

The development of fraternal love is helped by commitment and continuity, but these are not essential. Considering the way of the modern world, this may be just as well. As medical systems become increasingly complex and necessitate team-work, continuity of care becomes more difficult. Fortunately, healthcare professionals with great humanity can inspire trust quickly. Henri Nouwen explains:

Let us not diminish the power of waiting by saying that a life-saving relationship cannot develop in an hour. One eye movement or one hand-shake can replace years of friendship when man is in agony. Love not only lasts forever, it needs only a second to come about.[12]

(p. 67)

Education of healthcare professionals in the past has not always concentrated on empathic witnessing, being more aligned to fixing problems or training people to be scientific and objective.[7] If our relationship with the patient is strained, we may not find fraternal love within our hearts. In these circumstances, *caritas* (or charity) is the form of love to which we need to turn. Ian McWhinney writes:

Charity is not dependent on affection; charity can be shown even when there is a lack of affection. Charity is not an emotion; it is a commitment, an act of will. To love in this way is to seek the good of the person, unconditionally.[16]

(p. 85)

There is an important difference in these circumstances between affection for a patient, which is not always possible, and acceptance of a person and who they are. 'Difficult' people generally come from 'difficult' backgrounds. Exploring their past may not benefit the patient as much as the person who is trying to help them, to find some anchor of common humanity. Indeed, an understanding of what a person has been through may be the catalyst for the relationship to move from acceptance to affection. Doing our best for each patient is an important facet of professional virtue, and is based on affection when it is present, and acceptance when it is not. The relationship with the patient is central to healing power in healthcare. Eric Cassell summarised this well:

The most skilful practitioner raises the relationship to an art, not only encouraging its growth and promoting trust and faith on the part of the patient, but negotiating between intimacy and separateness, between empathy and objectivity. Access to the patient is necessary for successful treatment. Intimacy makes that possible. One of the skills in the art of great clinicians lies in coming as close as ethically possible to intimacy

– for the access to the patient that it provides – while maintaining independence of action. Therein lies the capacity for maximum therapeutic power on the patient's behalf.[10]

(p. 79)

The relationship between healthcare professional and patient is unique. We are given access to the bodies, minds, homes and darkest secrets of those who may be virtual strangers. In exchange for this privilege, as Cassell points out, we are expected to be 'warm, dignified, kind, open, trustworthy, giving (and forgiving), gentle, and perhaps to embody other characteristics usually associated with someone whom we love.'[17]

Self-knowledge

Some of the reasons for encouraging healthcare professionals to improve their self-knowledge were explored in Chapter 2. McWhinney has summarised the need for self-knowledge succinctly:

> We cannot begin to know others until we know ourselves. We cannot grow and change as physicians until we have removed our defences and faced up to our own shortcomings. Without self-knowledge, it is difficult to prevent unrecognised feelings toward the patient from entering into the relationship – the process known to psychoanalysis as counter-transference. Finally, without self-knowledge, it is all too easy for us to feel superior to our patients, especially those with obvious weaknesses and failures.[4]
>
> (p. 82)

Being critical of patients is one way for professionals to try to prove their superiority. Genuine acceptance of others relates closely to suspending judgement, or preferably avoiding it altogether. This is, of course, considerably easier to suggest than to do. Here is McWhinney again:

> How can we expect patients to grow in self-knowledge if we lack self-knowledge ourselves? Yet how difficult the pursuit of this knowledge is, how much easier to live a life of comfortable self-deception. To confront with complete honesty our own inner selves is a painful thing.... We develop our own defence mechanisms, designed to hide our errors from ourselves and to suppress our feelings of guilt.[4]
>
> (pp. 81–2)

Self-knowledge involves confronting our shadow, admitting our prejudice and owning up to our shortcomings and mistakes. Those whose vulnerability is shielded behind tough defences may be unable to deal with or even admit to mistakes. This is a serious handicap in healthcare, since mistakes are inevitable and so much of our learning stems from them. Defined in this way, it becomes obvious that self-knowledge is never complete. The process is both uncomfortable and difficult:

> It is at the mental level that we understand the meaning of a person's experience and the values he or she lives by. It is at this level that we

encounter the spiritual aspects of medicine, the things that give significance to a person's life.

For the transcendental, the way of knowing is contemplative and intuitive. Knowledge at this level cannot be expressed in words or attained by the intellect.

The kind of preparation that can give us both self-awareness and an insight into the lives of others cannot be a matter for the intellect alone. This kind of understanding comes from the heart. The first prerequisite is faith that there is a level of meaning beyond the reach of our senses. Without such faith, we are not likely to have the commitment to undertake the search for this understanding. The intellect and the heart are not – or should not be – in conflict. The understanding that comes from the heart can enrich the intellect, and the intellect can act on the heart's insights. Each form of understanding reflects a different kind of truth. For the intellect, truth is the truth of a proposition, to be established by logical argument. For the heart, truth is something that penetrates one's whole being and transforms one's life.[4]

(p. 67)

The wounded healer

The potential for personal suffering to facilitate the development of professional empathy was discussed in Chapter 4. Experience of suffering can help to strengthen the empathic bond between the healthcare professional and their patients. The idea that personal wounds help the healer is at least as old as Greek mythology, in which Chiron the centaur was wounded by Hercules' arrow. In the Talmud there is a legend that the Messiah will be recognised by the way he dresses his own wounds at the city gates:

> 'How shall I know him?'
> 'He is sitting among the poor covered with wounds. The others unbind all their wounds at the same time and then bind them up again. But he unbinds one at a time and binds it up again, saying to himself, "Perhaps I shall be needed: if so I must always be ready so as not to delay for a moment." '[18]

In Chapter 9, the ways in which healthcare professionals may behave if they have not accepted their own mortality were discussed. These included a tendency to over-treat and to steer away from discussions with their patients about dying.

Is a wound a prerequisite for healing? I think not. I have taught many young doctors who have not experienced major suffering, who are empathic, thoughtful and compassionate in their care. One would certainly not wish suffering upon them. Perhaps the point is that when suffering occurs we can use it to our advantage in deepening our empathy and compassion towards others. There is a depth of personality to those who have suffered which is hard to define but easy to feel. As we saw earlier in Chapter 5, the experience of serious illness may cause the cantankerous to mellow. Suffering engenders compassion, and such a quality encourages people to pursue occupations in which they can relieve or share the suffering of others. This is a noble cause and not something to feel ashamed of.

The way to use our wounds in healing is not to inflict our suffering on others. As Nouwen puts it:

> ... no suffering human being is helped by someone who tells him that he has the same problems.
>
> Making one's own wounds a source of healing, therefore, does not call for a sharing of superficial personal pains but a constant willingness to see one's own pain and suffering as rising from the depth of the human condition which all men share.[12]
>
> (p. 88)

Nouwen goes on to argue that healing involves setting aside a part of oneself for the benefit of others, in the same way that a guest room in a home might be made ready for strangers:

> What does hospitality as a healing power require? It requires first of all that the host feel at home in his own house, and secondly that he create a free and fearless place for the unexpected visitor.
>
> Hospitality is the ability to pay attention to the guest. This is very difficult, since we are preoccupied with our own needs, worries and tensions, which prevent us from taking distance from ourselves in order to pay attention to others.
>
> Paradoxically, by withdrawing into ourselves, not out of self-pity but out of humility, we create the space for another to be himself and to come to us on his own terms.
>
> It is healing because it takes away the false illusion that wholeness can be given by one to another. It is healing because it does not take away the loneliness and the pain of another, but invites him to recognise his loneliness on a level where it can be shared. Many people in this life suffer because they are anxiously searching for the man or woman, the event or encounter, which will take their loneliness away. But when they enter a house with real hospitality they soon see their own wounds must be understood not as sources of despair and bitterness, but as signs that they have to travel on in obedience to the calling sounds of their own wounds.
>
> Many people suffer because of the false supposition on which they have based their lives. That supposition is that there should be no fear or loneliness, no confusion or doubt. But these sufferings can only be dealt with creatively when they are understood as wounds integral to our human condition.[12]
>
> (pp. 92–3)

Healing and patient autonomy

The position of healer and of those who are ill or suffering is unlikely, by its very nature, to be equal. The experience of illness as discussed in Chapter 5 was one of loss of confidence, control, innocence and omnipotence. These losses make the patient vulnerable, and this vulnerability needs to be respected and honoured by the healthcare professional. Power needs to be used virtuously and with compassion.

The knowledge, skills and attitudes that we have gained in healthcare engender trust, and it is with this trust that the patient gives away some of their autonomy. Trust is put in us to use our expertise and judgement to choose the path that is in the patient's best interest. The trust that is given incorporates the risks inherent in treatment. Patients need to be informed and involved in decision making as much as possible, and to an extent determined by the patient, but ultimately their trust is on our shoulders and the power thus given needs to be used honestly and wisely. The more complicated medicine becomes, the more patients will rely on us to help them to make sensible decisions. When healing occurs, the patient resumes full autonomy and equality and the healthcare professional is no longer required.[19] Those patients who opt for complete autonomy throughout serious illness may maintain independence but suffer from isolation. As Alfred Tauber points out in *Confessions of a Medicine Man*, illness can be a lonely experience:

> In this sense, to suffer is to be alone, adrift in a sea of confusion and isolated by forces beyond one's comprehension and control. The most primitive experience of disease is precisely this very loss of autonomy, of self.[19]
>
> (p. 47)

Brody believes that physicians generally overestimate the extent to which patients want to be involved in decisions, and underestimate the extent to which patients seek out information about disease and its treatment.[7] He concludes:

> The goal, of course, is not to equalise power for its own sake: medicine is not arm wrestling. The goal is to use both powers – physician's and patient's – in tandem to produce, as efficiently as possible, the best and most skilled application of medical knowledge to the patient's problems to secure an outcome that best aids the patient in living out his life plan.[7]
>
> (p. 112)

As Glin Bennet argues in *The Wound and the Doctor*, it is healthcare professionals with too much status and power who may come to believe that they possess special wisdom, insight and competence:

> Everybody has the tendency to become idiosyncratic if not exposed to some kind of criticism or control, such as occurs naturally in relaxed family settings or in working relationships.[20]
>
> (p. 75)

Sharing information helps to reduce medical power, but Bennet believes that there should be sufficient trust for some secrets to be allowed. Bennet also has difficulty with the concept of equality in the doctor–patient relationship, because the patient usually initiates the transaction. Illness or suffering creates a personal need which the healthcare professional is in a position to help.[20]

So far, we have looked at power structures in healing and the importance of the relationship between the patient and the healthcare professional in promoting recovery. It is time now to move on more specifically to the skills that we need to acquire in order to improve our healing abilities.

Healing skills

The ability to heal has an ethereal nature that is difficult to define and even more difficult to teach. It has a magical and miraculous quality. However, that is not to say that learning about healing is impossible. Healing ability comes from within us, from that part of us that Nouwen calls 'hospitality'. We need to look inside ourselves to find healing power, but there are skills that we can work on to improve our effectiveness. My contention is that the neglect of healing has led to much of the modern discontent with professional healthcare. In ancient China, the Great Physician was the force that provided a stable harmony between inner being and outer knowledge. Here is Jacob Needleman writing in *The Way of the Physician*:

> In my opinion, modern medicine, modern science, modern man has more knowledge than he can possibly use. Or rather he has a certain level of knowledge, a certain quality of knowledge composed of a mass of information and techniques in which he wanders as in a labyrinth. Since it is knowledge plus vital energy that heals another, the more knowledge he obtains at the expense of acquiring access to the higher energies within himself, the worse his life and practice become. It has been said of modern medicine that it does not extend life, but merely prolongs death.[21]
>
> (p. 181)

If healing is accepted as an integral part of the work of healthcare professionals, what are the skills and qualities that need to be developed?

Empathic listening

The *Concise Oxford Dictionary* defines empathy as 'the power of identifying oneself mentally with (and so fully comprehending) a person or object of contemplation'.[22] Empathy in healthcare involves professionals using their imagination to try to understand, perceive and feel the illness experience in the same way that the patient does.[14] Empathy does not involve projecting oneself into the same situation. It is concerned with trying to understand how another person is experiencing it, and what their feelings are about their predicament. Empathy arises when judgement of others is abandoned. It reflects a genuine curiosity for the plight of others, and is hindered by absorption with oneself. The curiosity needs to be driven by a genuine desire to help the other person. The empathic healthcare professional shares the patient's human situation, including the shared possibilities of illness, suffering and death.[23] The struggle to understand others as accurately as possible is at the heart of empathy.

In healthcare, empathy is usually gained by listening to the patient's story or narrative. Empathic listening requires the healthcare professional to remain vulnerable to the suffering and anguish of others. Scientific training often emphasises the merits of striving for objectivity, whereas empathic listening demands subjectivity, the unique search to help another human being to find meaning in their suffering. By maintaining a vulnerable, open and honest approach, both the patient and the healthcare professional will be changed by the shared experience. Listening to the narrative throws light on the lived experience of illness as experienced by that particular person. Attentive listening to a patient's story is a major source of healing.

Empathic listening is not primarily concerned with the Freudian stereotype of a patient lying on a couch talking for lengthy periods while the professional takes copious notes. Empathic listening must not appear hurried, and it involves a dialogue. The communication skills that most healthcare professionals are now taught are an essential part of this process. Attentive listening, reflective questions, and open and closed questions are all part of the technique needed to help us to gain an understanding of the patient's experience. Appreciation of the importance of body language, eye contact and the appropriate use of touch is a very important part of empathic listening. Traditional clinical method is primarily a question-and-answer style, and can lead to early and unnecessary interruptions to the patient's narrative – a barrage of closed questions resembling an interrogation rather than a dialogue. Oliver Sacks describes a bruising encounter with his orthopaedic surgeon after he had injured his leg in a climbing accident:

> I was stunned. All the agonised, agonising uncertainties and fears, all the torment I had suffered since I discovered my condition, all the hopes and expectations I had pinned on this meeting – and now this! I thought, what sort of doctor, what sort of person, is this? He didn't even listen to me. He showed no concern. He doesn't listen to his patients – he doesn't give a damn. Such a man never listens to, never learns from, his patients. He dismisses them, he despises them, he regards them as nothing.[2]
>
> (p. 73)

Empathic listening is hard work, as skilled as wielding a scalpel and just as draining. Carl Rogers has given one of the best summaries of the skill in his book *A Way of Being*:

> Attentive listening means giving one's total and undivided attention to the other person, and tells the other that we are interested and concerned. Listening is a difficult work that we will not undertake unless we have deep respect and care for the other. As counsellors, we listen not only with our ears but with our eyes, mind, heart and imagination as well. We listen to what is going on within ourselves, as well as that which is taking place in the person we are hearing. We listen to the words of the other, but we also listen to the messages buried in the words. We listen to the voice, the appearance and the body language of the other.
>
> We are attentive listeners when we focus entirely upon what is said and the circumstances under which it is said. We do not use selective listening by hearing only what interests us and fits with our preconceptions. We simply try to absorb everything the speaker is saying verbally and non-verbally without adding, subtracting or amending. Attentive listening is a demanding process to be undertaken only if we truly care for the other person.[24]

As we have seen in Chapter 5, illness brings fear and a sense of isolation and alienation. Empathic listening is the way into the world of those who suffer, and is bound up with a message of hope – that they will not be alone and they will not be rejected or abandoned. In essence there is a yawning gulf between 'taking a medical history' and listening to the patient's story.

Facilitation of change

In Chapter 5 we looked at the experience of illness from different perspectives. Illness poses questions for the patient and their family, and serious illness is generally accompanied by a sense of loss. The most fruitful perspective from which to view illness is, in my opinion, as part of the inevitable change that constitutes life on earth. Suffering, illness, ageing and death are a guaranteed part of life, and helping patients to accept and adapt to these changes is an effective way to enable them to get over and beyond illness. Healing involves helping patients to find a new wholeness from that which is broken. As life progresses, we have to learn to adapt to the limitations that are increasingly imposed upon us. In order to help patients to develop a positive outlook, healthcare professionals need to work with their patients' feelings. Understanding these feelings is the first step, but helping patients to work with these powerful emotions is equally important. A patient who is immersed in self-pity or consumed by bitterness, guilt or anger may benefit from being challenged or even confronted once trust has become established. In other words, healing is not merely a matter of establishing and maintaining a status quo. Insight and imagination may be required to help patients to find ways to move on. It may, for example, be justified to challenge those who get stuck on the question of 'Why me?' by asking them the alternative question 'Why not me?'.

Since the healthcare professional may be a crucial catalyst for change, it is important not only that they understand the patient's experience but also that their advice can be understood by the patient. Talking in technical mumbo-jumbo is a perennial problem in medicine, and is intended to keep the uninitiated (the patient) at arm's length. Why we cannot use everyday and excellent terms such as heart attack, stroke and nervous breakdown, instead of dreaming up alternatives like myocardial infarction, cerebrovascular accident and depressive illness, is completely beyond me. I am in agreement with Bert Keizer, who writes:

> If we were to put these expressions in plain English, medicine would lose much of its mystique. The effect might be compared to the introduction of vernacular in the Roman Catholic Mass: like the priest, the doctor would have to turn round, face the congregation and tell them in plain English what he is doing.[6]
>
> (p. 41)

As Howard Brody points out in *Stories of Sickness,* healthcare professionals should be as careful with their words as the surgeon is with his scalpel.[25] Passing on medical truth can become almost vicious if it is handled tactlessly. Chronic illness or disability often forces patients to make major changes to the plans that they had for their lives. They must be given the time and the opportunity to adjust to these upheavals, and should be allowed to feel loss and grief for hopes that will never be realised.

Grace

The ability to heal is a gift. We saw in the last chapter how traditional healers are often marked out from an early age by unusual qualities. Scientific medicine has concentrated on the Aesculapian mode of healing power which, as we saw earlier, is readily transferable from one person to the next. Selection for healthcare professional training in developed countries is usually based primarily on academic ability, but there is a trend towards placing more emphasis on the ability to communicate and empathise. In the past, the recommended advice for those trying to enter the medical profession was to answer questions about motivation with talk of enjoying scientific challenge and intellectual stimulation, and to avoid all mention of wanting to help others.

The ability to understand and provide care for others, particularly strangers, is a sign of a human being who has made considerable progress along the path of spiritual enlightenment. It represents a move beyond self-absorption. The instruction to love your neighbour as yourself is a profoundly difficult task. Love may be easier to acknowledge with patients whom we have known for many years and with whom we have developed a professional friendship. We have already discussed the problem of loving the 'difficult' patient and those whose behaviour we find abhorrent. Identifying with the suffering of others brings a closeness, and handling this intimacy demands self-knowledge and professionalism.

Jacob Needleman comes close to the magic when he describes his feeling as an ill child being cared for by a much-respected physician:

> Your presence, your attention, your impersonal love for something in me that was higher and more intimate to me than my frightened ego is what remains in my memory of you. While caring for my body, you were also a kind of extraordinary educator siding with that in me that yearned for inner freedom, inner being. And I repeat what I wrote in my first letters: It was not what you said, it was what you were.[21]
>
> (pp. 96–7)

Inner loneliness may drive people into the caring professions, and their own needs may overshadow those of the sick and disadvantaged they have set out to help. This is clearly a grey area, as all of us have a need to be useful and to make a fulfilling contribution to the society in which we live. Perhaps the acid test is related to how we fare at home, on holiday, during illness and after retirement. If life without work seems meaningless, we may have a genuine problem. Alistair Campbell has made some useful observations on this problem:

> The over-committed helper appears to eschew all personal comfort and private interest in the name of service to others. The reality, however, is often quite other. The hidden rewards are so great that this seeming selflessness is a form of self-assertion, which seeks to deny the reciprocity in all acts of caring, and to keep the helper firmly in the ranks of the strong and need-free.
>
> It is often more blessed to care than to be cared for, and the ability to care is frequently made possible by the understanding and sensitivity of the needy person. Such reciprocity suffuses the relationship of caring

with a spontaneity, with a sense of grace which enriches carer and cared-for alike.

We feel cared for when *our* need is recognised and when the help which is offered does not overwhelm us but gently restores our strength at a pace which allows us to feel part of the movement to recovery. Conversely, a care which imposes itself on us, forcing a conformity to someone else's ideas of what we need, merely makes us feel more helpless and vulnerable. The experience of being cared for, rather than being 'managed', is summed up in the adjective 'graceful'. Graceful care refers to something which is not offered by anxious people trying to earn love, but by sensitive people who release us from bonds of our own making in spontaneous and often surprising ways.[11]

(pp. 106–8)

I suspect that grace has to do with being able to give *and to receive* – to have experience of being both powerful and powerless. In terms of healthcare, it is only when *we* become ill or suffer that our ability to receive help from others graciously is tested. This is perhaps why midwives who experience childbirth, or surgeons who 'go under the knife' may be irrevocably changed. However we arrive there, I suggest that our aim is to become graceful and gracious healers who are able both to give and to receive care from our fellow humans. Ian McWhinney summarises this:

In the end, people are healed by love. The healer's technique and insight are important, but without love his or her power is limited. It is sad but true that in the course of medical education, with its stress on objectivity, the need to concentrate on techniques and absorb information, and the suppression of feeling by which we defend ourselves, our hearts may become hardened without our knowing it.[4]

(pp. 84–5)

Healing tasks

If healing is a gift, what are we giving to those who are ill or suffering? I suggest that there are eight healing tasks.

Giving explanation, advice and prescription

Healing involves helping to answer those questions that illness poses for the patient. We saw in Chapter 5 that the major questions posed are as follows.

- What is wrong?
- Can it be treated?
- What will happen to me?
- Why me?

Healing involves working within the patient's own constructs to help to make some sense of their illness. Therapeutic solutions need to be negotiated and agreed with the patient. Although prognostication is often no more than inspired guess-work, patients may need an idea of the likely progress and outcomes of their illness.

Inspiring confidence

Patients need confidence in their professional attendants in the same way that those of us with leaking pipes need confidence in a good plumber. Cars are a complete mystery to me, and I have to judge mechanics by whether they listen to what I have to say, whether they fix faults quickly, and whether they seem to know what they are talking about. If attention to my clothes, manners and vocabulary helps to inspire trust among my patients, then I am happy to oblige. Complete honesty in moments of confusion can be alarming for the patient. Would the woman on whom I performed my first Caesarean section have been inspired by total candour? Did she understand the reason for my assiduous post-operative care? I sincerely hope not. There is an element of acting in the healthcare professions which is an integral part of our generic skills.

Lending strength

Recovery from suffering may involve borrowing strength from others. The de-pressed patient sees a world without hope of recovery and emphasising the certainty of improvement with treatment is a key part of the healer's role. Sometimes fellow sufferers can provide the necessary support when times are hard, as in organisations such as Alcoholics Anonymous.

Caring

When cure of illness is not possible, care of the patient becomes central to the medical effort. The phrase 'The doctor told me there was nothing else they could do for me' should have vanished decades ago. There is always something more we can do. I only realised recently that nurses are encouraged in training to talk to patients when they are tending to them after death. I had been surprised to be introduced by a nurse to a dead patient, but in fact this is a deeply humane act. I suspect that nurses have always understood more about care than doctors. Perhaps gender differences are having an effect here and things will change as the majority of doctors become female. Care for the experience of illness extends to the family, too, and help may be required to renegotiate roles and restore interpersonal rela-tionships.

Restoring control

We examined the sense of loss that accompanies illness in Chapter 5. Loss of con-fidence, loss of control and loss of an innocent sense of omnipotence are all threatened by severe illness. Strength from healthcare professionals, family and friends may allow patients to regain these losses and be restored to independence. Accepting change and the inevitability of ageing and death may allow a maturation of the personality and an opportunity to make the best of what life remains. Once control has been regained, patients may no longer require help from healthcare professionals. This restoration usually adds to self-respect, and is one reason why healthcare professionals who encourage dependence may be doing their patients harm.

Giving hope

I believe that it is cruel to take away all hope from patients, however ill they may be. Life is full of surprises. Some years ago a middle-aged woman presented with a craggy liver and massive weight loss. An ultrasound scan confirmed hepatic metastases and she was admitted to hospital to track down the site of her primary cancer, but further investigations were unhelpful. The pain was severe and bedsores developed, so she was commenced on morphine. She talked of her approaching death with her customary good humour. She was a fervent Catholic and also a tremendous fan of John Wayne. We discussed who might turn up at the end of her bed in the night when the time for her death drew near, hoping perhaps for a little Hollywood magic. The night after our discussion, one of her (many) photographs of John Wayne fell to the floor and smashed. After this she appeared to change. She began to put on weight and her pain lessened so that we were able to reduce her morphine and eventually stop it. Her liver appeared to decrease in size, and eventually a repeat ultrasound of the liver was reported as normal. She has since moved away, but my spies tell me that she is alive and well. Fortunately, the small statue of the Virgin Mary on her front lawn did nothing unusual in terms of shedding tears of blood, so our rural community was left relatively unscathed.

Giving equanimity

We considered in Chapter 4 the benefits of accepting our own mortality. This is not a panacea, nor is it universally applicable. Some people are better served by clinging to feelings of omnipotence. Acceptance of change associated with disability and debility can lead to a sense of hopeful resignation.

Maintaining humility

Healing requires humility. Once the power of healing is recognised and accepted, there is a moral responsibility to use it wisely and for the good of the patient. Howard Brody highlights the potential dangers of taking oneself too seriously:

> It may be largely out of this dual sense of power and humility that the physician's virtue and character can help ensure that power is used responsibly and that its abuses are avoided. Owned, aimed and shared power each arise naturally from this dual sense of power and humility engendered by the virtue of compassion.
>
> The physician who is painfully aware of how easy it is to be full of oneself is the one who is most likely to be more comfortable when power

is shared instead of monopolised. The physician who is inclined to be self-reflective and self-critical about such matters, who knows that the easy rationalisations lead to arrogance, will be more likely to own responsibility for the power that is used and to question carefully the goals towards which that power is applied.[7]

(pp. 260–4)

We shall return to compassion and virtue later in the book. The ability to heal is a gift which can be developed and worked upon. Healing involves working with the forces of natural recovery, and the healer needs to be aware that the power emanates from within the patient and not from within the healer. The benefits of healing are fundamental to healthcare and should be cherished by those who are fortunate enough to possess them. Here is Oliver Sacks writing in *The Man Who Mistook His Wife for a Hat*:

> I have known Jimmie now for nine years – and neuropsychologically he has not changed in the least. He still has the severest, most devastating Korsakov's, cannot remember isolated items for more than a few seconds, and has a dense amnesia going back to 1945. But humanly, spiritually, he is at times a different man altogether – no longer fluttering, restless, bored and lost, but deeply attentive to the beauty and soul of the world, rich in all the Kierkegaardian categories – the aesthetic, the moral, the religious, the dramatic.... Empirical science, empiricism, takes no account of the soul, no account of what constitutes and determines personal being. Perhaps there is a philosophical as well as a clinical lesson here: that in Korsakov's, or dementia, or other such catastrophes, however great the organic damage ... there remains the undiminished possibility of reintegration by art, by communion, by touching the human spirit, and this can be preserved in what seems at first a hopeless state of neurological devastation.[26]

(p. 37)

References

1 Rilke R (1993) *Letters to a Young Poet.* WW Norton & Co., New York.
2 Sacks O (1986) *A Leg to Stand On.* Pan Books, London.
3 Wisechild L (1988) *The Obsidian Mirror.* Seal Press, New York.
4 McWhinney I (1997) *A Textbook of Family Medicine* (2e). Oxford University Press, Oxford.
5 Doyle R (1998) *The Woman Who Walked Into Doors.* Vintage, London.
6 Keizer B (1996) *Dancing with Mister D.* Transworld Publishers, London.
7 Brody H (1992) *The Healer's Power.* Yale University Press, New Haven, CT.
8 Helman C (ed.) (2003) *Doctors and Patients.* Radcliffe Medical Press, Oxford.
9 Pellegrino E and Thomasma D (1981) *A Philosophical Basis of Medical Practice.* Oxford University Press, Oxford.
10 Cassell E (1991) *The Nature of Suffering and the Goals of Medicine.* Oxford University Press, Oxford.
11 Campbell A (1984) *Moderated Love.* SPCK, London.

12   Nouwen H (1979) *The Wounded Healer.* Doubleday, New York.

13   Berger E (1997) *A Fortunate Man.* Vintage, Random House, New York.

14   Kleinman A (1988) *The Illness Narratives.* Basic Books, New York.

15   Needleman J (1985) *The Way of the Physician.* Arkana, London.

16   McWhinney I (1997) *A Textbook of Family Medicine.* Oxford University Press, Oxford.

17   Cassell E (1985) *Talking with Patients. Volume 1.* MIT Press, Cambridge, MA.

18   The Tractate Sanhedrin. In: *The Talmud.*

19   Tauber A (1999) *Confessions of a Medicine Man.* MIT Press, Cambridge, MA.

20   Bennet G (1987) *The Wound and the Doctor.* Secker & Warburg, London.

21   Needleman J (1992) *The Way of the Physician.* Arkana, Penguin Books, Harmondsworth.

22   Thomson D (1995) *The Concise Oxford Dictionary* (9e). Oxford University Press, Oxford.

23   Spiro H (ed.) (1993) *Empathy and the Practice of Medicine.* Yale University Press, New Haven, CT.

24   Rogers C (1980) *A Way of Being.* Houghton Mifflin, Boston, MA.

25   Brody H (1987) *Stories of Sickness.* Yale University Press, New Haven, CT.

26   Sacks O (1986) *The Man Who Mistook His Wife for a Hat.* Picador, London.

Further reading

- Brody H (1992) *The Healer's Power.* Yale University Press, New Haven, CT.
- Campbell A (1984) *Moderated Love.* SPCK, London.
- Cassell E (1991) *The Nature of Suffering and the Goals of Medicine.* Oxford University Press, Oxford.
- Kleinman A (1988) *The Illness Narratives.* Basic Books, New York.
- McWhinney I (1997) *A Textbook of Family Medicine* (2e). Oxford University Press, Oxford.
- Needleman J (1992) *The Way of the Physician.* Arkana, Penguin Books, Harmondsworth.
- Nouwen H (1979) *The Wounded Healer.* Doubleday, New York.
- Sacks O (1986) *A Leg to Stand On.* Pan Books, London.

CHAPTER 12

Uncertainty, bewilderment and mystery

> Education is the path from cocky ignorance to miserable uncertainty.
> Mark Twain

> Study until twenty-five, investigate until forty, profession until sixty, at which age I would have him retired on a double allowance.
> Sir William Osler

> It is the burden of doctors to have great responsibility in a sea of doubt and uncertainty.
> Eric Cassell, *The Nature of Suffering and the Goals of Medicine*[1]

> Perhaps the most basic skill of the physician is the ability to have comfort with uncertainty, to recognise with humility the uncertainty inherent in all situations, to be open to the ever-present possibility of the surprising, the mysterious, and even the holy, and to meet people there.
> Rachel Naomi Remen, quoted in *Doctors and Patients*[2]

Introduction

Uncertainty is an inherent part of life as a healthcare professional. Biological systems are variable, complex and unpredictable, and our understanding of them is incomplete. Much of healthcare has to do with forecasting, planning or trying to alter future events, and is therefore uncertain by its very nature. Sir William Osler described medicine as 'a science of uncertainty and an art of probability'. One of the key attributes of a good healthcare professional is this ability to make sound decisions on the basis of inadequate information. Success in a sea of uncertainty demands reliance on a key quality that may be called 'gut instinct', 'intuition', 'sixth sense' or simply a 'hunch'. Primary care medicine in particular demands this quality, as there is neither the time nor the resources to fully examine and investigate each complaint. Careful listening, keeping an open mind and lateral thinking are all of critical importance. Trusting clinical instinct becomes easier with experience, and perhaps this is what Osler was referring to in the quotation at the start of this chapter.

Uncertainty and personality

Navigating in the fog of doubt is not an experience that all personalities are comfortable with, and it is hard to imagine an area of medicine where it does not apply. Even the cadaver and the histology slide can regularly pose questions to which there is no clear answer. There are perhaps two key personal qualities that make uncertainty a problem, namely fear of being wrong, and arrogance. It could be argued that these qualities are closely related, particularly if arrogance is perceived as a defence against a lifetime of assault on personal feeling. Being wrong in healthcare may cause unnecessary suffering and cost the patient their life, but there are many other occupations where this applies. Consider air-traffic controllers or nuclear-energy operatives, for example.

It is human to be arrogant when young, and it is natural to be anxious as an inexperienced healthcare professional. It is not the making of mistakes that is the problem here – healthcare professionals are human, and humans make mistakes. The problem is whether and how quickly we learn from our mistakes. The anxious lose confidence and sleep over even trivial mistakes, and struggle with the responsibility of inadvertently harming those they set out to help. Their anxiety drives them to over-investigate and over-treat patients, and the latter end up as apprehensive and exhausted as the healthcare professional. Unfortunately, harming patients as a result of mistakes is an inevitable consequence of the job. We will make errors and patients may die as a result. We carry our mistakes through our career like a cupboard of skeletons on our back.

The arrogant have a defensive shell that makes admitting to mistakes, even to themselves, a genuine problem. They show reluctance to face up to the reality of their errors, and are likely to come out fighting if confronted with them. Arrogance is a weakness, but it is not usually perceived as such. The interpersonal skills of the arrogant make them few friends, and in healthcare one needs as much help as one can get, not only from patients and their relatives, but also from colleagues. I find it helpful to imagine the arrogant as little boys and girls being humiliated by parents or by their peers in the playground. In reality, they almost certainly were. Their inability to show vulnerability reflects past wounds. Without vulnerability there is no love, and healthcare without love is a joyless experience. That vital ingredient, the sixth sense, is above all a *feeling*, and for the arrogant, feelings are locked away and gut instinct is likely to be ignored. The cure for arrogance is to grow older and to learn to trust and value the human race.

Learning from mistakes is a reflective skill that is at the heart of good healthcare, but we must balance this by remembering to learn from our successes as well. All of the patients we have productively helped along the way balance the heavy cupboard on our back. We need to remain humble but not disheartened. A certain level of confidence is required to motivate the healthcare professional to turn out of bed every morning, noon and night. In particular, when we examine our mistakes we should forgive ourselves if at the time we were doing the best we could and we had the patient's best interests at heart. This is ultimately what makes the cupboard of skeletons bearable. We are humans, not gods, and we can only do our best. We have our gift, which is steeped in our humanity, and we must learn to make the very best of it.

Uncertainty and medical orthodoxy

Healthcare provides itself with some official channels for coping with uncertainty. In his book *Mystery in Western Medicine*, David Greaves points out that medical terminology is designed to defy uncertainty. The word 'idiopathic' is a splendid example of medical blagging, not only sounding authoritative but also implying that an answer to the causation is just around the corner. Another traditional medical ruse when the patient perplexes the professional is to label their problem as psychosomatic and then to punish them by sending them to a psychiatrist. The implication here is 'I can't find out what is wrong with you, so you must be mad'. Alternatively, one can clutch recalcitrant symptoms together into a syndrome or disorder. Nightmares could become chronic recurrent nocturnal dysphoric disorder (or CRNDD for short). Greaves concludes:

> Terms such as idiopathic and syndrome are therefore an essential part of this process of converting mystery into an apparently soluble puzzle and as such are not neutral descriptions as is claimed, but symbols of hope and belief.[3]
>
> (p. 7)

At the heart of uncertainty is the problem that every person is different. Orthodox medicine gets around this issue by turning people into 'interesting cases'. The particular can then become generalised. The patient ceases to be an individual and instead becomes a case of phaeochromocytoma on legs.

Another tried and tested strategy for defeating uncertainty is to become certain instead.[1] As a junior doctor I worked for a physician whose main pleasure in life seemed to revolve around finding clinical signs that his junior staff had missed. I would return to patients after ward rounds trying to feel that elusive spleen or hear a recalcitrant murmur. My clinical confidence only returned after attending post-mortem examinations of these patients, which showed mercifully normal organs and pristine heart valves. As a student I worked with another physician who was as deaf as a post. He had a legendary ability to hear murmurs that no one else could, and once lent me his stethoscope to listen in. His registrar muttered *sotto voce* 'Be careful, young man, that stethoscope has a built-in diastolic murmur.'

The final medical strategy for banishing uncertainty is to blame the patient. The wound that fails to heal is due to the patient interfering with it. Hypertension that fails to respond to treatment is caused by non-compliance.

Coping with uncertainty

Accepting uncertainty is the first step in finding a legitimate way to deal with the problem of doubt, without necessarily burdening the patient. Complete honesty about our confusion at all times would be a cruel abrogation of responsibility to the patient. Eric Cassell points this out in *The Healer's Art*:

> In caring for patients, the doctor must learn to deal with, and conceal, the doubts and fears by some mechanism or another. The sick patient has enough troubles and he doesn't need his doctor's doubts.[4]
>
> (p. 141)

Indeed, one could go further and suggest that we should welcome uncertainty, as it is the individuality and diversity of human nature that prevents us from becoming bored with healthcare. Those who feel that 'they have seen it all before' need to be retired before they do someone damage. When the pioneering psychologist Abraham Maslow studied the psychology of the healthy individual, he found that comfort with uncertainty was a defining characteristic of the successful personality. In *Motivation and Personality* he writes:

> Studies of psychologically healthy people indicate that they are, as a defining characteristic, attracted to the mysterious, to the unknown, to the chaotic, unorganised, and unexplained.[5]
>
> (p. 24)

I suggest that there are at least six constructive ways of dealing with uncertainty:

1 knowledge and experience
2 thoughtful investigation
3 evidence, protocols and guidelines
4 patience
5 lateral thinking
6 honesty.

Knowledge and experience

Confidence comes with increasing knowledge and experience, and it is right for the healthcare professional to make every effort to keep up to date in order to minimise the uncertainty that stems from lack of information or expertise. On the other hand, patients understand the problem of ever-expanding medical information, and most are at ease with an admission of ignorance provided that it is coupled with a commitment to find out the necessary information or to seek help from a colleague. Instantaneous access to the Internet, to guidelines and to decision support means that increasingly help can be sought within the confines of the consultation. As expertise develops, protocols and guidelines become less useful and their limitations become more apparent.

As we discussed earlier, there is a difference between having an experience and learning from it. Dogma, prejudice and preconceptions all block the route to learning. This is why the realisation of ignorance is such a critical part of the learning process. The Buddhist says that 'when the pupil is ready, the master appears.' I suspect that TS Eliot was thinking along similar lines in the *Four Quartets* when he wrote:

> We shall not cease from exploration
> And the end of all our exploring
> Will be to arrive where we started
> And know the place for the first time.[6]
>
> (p. 59)

Indeed it is the understanding that all knowledge is uncertain that is central to learning. In science, once a hypothesis fails to explain certain facts it is discarded and replaced by another. Textbooks are out of date before they are printed. Be open to new experiences and do not discard their lessons because they seem to be at variance with the perceived wisdom of the day. Healthcare professionals tend to listen to those things which patients tell them that make sense within the medical model, and to ignore everything else. Listening openly to the patient's story can unravel many medical mysteries, whether or not it makes sense at the time.

Thoughtful investigation

Investigations can prove useful in determining the answers to those questions that illness poses for the patient which, as we saw in Chapter 5, include 'What is wrong?', 'Can I be treated?', 'What will happen to me?' and 'Why me?'. However, it is important to remember that most diagnoses are made from the history, and that the contribution made by physical examination and investigations is much less important. In addition, it is crucial to realise that undertaking thoughtless batches of tests can merely add to the general confusion.

Before doing any test, ask yourself what difference the result of the test will make to the management of the patient. This is why routine health checks with their standard battery of tests cause such mayhem. One slight abnormality on a 'routine' test leads to a profusion of further tests (often invasive) to which the patient is then subjected. A classic example is the use of sophisticated urinalysis tests on the general population. Microscopic haematuria fulfils none of the criteria for a productive screening programme. If the test result is positive, do we ignore it or do we subject the patient to intravenous urography and outpatient cystoscopy? In the culture of blame in which we are immersed, can we afford not to investigate this fully? This dilemma is central to why private medical systems love screening (it is good for business) and why doctors generally disapprove of it (it is a waste of time and limited resources). Health checks fit in well with the mechanistic view of the body as a machine that needs regular servicing and checking.

Central to the problem of uncertainty in investigation is the problem of individual variation around the mean. Measure any biological variable and a normal population will show a bell-shaped Gaussian distribution. The cut-off points of normality are arbitrarily set at +2 or −2 standard deviations from the mean. The end result of this is that when a biological measurement is made of 100 normal people, approximately five of them will be defined as having an abnormal result. In my view, this is why there should be no such thing as a 'routine' test. Investigating patients in order to provide reassurance (either for the patient or for the doctor) is fraught with a tendency for the whole scheme to backfire. The stethoscope picks up a slight murmur, the ECG shows right bundle branch block, the echocardiogram shows a floppy mitral valve, the exercise test is ambiguous and, before you know it, someone is poking around in the patient's coronary arteries. Being told at the end of all this that there is nothing wrong with the heart can take some swallowing, and some patients never fully recover from the experience. What is more, these risks take no account of poorly calibrated instruments, observer bias and error, or the general difficulty of interpreting test results.[3]

As Greaves points out, the march of technology distances the healthcare professional from the patient. Prior to the stethoscope it was customary for the physician to rest his ear on the bare chest or breast of the patient, a manoeuvre that might raise a few eyebrows today. As technology becomes more and more impressive, the investigation tends to assume greater prominence than it truly deserves. Physical examination becomes less valued and the medical history becomes a distant memory.[3] Taken to its logical conclusion, this model would make the diagnostic skills of the healthcare professional redundant. For each new symptom the patient would merely hop into a body scanner and the answers to the four crucial questions could be provided on a tear-off slip or perhaps emailed to their mobile phone.

The evidence to date that technology can dispel medical uncertainty is slim. It is still not possible to get a computer to reliably read an ECG as well as I can, and (take it from me) that is a damning indictment. Perhaps the appreciation of electric waveforms is an art rather than a science.

The enthusiasm for investigation also shows a Gaussian distribution, perhaps with the over-anxious and fearful healthcare professional at one end and the arrogant one at the other. Investigations are an essential part of medicine, but careful thought should be given to every request for a test.

Evidence, protocols and guidelines

Evidence-based medicine (EBM) is the Holy Grail of the healthcare professional who is uneasy with doubt. It appeals to the young who plead to be spared debate and 'just be given the facts'. The lifeblood that fills the cup is the hallowed randomised controlled clinical trial (RCCT). Thus the limitations of the controlled clinical trial are the same as those that apply to EBM. I am not arguing here that EBM has no useful place in modern medicine, or that the RCCT should be abandoned, but merely that neither represents the absolute truth, and both need to be examined with a critical eye.

Controlled clinical trials still have much to do with teaching hospitals. When I was a medical student in the 1970s, the teaching hospital had more professionals than patients and admission could only be gained if you were 'an interesting case'. The general riff-raff of an emergency take was not allowed in. Power and prestige still revolve around the teaching hospitals. This is where the professors hang out, and their task is to joust with each other in regular gladiatorial contests. As a general rule, the closer you are to patients the busier you become and the less time you have available for clinical research.

Broadly speaking, the RCCT wants cases rather than patients. If you are investigating one disease you do not want them to suffer from four others and be on six different medications. This alone rules out the majority of patients I see in clinical practice. Take a look at a list of patients in primary care suffering from a particular disorder, and estimate how many might be prepared to come to the surgery on four or five extra occasions to help you to investigate a new treatment versus a placebo. If one in ten of the list seems likely, you will be doing well. This means that the results of a trial would not apply to 90% of your patients. The reasons for exclusion would include all kinds of factors – too busy, too ill, too stressed, too complicated, too anxious, and so on. The world of the RCCT is essentially unreal.

If medical intervention is having a modest impact, huge numbers of patients may be required in a trial. Pharmaceutical companies sponsor much research, and this means that very few head-to-head comparisons of competing treatments are performed. Large trials of cheap generic drugs are unlikely. Researchers and drug companies generally prefer results stated as a *percentage reduction in risk* rather than the more meaningful *number needed to treat*. A 50% reduction in fracture sounds far more impressive than 100 patients needing to take a treatment for 10 years in order to prevent one fracture.

The expression of risk might seem a reliable way to help patients to reach a decision about the correct course of action. My computer terminal can automatically tell me that the patient sitting beside me has a 20% risk of having a heart attack or stroke in the next 10 years. On the other hand, they may already be 74 years old. What is more to the point, is this particular patient the one in five who is going to have an event, or one of the four in five who are not?

The outcomes of clinical trials form the backbone of protocols and guidelines, and this seems reasonable. Anyone who has a strong faith in guidelines would do well to attend the meetings when they are being prepared. Arrange for ten eminent and enthusiastic experts to meet together and agree on a simple set of guidelines for best practice. A quick job? I think not. The end result is usually delayed, often for years, and has more to do with egos, commerce and blind faith than to do with science and logic. I suspect that if Moses had not rejected a committee structure, there would have been more than ten commandments (with plenty of room for caveats, opt-outs and provisos). O'Neill quotes Wiggins as having referred to a system of rules that might spare 'the agony of thinking and all the torment of feeling that is actually involved in reasoned deliberation'.[7]

The essence of my argument here is not that we ignore RCCTs and EBM, but merely that we take them with a large pinch of salt and let them inform, but not make, our clinical decisions.

Patience

Patience is a key quality in the struggle against uncertainty. It is easier to develop in primary care, where repeated visits can easily be arranged. Most puzzling presentations become clearer with time, or else simply disappear. Follow-up can often be left to the patient, with instructions to return after a determined period if symptoms have not resolved. Instructions to return if new symptoms develop or the patient's general condition deteriorates are almost a compulsory element of primary care medicine, particularly in childhood illness. Jacob Needleman has described this as a 'special quality of inspired patience and watchfulness in treatment', and worries that today's doctors have had this option taken away from them.[8]

Lateral thinking

Mistakes can often be compounded if healthcare professionals insist on sticking to their original formulation of the problem. If symptoms remain persistently problematic or fail to respond to treatment, the best strategy is to go back to basics. Is the diagnosis wrong? A child who seemed alert and well this morning may not seem alert and well two hours later. When problem cases are discussed among colleagues, there is often a sense of having headed off in completely the wrong direction. When there is one obvious cause for symptoms it can be difficult to keep all the other causes in mind. My sister felt profoundly weak and tired during her course of chemotherapy for breast cancer, and it was many months before severe hypothyroidism was detected.

Ignore the patients' or relatives' opinion at your peril. Exploring the patient's formulation of the problem can save hours of useless pondering. I remember asking one women what she thought might be wrong when she brought out a children's guide to pigeon-fancying: 'Could it be psittacosis, doctor?'. Indeed it could, and indeed it was! In healthcare we need all the help we can get. Uncertainty demands true humility, a modesty that tells you to throw out your previous decision and formulate another one. If you make a mistake or change your mind, ring up the patient and tell them so. I have never known a patient take offence at this strategy; perhaps because it signifies that considerable thought has been given to their problem long after leaving the consulting room. If your mistake has caused grievous harm, apologise face to face. In general patients are very forgiving, even if your mistake may cost them their life. This is particularly true if at all times you have tried to do your best for them. Above all, learn from your mistakes.

In summary, don't think in straight lines – think sideways.

Honesty

As we discussed earlier, it is unfair to share all doubt and confusion with the patient. Phrases such as 'I haven't the foggiest idea' are best avoided. As a young doctor I once told a patient that I was 99% sure he was not having a heart attack. Fortunately, I felt able to revise the mathematical estimate when he rang back two hours later, and I am glad to say some 20 years later that he is still alive and well. I put that one down to the arrogance of youth! At other times, however, sharing our uncertainty can be justified. It can be reasonable to explain after extensive tests that no serious cause for a symptom has been found, even if an explanation for the symptom is not forthcoming. Mechanics find this a difficult concept – a mechanic who cannot fix a car is clearly a scoundrel. Many puzzling symptoms resolve with time and without explanation. Others sneak up on you and turn out to be one of those conditions that are difficult to diagnose, such as primary Sjögren's syndrome or multiple sclerosis.

Having looked at some legitimate and illegitimate ways of dealing with uncertainty, we next need to consider the role of the healthcare professional in helping patients to make good decisions. The key to making good decisions in uncertain situations is judgement or, as Aristotle called it, practical wisdom.

Practical wisdom

Judgement in healthcare is a fundamental but curiously neglected asset. Those who lack good judgement flounder in the sea of uncertainty, grasping at ESRs and other such medical straws. Eric Cassell conveys this well in *The Nature of Suffering*:

> One can say that the function of the doctor in making medical science work for particular patients is not tacit or invisible at all. Rather, it is judgement, and everybody knows that doctoring requires judgement. This is correct, but think how little is known about judgement aside from the fact that experience is necessary to acquire it, and that some people (including some doctors) never have it.[1]

(p. 106)

One thing can safely be said about judgement – it is complex. James Nelson takes us back to Aristotle's view:

> Aristotle's idea was that the competent maker of moral decisions possesses a faculty he called *phronesis*, typically translated as 'practical wisdom.' Phronesis involves the ability to discern the best course of action in a given instance of choice. It is decidedly not a mastery of algorithmic decision procedures, although of course a person of practical wisdom will have to know a great many general things, both about the world and about its value. Among these will be certain rules and principles and how to draw valid inferences. But seeing where right action lies between vicious extremes is not a matter of deducing conclusions from premises; it is, as we say, a matter of judgement.
>
> Excellence in them [moral decision making] is achieved not by memorising formulae but by developing a highly nuanced sense of what is fitting given the particularities of the presenting situation.[9]
>
> (pp. 48–9)

Nelson goes on to define two approaches to decision making. He calls the approach that relies on outcomes research and generates clinical guidelines the *formal evidence model*, and he refers to its champions as *formalists*. The second approach, which he calls the *expert judgement model*, rests on making good clinical decisions by integrating scientific information and models with clinical experience, cultural understanding and life experiences:

> This conglomeration gives rise to an individual's ability to see clinically relevant particulars in a way enlivened by their own interplay, and their interplay with an unruly mixture of general ideas and experiences that can suggest fruitful analogies and illuminate the contours of useful patterns.[9]
>
> (pp. 52–3)

In healthcare these analogies and patterns might, for example, be the experience and views of the patient which allow us to communicate and reach decisions in a way that makes sense and resonates with the patient's world view and their personal system of faith and belief. Nelson goes on to quote Wittgenstein's discussions on 'expert judgement':

> Is there such a thing as 'expert judgement' about the genuineness of expressions of feeling? – Even here, there are some whose judgement is 'better' and those whose judgement is 'worse.'
>
> Correcter prognoses will generally issue from the judgements of those with a better knowledge of mankind.
>
> Can one learn this knowledge? Yes; some can. Not, however, by taking a course in it, but through *'experience.'* Can someone else be a man's teacher in this? Certainly. From time to time he gives him the right *tip*. This is what 'learning' and 'teaching' are like here. What one acquires here is not a technique; one learns correct judgements. There are also

rules, but they do not form a system, and only experienced people can apply them right.[10]

(p. 63)

I suspect, too, that the best way to learn this skill is in a position of apprentice – a one-to-one relationship with the master. This, of course, begs the question of how we identify an expert judge. How, come to that, do we choose our role models? I suspect that it has to do with how accurate and reliable a person's judgements turn out to be. I have no way of assessing the competence of a mechanic, as the workings of a car are a complete mystery to me. Over time the wisdom or otherwise of the mechanic's predictions and advice become apparent. In the same way, our patients assess our skill in judgement. Did the illness behave in the way we predicted? Did the course of action we suggested prove to be the right one? Did the loved one die in the dignified way we had forecast? Judgement relates to the future accuracy of our treatment, predictions and advice.

There is clearly a marked difference between knowledge and wisdom. Wisdom cannot readily be taught on a course, and it cannot easily be measured. Knowledge relates to accumulated facts from the past, whereas wisdom relates to the accuracy of prophecy of the future. The wise person is not always right in their prophecy, but they are more usually right than wrong. The judgement of the wisest healthcare professional is therefore not infallible.

There is another conundrum here. As Eric Cassell points out, the closer we come to another human being the greater our uncertainty becomes. This may be the reason why looking after the healthcare of family and friends is so difficult. Here is Cassell in *The Nature of Suffering*:

> Withdrawal from the patient is rewarded with certainty and punished by sterile inadequate knowledge; movement toward the patient is re-warded with knowledge and punished with uncertainties. The fact remains, however, that to disengage from the patient is to lose the ulti-mate source of knowledge in medicine.[1]

(p. 232)

There are other tensions, too, in this complicated field. There is always an element of time in healthcare encounters. Finding out about the patient's world takes time and an innocence of approach, whereas concluding one consultation and moving on to the next one calls for closure and maturity of experience.[3] Being trained to be scientific and objective can hamper the development of the subjectivity inherent in entering into another's suffering. Howard Brody, in his book *The Healer's Power*, emphasises the importance of balancing power and powerlessness. As soon as the healthcare professional becomes full of him- or herself, humility is lost and danger looms. Wisdom is elusive, and those who believe that they have it may well be a hazard to health. Brody writes:

> He is most likely to fail on those bad days when he is too full of himself and hence unable either to attend carefully to the anguished patient or else too wrapped up in himself to be open to the experience of anguish in the other.[11]

(p. 262)

Brody identifies a combination of genuine concern for patients together with a self-critical humility as the best way forward. He proposes that those healthcare professionals who are happy to share power with the patient are those least likely to abuse it. He concludes:

> It may be largely out of this dual sense of power and humility that the physician's virtue and character can help ensure that power is used responsibly and that its abuses are avoided. Owned, aimed and shared power each arise naturally from this dual sense of power and humility engendered by the virtue of compassion.[11]

(p. 260)

It is to the subject of compassion that we shall now turn.

References

1   Cassell E (1991) *The Nature of Suffering and the Goals of Medicine.* Oxford University Press, Oxford.
2   Helman C (ed.) (2003) *Doctors and Patients: an anthology.* Radcliffe Medical Press, Oxford.
3   Greaves D (1996) *Mystery in Western Medicine.* Avebury, Aldershot.
4   Cassell E (1985) *The Healer's Art.* MIT Press, Cambridge, MA.
5   Maslow A (1970) *Motivation and Personality* (3e). Harper & Row, New York.
6   Eliot TS (1943) *Four Quartets.* Faber & Faber, London.
7   O'Neill O (2000) *Bounds of Justice.* Cambridge University Press, Cambridge.
8   Needleman J (1992) *The Way of the Physician.* Penguin Books, Harmondsworth.
9   Nelson J (2001) 'Unlike calculating rules'? Clinical judgement, formalised decision making, and Wittgenstein. In: C Elliott (ed.) *Slow Cures and Bad Philosophers.* Duke University Press, Durham, NC.
10 Wittgenstein L (1953) *Philosophical Investigations.* Translated by G Anscombe. Basil Blackwell, Oxford.
11 Brody H (1992) *The Healer's Power.* Yale University Press, New Haven, CT.

Further reading

* Brody H (1992) *The Healer's Power.* Yale University Press, New Haven, CT.
* Cassell E (1985) *The Healer's Art.* MIT Press, Cambridge, MA.
* Cassell E (1991) *The Nature of Suffering and the Goals of Medicine.* Oxford University Press, Oxford.
* Elliott C (ed.) (2001) *Slow Cures and Bad Philosophers.* Duke University Press, Durham, NC.
* Greaves D (1996) *Mystery in Western Medicine.* Avebury, Aldershot.

CHAPTER 13

Compassion

Make your heart like a lake,
with a calm, still surface,
and great depths of kindness.

Nurture your true nature.
Make love your gift to others.
Only talk the truth.

Lao Tzu, *Tao Te Ching*[1]

This is a melting heart, and a troubled heart, and a wounded heart, and a broken heart, and a contrite heart; and by the powerful working of thy piercing Spirit such a heart I have

John Donne, *Devotions upon Emergent Occasions and Several Steps in my Sickness*[2]

Break off my arms, I shall take hold of you
and grasp you with my heart as with a hand;
arrest my heart, my brain will beat as true;
and if you set this brain of mine afire,
upon my blood I then will carry you.

Rainer Maria Rilke, *Poems from the Book of Hours*[3]

… my heart has melted with tenderness for all sheltering creatures, and I have passionately loved the vagabonds of the earth.

André Gide, *Fruits of the Earth*[4]

A ragged urchin, aimless and alone,
   Loitered about that vacancy, a bird
Flew up to safety from his well-aimed stone:
   That girls are raped, that two boys knife a third,
   Were axioms to him, who'd never heard
Of any world where promises were kept,
Or one could weep because another wept.

W H Auden, *The Shield of Achilles*[5]

The sound human understanding is an occasion of grace, not heroic triumph.

J Edwards, *Ethics Without Philosophy*[6]

Medicine can never be taught only intellectually. Medicine is not science in that sense. Or rather, it is real science – science rooted in the mind of the heart.

J Needleman, *The Way of the Physician*[7]

Introduction

Compassion is at the very core of humanity in medicine. In this chapter the need for compassion in healthcare will be explored and ways of developing this personal quality will be examined. In compassion, the world of feelings meets the world of action. Feeling sorry for others is not enough. The person who has learned to take action selflessly for the benefit of those who suffer enters a state of grace. Grace is all around us and is no respecter of age, rank or prestige. To find grace, watch a 16-year-old carer feeding an 85-year-old woman with severe dementia, but pass by those in the office writing care plans.

The world of feelings can be a confusing place. There are important differences between the emotions of sympathy, empathy and compassion. It may be easiest to illustrate these differences by looking at examples. An elderly woman in a ward needs a bedpan. A patient in the next bed rings for the nurse, who eventually arrives. The nurse may feel sorry for the old woman; she may also understand what wanting to urinate is like and feel sympathy. She may be so tuned into the suffering of others that she can mentally put herself in the elderly woman's shoes – she demonstrates empathy. A compassionate nurse stops what she is doing and immediately fetches a bedpan, pulls curtains around the elderly patient and gently helps her onto the bedpan. Absence of compassion leads the nurse to keep the patient waiting for 20 minutes. It may be caused by lack of care or thought, by inappropriate exercise of power, or by frank cruelty or abuse. Being busy is not a legitimate excuse for lack of compassion.

Migrating geese provide another example. Strong geese take turns at the front of the formation where the air resistance is greatest. Young, frail and old birds fly in the body of the aerodynamic wedge. If a bird is injured or too tired to continue, stronger birds accompany it down to a resting place and then help it to rejoin the flock circling overhead.[8] Sympathy involves feeling concern for others who suffer. Empathy involves the ability to appreciate the suffering of others as if it were your own. Compassion involves doing something positive to share and help to relieve the suffering of others. The act of compassion can involve sitting in silence and not moving a muscle. However, this is not inactivity – it is the difficult art of active listening and silent witnessing. It is the act of *being there* for the stranger who suffers. Compassion is central to the teachings of most religions. It is no coincidence that, when asked about a sure path to heaven, Jesus talked to a lawyer of loving his neighbour and shared the parable of the Good Samaritan.

Compassion for all living things is at the core of Buddhist philosophy, and the Dalai Lama has written extensively about it. He states that 'the true aim of cultivating compassion is to develop the courage to think of others and to do something for them.'[9] This is an important definition because it highlights the need for passion and bravery in acts of compassion. Anyone can sit in an armchair and watch the distant suffering of others on television. In Western society, suffering is in danger of becoming a spectator sport, or a public relations opportunity for celebrities.

Compassion, on the other hand, drives us to *do something* about the suffering of others. Oliver O'Donovan has written of compassion that it 'circumvents thought, since it prompts us immediately to action.'[10] Indeed, as compassion develops, the suffering of others becomes part of oneself. The nineteenth-century American poet Walt Whitman not only wrote of compassion but also lived a compassionate life. In his major opus *Song of Myself* he writes:

> I am the man, I suffer'd, I was there.
>
> The disdain and calmness of martyrs,
> The mother of old, condemn'd for a witch, burnt with dry
>   wood, her children gazing on,
> The hounded slave that flags in the race, leans by the fence,
>   blowing, cover'd with sweat,
> The twinges that sting like needles his legs and neck, the
>   murderous buckshot and the bullets,
> All these I feel or am ...
>
> Agonies are one of my changes of garments,
> I do not ask the wounded person how he feels, I myself
>   become the wounded person,
> My heart turns livid upon me as I lean on a cane and observe.[11]

(pp. 27–8)

Compassion in medicine

A traditional scientific training in the healthcare professions can be antipathetic to the development of compassion. As Howard Spiro has pointed out, it can be difficult to maintain emotional openness as a medical student if the first task is to dissect a dead body.[12] I clearly remember the dread with which I entered the huge anatomy room at medical school with 160 compatriots, walking past rows and rows of sprawling naked bodies on trolleys before settling down in small groups to start dissecting them. Fortunately, most of these bizarre initiation rites were abandoned long ago. Spiro identifies other factors that help to extinguish empathy:

> Isolation, long hours of service, chronic lack of sleep, sadness at prolonged human tragedies, and depression at futile and incomprehensible therapeutic manoeuvres turn even the most empathic of our children from caring physicians into tired terminators. No wonder we have little empathy for the defeated, the humble, the dying, those who have not made it to the top of the heap, and even for the sick. Our energy gets us into medical school and after that little time remains for contemplation.[12]

(p. 844)

Alastair Campbell writes with skill and perception about the role of compassion in professional life in his book *Moderated Love*, and most of the ideas in this chapter stem from this excellent text. Those who are uncomfortable with the word 'love' might prefer to substitute 'friendship'. Campbell writes:

The secret of medical dominance is knowledge (or at least the imputation of knowledge). I have been suggesting that medical knowledge, when incarnated in individual and society, can serve the purposes of love, in the sense that it can overcome fear, hostility and ignorance, and it can open a path to the enhancement of human well-being in a non-discriminating manner. In terms which will become more familiar as this book progresses, I regard medical knowledge as serving both *philia* (friendship based on mutual understanding and respect) and *agape* (concern for all humankind).[13]

(p. 32)

This touches on the sacred nature of the tasks that healthcare professionals perform. Hippocrates emphasised this aspect of care in his oath when he included the phrase 'Pure and holy will I keep my Life and my Art.' This facet of our responsibility brings us into the realms of personal virtue, or goodness, and we shall consider professional virtue in greater detail in Chapter 15. Campbell explains the need for virtue when he writes:

... the need to trust those who deal with one's body or one's personal problems gives continued force to the hope that there is more to the practice of medicine, nursing and social work than the pursuit of money and status.[13]

(pp. 70–1)

As Campbell points out, there is a tension here between egotism (selfishness), which concerns itself with personal enrichment and glorification, and altruism, which is action performed for the benefit of others. Selfishness may pose as altruism in those who help others in order to dominate them, often as a means of trying to compensate for low self-esteem. On the other hand, altruism is prone to denigration in a materialistic and individualistic culture. The argument runs that people only think of others in order to make themselves feel better. People may be categorised as 'chronic helpers'. Popular healthcare professionals may be viewed by colleagues as needing their patients more than their patients need them, but this attitude may simply represent professional envy.

The line between altruism and selfishness is a difficult and sensitive area of our shadow. The Dalai Lama argues that happiness is only possible if one's life is spent trying to benefit others and not to harm them, and Buddhists seem to have less suspicion of the motives of a good person. In *Ancient Wisdom, Modern World*, he writes:

the more we truly desire to benefit others, the greater the strength and confidence we develop and the greater the peace and happiness we experience. Through love, through kindness, through compassion we establish understanding between ourselves and others.[14]

(p. 135)

The key factor here may be our motivation to help others. Those who seek inner contentment from their actions act virtuously. Those who seek personal fame, power or fortune as their primary goal are probably less virtuous. However, it seems to me that none of us can put hand on heart and say that our motives for becoming healthcare professionals were entirely virtuous. Our shadow is always with us and we are humans, not gods. Our motives, like our morals, are mixed. The best strategy might be to concentrate on judging our own motivation and not casting aspersions on that of others.

Talk of love of patients tends to make healthcare professionals jittery. This stems partly from the various meanings of the word 'love', particularly in a society where romantic and erotic love is rated far above other forms of love. Earlier I suggested that the word 'friendship' might be a reasonable substitute, but there are limitations to this approach. Passion is needed for compassion to occur. Compassion drives us to do our best for those who suffer, irrespective of whether we happen to like them or not. Campbell reminds us of the *Prayer of a Physician* by Maimonides:

> Endow me with strength of heart and mind so that both may be ever ready to serve the rich and the poor, the good and the wicked, friend and enemy.[13]
>
> (p. 74)

Campbell stresses other important characteristics of professional love:

> Thus a morality based on love must be carefully delineated to show its power to oppose hatred. Sympathy points the way. Moral goodness consists in the love of all our fellow human beings, through empathy, identification, but especially by bringing forth the values they themselves possess. Where hatred constantly seeks to disvalue our fellow humans, love constantly seeks to enhance their value.[13]
>
> (p. 77)

A clear understanding of boundaries is necessary for the virtuous development of compassion. A compassionate approach will open doors into the inner world of those who suffer, but there will be secrets that individuals will not wish to share, and these must be honoured. There is a fine line between striving for understanding of others and taking a voyeuristic pleasure in plumbing the murky depths of their shadow. As Campbell puts it, 'The value to be enhanced is the value of other people *in all their inner secrecy.*'[13] At other times inner secrets need to be shared, and it is then crucial to maintain one's composure and to suppress feelings of disgust if these occur.

The nature of the relationship between the compassionate healthcare professional and those who suffer is complex. Those who are cold and aloof are too distant to help. Those who become too close lose what Campbell terms the 'critical distance', and can no longer provide the objective point of view that is necessary. This is precisely the problem that occurs when healthcare professionals try to look after their family when they become ill. Thus the professional relationship is not a friendship. The patient comes when help is needed, and contact is not expected until the next episode when help is required. Those who immerse themselves in the suffering of others are in danger of losing themselves. Sharing the suffering of others causes emotional distress, and this needs to be acknowledged and dealt with. This form of love is known as *agape* – the love which risks self in order to enhance value.[13] Campbell writes:

The requirements of *agape* are, I believe, at the root of the atmosphere of purity and dedication which permeates professional ethics. We must recognise that its requirements are more than can reasonably be expected.

Thus I would see altruism, in all its complexity now laid out, as entirely appropriate to, indeed necessary for, professional helping. Yet I concede that it is elusive, perhaps possible only as a commitment which is frequently not honoured.

... professional helpers represent more than human attempts to care. Their opposition to illness, pain and social disadvantage symbolises the 'impossible ideal' of *agape*, a love which restores full value to every individual, however damaged, however oppressed, however bereft of hope. In this sense the professional commitment is a religious one, though this need not imply that the practitioners see themselves as believers. Their *actions* and *attitudes* look for an ultimate conquest of suffering.[13]

(p. 83)

Professional compassion is a difficult and demanding quality to develop, but also one that offers the individual practitioner great benefits. These have been well summarised by the Dalai Lama in *The Art of Happiness*:

If you maintain a feeling of compassion, loving kindness, then something automatically opens your inner door. Through that, you can communicate much more easily with other people. And that feeling of warmth creates a kind of openness. You'll find that all human beings are just like you, so you'll be able to relate to them more easily.[15]

(p. 27)

Suffering and compassion

We examined the meaning and experience of suffering in Chapter 4. We also looked at how suffering can benefit the individual if it helps to develop a sense of compassion for others. Suffering can cause loneliness and silence, and compassion drives others towards us in our hour of need. In the world of grace there are two crucial skills. One is to give help selflessly to another in need, and the other is to ask for and receive help willingly when our own suffering demands it. Sometimes those who give help to others readily can struggle when circumstances change and receiving kindness from others becomes a necessity. For the healthcare professional in need, colleagues and patients can provide much-needed succour and understanding. At least, that is my personal experience.

On earth there is no shortage of misery, as John Donne points out in his reflections on recovery from serious illness:

... his misery, as the sea, swells above all the hills, and reaches to the remotest parts of this earth, man; who of himself is but dust, and coagulated and kneaded into earth by tears; his matter is earth, his form misery.[2]

(p. 50)

It is compassion that binds one being to another and that fights for justice within society and the world. It is compassion that strives to ensure that people do not suffer or die alone. Campbell writes:

> Although we may feel intensely individual and at times acutely alone, we are social beings from the moment of conception to the moment of death. To be a creature is to be born of others, to know ourselves through them, to depend upon them and finally to be the instance of that pain to others.[13]

(p. 96)

This, of course, is also the sentiment behind John Donne's famous passage on hearing the church bells of another's funeral:

> Who bends not his ear to any bell which upon any occasion rings? But who can remove it from that bell which is passing a piece of himself out of this world? No man is an island, entire of itself; every man is a piece of the continent, a part of the main. If a clod be washed away by the sea, Europe is the less, as well as if a promontory were, as well as if a manor of thy friend's or of thine own were: any man's death diminishes me, because I am involved in mankind, and therefore never send to know for whom the bell tolls; it tolls for thee.[2]

(pp. 108–9)

Compassion drives us to care for strangers. It turns us into good companions on the journeys of others. Here is Campbell again:

> Companionship arises often from a chance meeting and is terminated when the joint purpose which keeps companions together no longer obtains. The good companion is someone who shares freely, but does not impose, allowing others to make their *own* journey.
>
> The skill of companionship lies in sensing the need of the other person and accommodating oneself to the other's idiosyncrasies. Skilled nursing care depends upon such sensitivity. The body of the other person is handled in a way that overcomes embarrassment, and a sense of privacy is left intact. Nursing is a companionship which helps the person onward. Whether the destination is recovery or death, a companion helps the hardness of the journey. So the good companion looks ahead and encourages when all seems lost.
>
> Companions are with one for a while, but they have their own lives to lead, too.[13]

(pp. 49–50)

Reich has also highlighted the close links between suffering and compassion. He proposes three phases of suffering which in turn generate three types of compassion. The first phase he calls *mute suffering*, when the sufferer is overwhelmed by the experience and cannot find words to express it. The second phase is *expressive suffering*, when the sufferer uses language to describe and enhance understanding and control of the experience. The third phase is *new identity in suffering*, during which understanding of the experience brings about individual change and a new sense of identity. Reich's corresponding phases of compassion include *silent compassion*, when the companion spends time with the sufferer without attempting to control, rationalise or intellectualise the experience. *Expressive compassion* is when some limited attempt is made to broaden the sufferer's perceptions, so that they become conscious of and connected with a wider spectrum of meaning and value. Finally, *new identity in compassion* occurs when the companion is also changed by the shared experience of suffering.[16] It is during this important third phase that the healthcare professional can grow as a person by learning from the vicarious experience of another's suffering.

Cultivating compassion

If we accept that compassion is a crucial part of humane healthcare, how can we learn to develop this personal quality? First of all, we need to abandon narcissism. Thinking only of oneself and ignoring the suffering of others is a complete bar to developing a compassionate nature. Secondly, we must lay ourselves open to the world of feelings. Sometimes the world of feelings can prove to be something of a Pandora's Box. Inner feelings include love and tenderness but also the 'deadly sins', those aspects of our shadow that it is more comfortable to ignore or deny. Why is opening this box necessary? Imagine, perhaps, a healthcare professional who is caring for a homosexual patient dying of AIDS when there is inner conflict and denial about their own sexuality. Most patients who arouse strong feelings of antagonism within us may be pointing up areas of subconscious conflict. The lazy, the promiscuous, the dishonest, the cruel, the violent and the addicted may all trigger resonance with our own internal discomfort. Allowing our feelings to surface so that our prejudices and internal conflicts can be recognised is an uncomfortable task.

In recognising our own internal contradictions we come to accept the outward behaviour of others. As humans we can be kind or cruel, brave or cowardly, ruthless or merciful, and tolerant or bombastic. In his book *The Wounded Healer*, Henri Nouwen writes:

> For a compassionate man nothing human is alien: no joy and no sorrow, no way of living and no way of dying.
>
> Thus the authority of compassion is the possibility of man to forgive his brother, because forgiveness is only real for him who has discovered the weakness of his friends and the sins of his enemy in his own heart and is willing to call every human being his brother.[17]
>
> (p. 41)

In this sense, compassion tends to bring a sense of peace to an individual's view of the world. By endeavouring to understand others and by accepting the contradictions within both ourselves and them, condemnation of the nature of others begins to evaporate. I think that this is what Yeats is referring to in his poem *The Second Coming*:

> The blood-dimmed tide is loosed, and everywhere
> The ceremony of innocence is drowned;

The best lack all conviction, while the worst
Are full of passionate intensity.[18]

(p. 235)

As we open up our inner feelings, we also allow ourselves to be vulnerable to the love and suffering of others. Those with the most difficult task come from a background where, whenever they opened themselves up to others, pain, neglect or humiliation promptly followed. In these circumstances, as with the hermit crab, the best policy is to retreat into a tough shell for safety.

Once our personal vulnerability is offered, compassion grows so that sensitivity to the suffering of others is enhanced. In his book *Ancient Wisdom, Modern World*, the Dalai Lama writes:

> when we enhance our sensitivity toward others' suffering through deliberately opening ourselves up to it, it is believed that we can gradually extend our compassion to the point where the individual feels so moved by even the subtlest suffering of others that they come to have an overwhelming sense of responsibility toward those others. This causes the one who is compassionate to dedicate themselves entirely to helping others overcome both their suffering and the causes of their suffering.[14]

(p. 128)

He goes further in *The Art of Happiness*:

> Compassion can be roughly defined in terms of a state of mind that is non-violent, non-harming and non-aggressive. It is a mental attitude and is associated with a sense of commitment, responsibility, and respect towards others.
>
> ... the more fully one understands suffering, and the various kinds of suffering that we are subject to, the deeper will be one's level of compassion.[15]

(p. 135)

This is very much a spiritual aspect of healthcare, and I argue that this sense of the spiritual is an integral part of any healthcare system that treats fellow humans with kindness, tolerance, patience, dignity and respect. These qualities should also be shown to those who work within the system. This spirituality is not necessarily religious in the usual sense – it has to do with an inherent belief in the goodness of human beings, in connectedness and in valuing others and treating them with kindness. By developing our compassion we become more tolerant and loving. Here is the Dalai Lama again:

> Since love and compassion and similar qualities all, by definition, presume some level of concern for others' well-being, they also presume ethical restraint. We cannot be loving and compassionate unless at the same time we curb our own harmful impulses and desires.[14]

(p. 27)

This is not to argue that we become saints. It is to suggest that we should try to behave ethically. Anger is permitted, not towards our patients, but towards systems and institutions that bring about illness and suffering. The Dalai Lama finishes his book *Ancient Wisdom, Modern World* with the following appeal:

> Relinquish your envy, let go of your desire to triumph over others. With kindness, with courage, and confident that in doing so you are sure to meet with success, welcome others with a smile. Be straightforward. And try to be impartial. Treat everyone as if they were a close friend.
>
> If you cannot, for whatever reason, be of help to others, at least don't harm them.
>
> Try not to turn away from those whose appearance is disturbing, from the ragged and unwell. Try never to think of them as inferior to yourself. If you can, try not even to think of yourself as better than the humblest beggar.[14]
>
> (pp. 245–6)

Grace

I have argued that to strive to cultivate compassion for the suffering of others is a noble and rewarding commitment. Those who have made headway in this direction may find themselves starting to enter a state of grace. Grace has to do with the manner of giving and receiving. It is a gift and a quality of great beauty. It can be easier to recognise than to describe. Those who treat us with kindness and want absolutely nothing in return have given graciously. Those who accept our thanks or our help willingly and without fuss have learned to receive with grace. In gracious transactions both the helper and the helped feel enriched. Michael Ignatieff describes the territory in his book *The Needs of Strangers*:

> It is the manner of giving that counts and the moral basis on which it is given: whether strangers at my door get their stories listened to by the social worker, whether the ambulance man takes care not to jostle them when they are taken down the steep stairs of their apartment building, whether a nurse sits with them in the hospital when they are frightened and alone. Respect and dignity are conferred by gestures such as these. They are gestures too much a matter of human art to be made a consistent matter of administrative routine.[19]
>
> (p. 16)

Thus grace has little to do with duties or rights, with which modern Western society is more familiar. Campbell has this to say:

> Graceful care refers to something which is not offered by anxious people trying to earn love, but by sensitive people who release us from bonds of our own making in spontaneous and often surprising ways. The gracefulness in caring is as closely connected to bodily expression as it is to an intellectual understanding or emotional awareness. The body gracefully offers and gracefully receives, in harmony with thought and feeling. Here especially spontaneity (or lack of it) is seen.

The need to be touched, held and nurtured is with us from the very beginning to the very end of life. There is something very basic, then, in the experience of being cared for. Each of us knew it in the tender embrace of our mother – that is our first (and perhaps our most important) bodily awareness of grace. For the professional person, offering care to a wide variety of people within the context of specific needs, there can rarely (if ever) be the closeness and constancy of a mother's love. This would be inappropriate in most circumstances and would lose sight of the autonomy and coping capacity of the person helped.

The 'sacrament' of caring is the use of the physical closeness of bodies to a therapeutic end, the overcoming of weakness and the restoration of hope which another human presence makes possible.[13]

(p. 111)

The closeness of physical bodies is perhaps most apparent in the field of nursing and it is here that the grace of a mother and baby is recalled. Examples include help with eating, washing, toileting and bodily comfort. Here is Campbell again:

These features of the nursing relationship make the care which nurses offer their patients an especially powerful means for good or ill. The nurse as companion possesses that gracefulness which we have identified at the heart of caring. There is a sensitivity in companionship which shares without invading privacy, and which helps in the other's journey without attempting to dominate and create crippling dependency.[13]

(p. 112)

Here, too, comes an idea of the complexity and difficulty of striving for grace in healthcare. As Nouwen points out, skills are needed in good communication, in compassion and in finding the time for inner contemplation in a busy occupation. He writes:

The contemplative is not needy or greedy for human contacts, but is guided by a vision of what he has seen beyond the trivial concerns of a possessive world.[17]

(p. 41)

Grace is a gift, and it stems from the commitment to help our patients to the best of our abilities. It demands that we offer our vulnerability and a particular form of love which is hard to define. Campbell calls it 'moderated love'. He quotes from Day Williams:

Love means willingness to participate in the being of the other at the cost of suffering, and with the expectation of mutual enrichment, criticism and growth.[13]

(p. 101)

Even then the task is not complete. We must show concern and foster hope in the confusion of illness. We must find the delicate balance between involvement and detachment.

If grace is accepted as being important, where can we find it? Grace is a special quality, and when we are touched by it we, too, feel special. My heroes and role models made me feel special, unique and important, and I know that they made many others feel the same way. At times we stumble upon compassion and grace in unlikely places. John Steinbeck described them in the closing passage of his greatest work, *The Grapes of Wrath*, in which a young mother agrees to breastfeed a starving stranger:

> For a minute Rose of Sharon sat still in the whispering barn. Then she hoisted her tired body up and drew the comforter about her. She moved slowly to the corner and stood looking down at the wasted face, into the wide, frightened eyes. Then slowly she lay down beside him. He shook his head slowly from side to side. Rose of Sharon loosened one side of the blanket and bared her breast. 'You go to,' she said. She squirmed closer and pulled his head close. 'There!', she said, 'There.' Her hand moved behind his head and supported it. Her fingers moved gently in his hair.[20]
>
> (p. 416)

Compassion acts as a force for virtue, and we shall examine this in more detail in Chapter 15. The Dalai Lama writes:

> … where love of one's neighbour, affection, kindness and compassion live, we find that ethical conduct is automatic. Ethically wholesome actions arise naturally in the context of compassion.[14]
>
> (p. 136)

What is more, compassion makes life meaningful. After a life spent in contemplation, Thomas Merton wrote:

> The pleasure of a good act is something to be remembered – not in order to feed our complacency but in order to remind us that virtuous actions are not only possible and valuable, but that they can become *easier* and more delightful and more fruitful than the acts of vice which oppose and frustrate them.[21]
>
> (p. 33)

Compassion is a two-way process, and in benefiting others we also benefit ourselves. The Dalai Lama writes:

> It is the source of all lasting happiness and joy. And it is the foundation of a good heart, the heart of one who acts out of a desire to help others. Through kindness, through affection, through honesty, through truth and justice towards all others we ensure our own benefit. This is not a matter for complicated theorising. It is a matter of common sense.[14]
>
> (p. 242)

For the healthcare professional who wants to work in a compassionate manner it is important to realise that the demands of compassion can become overwhelming.

The organisation in which they work needs to provide a framework within which others can empathically support the professional as they attend to the sufferings of their patients. Perhaps most importantly of all, we need to learn how to be compassionate towards ourselves.[22]

References

1   Lau Tzu (reprinted 1995, trans T Freke) *Tao Te Ching*. Judy Piatkus, London.
2   Donne J (1959) *Devotions Upon Emergent Occasions.* Ann Arbor, University of Michigan Press, MI.
3   Rilke RM (1899–1901, reprinted 1975, trans B Deutsch) *Poems from the Book of Hours.* New Directions, New York.
4   Gide A (1970) *Fruits of the Earth.* Penguin Books, Harmondsworth.
5   Auden WH (1968) *Selected Poems.* Faber & Faber, London.
6   Edwards J (2001) Ethics without philosophy. In: C Elliot (ed.) *Slow Cures and Bad Philosophers.* Duke University Press, Durham, NC.
7   Needleman J (1992) *The Way of the Physician.* Penguin Books, Harmondsworth.
8   Maori narrative quoted by Campbell A (1995) *Health as Liberation: medicine, theology and the quest for justice.* Pilgrim Press, Cleveland, OH.
9   Bunson E (ed.) (1997) *The Dalai Lama's Book of Wisdom.* Rider Books, London.
10 Hauerwas S (1990) *God, Medicine and Suffering.* WB Eerdmans, Grand Rapids, MI.
11 Whitman W (1855–1881) *Song of Myself.* Reprinted in *Walt Whitman* (1996) Everyman's Poetry, London.
12 Spiro H (1992) What is empathy and can it be taught? *Ann Intern Med.* 116: 843–6.
13 Campbell A (1984) *Moderated Love: a theology of professional care.* SPCK, London.
14 Gyatso T (2001) *Ancient Wisdom, Modern World.* Abacus, London.
15 Gyatso T and Cutler H (1999) *The Art of Happiness: a handbook for living.* Hodder & Stoughton, London.
16 Reich W (1989) Speaking of suffering: a moral account of compassion. *Soundings*. 72: 83–108.
17 Nouwen H (1979) *The Wounded Healer.* Doubleday, New York.
18 Yeats W (1992) *The Poems.* Everyman's Library, London.
19 Ignatieff M (1994) *The Needs of Strangers.* Vintage, London.
20 Steinbeck J (1951) *The Grapes of Wrath.* Penguin, Harmondsworth.
21 Merton T (1958) *Thoughts in Solitude.* Burns & Oates, London.
22 Brody H (1992) *The Healer's Power.* Yale University Press, New Haven, CT.

Further reading

Campbell A (1984) *Moderated Love: a theology of professional care.* SPCK, London.
Gyatso T (2001) *Ancient Wisdom, Modern World.* Abacus, London.
Gyatso T and Cutler H (1999) *The Art of Happiness: a handbook for living.* Hodder & Stoughton, London.
Ignatieff M (1994) *The Needs of Strangers.* Vintage, London.
Nouwen H (1979) *The Wounded Healer.* Doubleday, New York.

CHAPTER 14

Professional fulfilment

Nothing will sustain you more potently than the power to recognize in your humdrum routine, as perhaps it may be thought, the true poetry of life – the poetry of the commonplace, of the ordinary man, of the plain, toil-worn woman, with their loves and their joys, their sorrows and their griefs.

William Osler, *The Student Life*[1]

Our acts are attached to us as its glimmer is to phosphorus. They consume us, it is true, but they make our splendour.

André Gide, *Fruits of the Earth*[2]

Morality is character, character is that which is engraved; but the sand and the sea have no character and neither has abstract intelligence, for character is really inwardness.

Soren Kierkegaard, *The Present Age*[3]

The good person builds the human by being committed to someone or something beyond self.

James Drane, *Becoming a Good Doctor*[4]

Introduction

It might be reasonable to assume that most healthcare professionals love their work. Their labour is inherently meaningful, they generally do good for others and their customers are usually glad to see them, particularly in a crisis. The work of the healthcare professional is varied, interesting and demanding. Their status is high, their incomes are good, their pensions are generous and their job security is outstanding.[5]

In this chapter we examine why job satisfaction can prove elusive and how conflicting demands on the time of the healthcare professional may frustrate attempts to live balanced, fulfilling and harmonious lives. As well as outlining some of the difficulties and frustrations that can occur, strategies to overcome them are discussed.

Healthcare professionals have an inherent interest in appearing busy and tired, as Glin Bennet explains in his book *The Wound and the Doctor.* Allowances made by the public can lead to prompt attention for the daily needs of the healthcare professional, and help to furnish the heroic image with which the public likes to adorn them. If tiredness and busyness weigh down the life of the healthcare professional, they may have only themselves to blame. At times they may feel like hamsters in a wheel, but the speed of the wheel can frequently be influenced by their attitudes.[5] Over-commitment at work can lead to anxiety, brusqueness of manner or neglect of the need to continuously update knowledge and skills. How do healthcare professionals fall into this trap of doing too much?

Competing demands

I need to start by apologising to whoever thought up the very useful model which I am about to describe. The concept stayed with me, but where I first saw it has escaped me. The idea is that healthcare professionals are pulled by three opposing needs, namely time off, money and good clinical care. These demands pull in different directions and the healthcare professional needs to keep them balanced if harmony and professional fulfilment are the aim.

Time off

Adequate time away from work is an essential requirement for a balanced life. This time is needed for domestic duties, exercise and sleep, for time to oneself and for time with family and friends. Too much devotion to the pursuit of money or fame, or to the demands of excellence in clinical care, erodes time off and can strain loving relationships to breaking point. Assertiveness and internal discipline are required to protect this valuable asset.

Most people in the Western world who work too hard are hooked into a lifestyle that they cannot afford. Sometimes workaholics have suffered parental denigration and are trying to prove something to themselves or to the world. Some struggle with interpersonal relationships and find work easier than being at home. Occasionally people love their work so much that they cannot bear to be away from it; this becomes another manifestation of selfishness. Excessive hours of work not only deny the family the necessary attention, but also threaten the health of the sufferer. Naturally there are plenty of circumstances where people are worked too hard in organisations that are beyond their control. Healthcare professionals in poorer countries may be overwhelmed by medical need and have no option but to do their best in difficult circumstances. Family illness or misfortune may suddenly alter personal circumstances so that there is no short-term alternative but to work too hard. On the whole, however, cutting expenditure and expectations is the usual prescription for change. This may involve the whole family reassessing their desires and aspirations.

Money

Ecclesiastes has much to say about the follies of life. On money there is this:

> No one who loves money can ever have enough, and no one who loves wealth enjoys any return from it.
> It is better to be satisfied with what is before your eyes than to give rein to desire.[6]

André Gide advises likewise in his hymn to youth, *Fruits of the Earth*:

> Welcome everything that comes to you, but do not long for anything else.
> There are extravagant illnesses
> Which consist in wanting what one hasn't got.[2]

(p. 32)

Good clinical care

Taking pride in one's work is a worthy aim. Those who suffer deserve our help, and it can be difficult to know when to stop. There are often unexpected crises in healthcare that demand our immediate attention. There are tasks that cannot be hurried, such as breaking bad news or comforting the bereaved. All of these problems take our time and drain our emotional energy. Patients and our families generally understand these problems, but there is a fine line between commitment and over-commitment. Exhausting our energy at work means arriving home with nothing to offer. Families and colleagues usually recognise when devotion to duty is getting out of hand.

At the other end of the spectrum are those who maximise their income and time off by minimising time spent on clinical care. In *The Diving-Bell and the Butterfly*, Jean-Dominique Bauby writes:

> He was the very model of the couldn't-care-less doctor, arrogant, brusque, sarcastic, the kind who summons his patients for 8.00am, arrives at 9.00, and departs at 9.05 after giving each of them 45 seconds of his precious time.[7]

(pp. 61–2)

This approach can lead to riches, power and fame, although inner contentment is less likely. As Peter Toon puts it:

> To seek only the external goods and do no more than the minimum required to keep out of trouble is not so much a failure of duty as a self-defeating strategy, just as those who cheat at games are self-defeating.[8]

(p. 39)

Colleagues and team members are also cheated when working with those who skimp on clinical effort. Clinical laziness leads to poor morale, failures of leadership and an inevitable dumping of work on to other team members. Patients become disheartened with lazy healthcare professionals who seem disinterested in their concerns, and steadily drift over to other members of the team. Lazy colleagues are often charming and likeable, and their interior deception can make them incredulous and slippery when challenged.

Some professionals have the happy knack of working quickly but appearing to have all the time in the world. Patients know that our time is limited and appreciate efforts to give them undivided attention. The length of the working week for healthcare professionals, particularly for doctors, is steadily decreasing. This is an inevitable change that is good for the professional. However, there is a resulting reduction in experience and a threat to continuity and trust between healthcare professional and patient.

A sense of vocation

Work can be crucial to giving our lives meaning and identity. It is good for the soul. The Dalai Lama writes:

> The work of a person labouring in some humble occupation is no less relevant to the well-being of society than that of, for example, a doctor, a teacher, a monk or a nun. All human endeavour is potentially great and noble. So long as we carry out our work with good motivation, reminding ourselves that 'My work is for others', it will be of benefit to the wider community. But when concern for others' feelings and welfare is missing, our activities tend to become spoiled.[9]
>
> (p. 180)

Work that is suited to the individual should create satisfaction and pleasure. André Gide has this to say:

> Every perfect action is accompanied by pleasure. That is how you can tell that it was right for you to do it. I don't like people who pride themselves on working painfully. If their work was painful, they had better have done something else. The delight one takes in one's work is the sign of its fittingness.[2]
>
> (p. 32)

If particular dedication is required to work at a particular occupation, or if the employment sits particularly well on the shoulders of an individual, the job becomes a vocation. Sometimes people feel an urge or a calling to join a particular trade or profession. Thomas Merton writes of vocation in his book *Thoughts in Solitude*:

> A man knows he has found his vocation when he stops thinking about how to live and begins to live.
>   When we are not living up to our true vocation, thought deadens our life, or substitutes itself for life, or gives in to life so that our life drowns out our thinking and stifles the voice of conscience. When we find our vocation – thought and life are one.[10]
>
> (p. 85)

In vocation, work becomes an art that is loved and makes us loved. We feel satisfied and fulfilled. Our place of work becomes important and the quality of our surroundings matters. Ideally we should work with others who share our enthusiasm, commitment and sense of mission. Our tools should be top quality and cherished. We should find beauty in our work and strive to create it in our workplace.[11]

Threats to fulfilment

The greatest threat to job satisfaction for the enthusiast in healthcare is burnout. This is unlikely to affect the lazy brigade who never really caught fire in the first place. The term 'burnout' was first coined by Freudenberger in 1974 to describe the emotional and physical exhaustion that overtakes dedicated healthcare professionals who deal directly with patients with difficult or intractable problems.[12] What are the pressures that cause the threat of burnout? There are clearly personality factors that make burnout more likely. Some causes of workaholism have already been outlined. Those with perfectionist tendencies and those who cannot tolerate uncertainty or the consequences of their own clinical errors are at most risk. Inability to accept help from others or to work well in a team leads to a lack of the mutual help and support that are so crucial in times of personal need. Delusions of indispensability are risky.

In addition to particular types of personality that are poorly equipped for working in healthcare, there are some particular aspects of healthcare that generate their own stress.

Witnessing suffering

We have already seen how suffering sits at the very heart of healthcare. The compassion felt by the healthcare professional drives them to alleviate, or at least to share in, the misfortunes of others. Remaining distant and aloof protects the professional but hampers their effectiveness. In this scenario the patient is seen as 'one machine that can be investigated by another'.[13]

We have previously discussed how openness and vulnerability to the suffering of others is a prerequisite for effective healing, and how this experience changes both parties in the transaction. Here is Kenneth Sanders writing about psychotherapy:

> The doctor needs to be more than just a convenient receptacle for other people's pain and anguish. There is a desire to be nourishing, for creativity, to be active in the repair of something that is broken.
>
> The removal of something unpleasant from the patient's mind and the gift of something good and valuable, that is not only relief from pain, but also renewal of hope, may win thanks and even friendship.
>
> The conflict is then seen to be not between love and hate, but between passionate, turbulent feelings which really hurt, and indifference which is pain free.[13]
>
> (p. 10)

Hauerwas mirrors this when he writes from the perspective of the patient:

> The physician cannot help but be touched, and thus tainted, by the world of the sick. Through their willingness to be present to us in our most vulnerable moments that are forever scarred with our pain – a pain that we the healthy want to deny or at least keep at arm's length – they have seen a world we do not want to see until it is forced on us, and we will accept them into polite community only to the extent they keep

that world hidden from us. But when we are driven into that world we want to be able to count on their skill and their presence, even though we have been unwilling to face that reality while we were healthy.[14]

(p. 79)

The lived experience of another's suffering enriches us but also takes its toll. Here is Eric Cassell in *The Healer's Art*:

> The doctor is in and out of the lives of others. Where serious or terminal illness is an issue, he may become a family intimate for days, weeks or months, again becoming external to their lives when trouble ends. From this unique perspective he watches people and their families grow, some members maturing, others dying, all simultaneously with the growth of his own family; his own life provides the touchstone of empathy with which he observes his patients and hears what they tell him.[15]

(p. 96)

The closer we become to our patients, the greater the threat of pain, sorrow and loss. This is a point identified by John Berger in *A Fortunate Man*:

> The suffering which certain doctors witness may be more of a strain than is generally admitted.
> What is the effect of facing, trying to understand, hoping to overcome the extreme anguish of other persons five or six times a week?
> I speak of the anguish of dying, of loss, of fear, of loneliness, of being desperately beside oneself, of the sense of futility.[16]

(pp. 112–13)

Berger also identifies the sense of impotence that regularly confronts us:

> There are occasions when any doctor may feel helpless: faced with a tragic incurable disease; faced with obstinacy and prejudice maintaining the very situation which has created the illness or unhappiness; faced with certain housing conditions; faced with poverty.[16]

(p. 132)

Difficult patients

Good relationships with patients are central to enjoyment and fulfilment for the healthcare professional. We cannot get on with all of the people all of the time, but the more clinical friendships we build, the more satisfying our work becomes. There are some patients who are more difficult to like, and it is worth putting in extra effort to unlock some shared territory in difficult cases. The more stressed the healthcare professional becomes, the more difficult patients appear to be. The relationship between professional and patient is just one of many. Patients who appear unreasonable when ill are often seen to have dysfunctional interpersonal skills generally. The same applies to the healthcare professional. Friction with colleagues, team members and family often accompany problems in working with patients.

Sanders found inspiration from taking an interest in the people who exasperated him the most. Talking of a particular case, he writes:

> She was extremely adhesive,
>> There was no way of ending the consultation other than by escorting her to the door and propelling her through it.
>> She aroused my anxiety, as well as my dislike.
>> I felt guilty that I had departed from my ideal of myself as a doctor.

By taking the time to find out more about the person, a change occurred – not in the patient, but in the way he felt about her:

> I was moved, not only by her story, but by the transformation.
>> I felt my identity had improved from a fraudulent street vendor to a friendly milkman.
>> I began to feel that she was in some way related to me, perhaps an eccentric aunt for whom I had become partly responsible.[13]
>>
>> (pp.12–13)

I, too, have found great benefit from this approach. It can be surprising how much of a transformation follows disclosure of unexpected information. A paradigm shift occurs and our humanity and compassion suddenly flow out. An elderly woman tells you that her husband was killed in the war only months after their marriage. An only child died of leukaemia. A wife was electrocuted while turning on the television. Teenage years were spent in the Gulag Archipelago. Strive to get behind the insoluble medical symptoms. It is like mining deep underground for a golden nugget. Put on your headlamp and keep going. This is Balint territory, and it is dealt with in excellent and extensive literature elsewhere.

Difficult patients exist, and however clever your strategy, they will always be a problem. Work in inner cities is very different from that in leafy suburbs. As we saw in Chapter 3, poverty and social injustice put a much greater strain on healthcare workers, who may rightly feel that they are acting more like social workers. Violence and other abuse towards healthcare workers can be a particularly severe occupational stress.

Over-commitment

We have already discussed some aspects of personality in healthcare professionals and some special dimensions of our work that contribute to the risk of burnout. There is also the issue of why healthcare professionals put themselves forward for this line of duty in the first place. The desire to work with the sick and suffering may stem from family experience of illness or disturbed family dynamics. Here is Alistair Campbell writing in *Moderated Love*:

> The choice of a career of caring for people in need presumably stems from some needs in the helper, which gain satisfaction when one's working life is spent in an encounter with illness or social disability. The needy person obviously needs to be helped, but that help likely comes from

someone who needs to be needed. Unless we recognise the element of personal need leading people into professional caring, we shall fail to see how damaging some forms of over-commitment can be.[17]

(p. 105)

This aspect of neediness can be over-emphasised in a puritanical or individualistic culture where all acts of benevolence are viewed with cynicism and suspicion. Campbell rightly emphasises its importance, however, in those who over-commit:

> The over-committed helper appears to eschew all personal comfort and private interest in the name of service to others. The reality, however, is often quite other. The hidden rewards are so great that this seeming selflessness is a form of self-assertion, which seeks to deny the reciprocity in all acts of caring and to keep the helper firmly in the ranks of the strong and the need-free.[17]

(p. 106)

This is the thin line that can separate 'martyrdom to the cause' from grace. Campbell concludes:

> It is often more blessed to care for than to be cared for, and the ability to care is frequently made possible by the understanding and sensitivity of the needy person. Such reciprocity suffuses the relationship of caring with a spontaneity, with a sense of grace which enriches carer and cared-for alike.[17]

(p. 107)

Over-commitment can lead to a family life in which no meal, special occasion or holiday is uninterrupted by clinical demands, and children and partners feel un-loved and neglected. To be a good healthcare professional you need to be a good human being, a good spouse, a good colleague, a good customer at the shops, and a good driver on the roads.[18] All good healthcare professionals are in danger of becoming over-committed. Here is the paediatrician Peter McMullin looking back over his career:

> Although I had studied art, literature and philosophy, although I had the gift of tongues and of clear thinking, if not of clairvoyance, I found the milk of human kindness was leaking out of my soul, squeezed out by the pressures of work, of financial anxiety, of a wife and five children to care for and keep happy, of nights broken by the cries of my own children or the urgent clinical needs of others, of committee work and administrative responsibilities. I became less patient with my patients, less tolerant of the foibles of the human race. Less willing to listen, less able to care.[19]

(p. 714)

Fortunately there is much more attention paid today to preserving our strength and energy. As teachers we have an important role not only in talking about these problems, but also in sharing our limitations and difficulties honestly with younger colleagues.

Management

Healthcare professionals tend to worry unduly about management interference in their activities. Considering that the bulk of healthcare costs is borne by compulsory insurance premiums or taxation of the general public, it should come as little surprise when financial accountability is demanded. Governmental bureaucrats or health maintenance administrators can certainly add to job stress, but in a system where the money available will never be sufficient for doing 'everything for everybody', it is inevitable that limitations will be imposed in one way or another. If rationing decisions have to be made at the bedside or in the healthcare professional's office, the relationship between patient and professional becomes strained. Far better to blame faceless bureaucrats in some far-off agency.

Doctors in particular complain of loss of autonomy and professional freedom. The days of healthcare professionals paddling their own canoes is over. As evidence mounts about best methods of treatment, guidelines help to disseminate and establish best practice. Those who hold idiosyncratic views and use outmoded therapies will become increasingly isolated. So, too, will those professionals whose standards and performance do not match those of their colleagues. As data are increasingly demanded to monitor our performance, those who use computers willingly will greatly benefit, as data collection becomes a simple and paper-free exercise. As monitoring of clinical activity becomes more sophisticated, the lazy brigade may start (at last) to earn less money.

Bureaucrats, insurers and politicians may sometimes get their initiatives wrong, and it is then the professional's job to let them know. Usually the threat of change is more stressful than the change itself. On the whole, work as a family doctor in the UK has remained largely unchanged over the 25 years of my career. The changes that have occurred are mostly improvements on the old. Life is busier, but on-call has decreased beyond all recognition. Many new and effective treatments have appeared in circumstances where we were previously unable to help. Computers make clinical organisation and keeping up to date much easier.

Trying to ignore politics in healthcare completely is impracticable. Here is Glin Bennet again:

> Many doctors like to avoid political issues and concentrate on the work they were trained to do. They can avoid medical politics or even party politics, but they cannot avoid politics in the wider sense, because the circumstances of most people's lives are determined by political decisions. The amount of money spent on housing, on education, on health services, is all as a result of political decisions, and no doctor working with ordinary people can disregard this fact.[5]

(p. 251)

Complaints and malpractice

Complaints from patients can be traumatic, particularly if they are fabricated or vexatious. Speaking to other professionals such as solicitors (attorneys) and the like, it seems that healthcare professionals get unduly worried by complaints. Perhaps perfectionism or a need to be loved makes them harder to bear. Stories of medical 'bad news' are common in the media, but so are 'medical triumphs'. On the whole, trust in the medical profession today is probably no worse than the historical average.

Experience has shown that complaints from patients are more common in times of personal stress or over-commitment. Dysfunctional relationships with patients are more likely to occur when interactions are hurried or curt. I learned from my senior partner as a young doctor that when mistakes are made, the best policy by far is to visit the patient in hospital or at home and apologise personally. Check beforehand with a defence organisation for appropriate wording if you feel that this is necessary. Patients understand that we are human, and often their major goal in making a complaint is to ensure that lessons are learned. This is part of the territory of being open and vulnerable. Denial of our shortcomings may be less painful, but it is also less educational. If our manner has been rude or abrupt, this is the time to show a better side to our nature.

At the end of the day, healthcare professionals have to accept that complaints and legal action are a fact of life in Western society. However virtuous or marvellous we are, and even if we were to cave in to every unreasonable demand, the prolonged stress of a complaint or legal case is an inevitable accompaniment to our careers.

The philosophy of fulfilment

There are aspects of personal philosophy that make fulfilment more likely. The American psychologist, Abraham Maslow, devoted much of his life to the study of happy, creative and fulfilled human beings. He studied people whom he considered to be psychologically healthy, and published his results in his seminal book *Motivation and Personality.* Maslow looked at human needs and concluded that human beings have an innate tendency to move towards higher levels of health, creativity and self-fulfilment. He described the process of fulfilling potential as *self-actualisation.* Self-actualisers appreciate values such as truth, creativity, beauty, goodness, wholeness, aliveness, uniqueness, justice, simplicity and self-sufficiency.[20] He writes:

> Our healthy individuals find it possible to accept themselves and their own nature without chagrin or complaint or, for that matter, even without thinking about the matter very much.
> ...they can take the frailties and sins, weaknesses and evils of human nature in the same unquestioning spirit with which one accepts the characteristics of nature. One does not complain about water because it is wet, or about rocks because they are hard, or about trees because they are green.[20]
>
> (pp. 130–1)

If fulfilment is defined in terms of meeting our needs, then what are those needs? Michael Ignatieff writes:

> I will tell you that I need the chance to understand and be understood, to love and be loved, to forgive and to be forgiven, and the chance to

create something which will outlast my life, and the chance to belong to a society whose purposes and commitments I share.[21]

(p. 28)

In healthcare I believe this translates into two rather separate concepts. We need to accept human nature and our patients as they are. We also need to try to encourage them to fulfil their potential, even if suffering or disease has limited their options. Here is Ruth Wilkes addressing social workers:

> ... it is an approach that calls for humility, patience, an attitude of respect towards the world, and an awareness of its infinite mystery and complexity. This way of helping is difficult because it requires a detachment that does not come naturally. The inclination in any relationship is to meddle.... If, however, we can detach ourselves from other people in an attitude of non-possessive concern, we leave them free to change in their own way.... They are separate beings linked to others through the eye of imagination ...[17]

(p. 16)

Alastair Campbell summarises this approach:

> The power of medicine then becomes the power of *letting go* control, using knowledge of the limitations of medical work to encourage the patient to take part in the shared task of trying to understand and deal with the illness as it affects his or her being. The doctor as God must be replaced by the fallible human being, whose knowledge is incomplete and whose will is corruptible.[17]

(p. 28)

This is the central tenet of 'patient-centred' medicine, about which much that is excellent has been written. At the heart of this is faith in the value of life. Henri Nouwen writes:

> But for a man with a deep-rooted faith in the value and meaning of life, every experience holds a new promise, every encounter carries a new insight, and every event brings a new message.[22]

(p. 74)

It is difficult to envisage fulfilment without some sense of purpose, of values or of belonging to the whole. Certainly healthcare without spirituality is likely to be a rather two-dimensional affair. It is the difference between viewing the next patient as another routine hindrance and seeing them as another step into the unknown. If we take the Dalai Lama's definition of spirituality, healthcare without it would be decidedly bland:

> Spirituality I take to be concerned with those qualities of the human spirit – such as love and compassion, patience, tolerance, forgiveness, contentment, a sense of responsibility, a sense of harmony – which bring happiness to both self and others.[9]

(p. 23)

Merton argues that one's life is either spiritual or not:

> A life is either spiritual or not spiritual at all. No man can serve two masters. Your life is shaped by the end you live for. You are made in the image of what you desire.[10]
>
> (p. 55)

Clearly there is room on the planet for those with and those without spirituality. If there is any choice in the matter, working with people and in an environment that shares your ethos has a lot to commend it.

In a materialistic culture, finding happiness through accumulation becomes the major goal in life. Maslow feels that this produces 'a transient ecstasy followed by discontentment and a grumble for more', and he advises us to resist this by counting our blessings and being grateful for them. Self-actualisation is characterised by an awareness of 'undeserved good luck, of gratuitous grace, which guarantees for them that life remains precious and never grows stale'.[20] Merton again argues that there is no middle ground:

> There is no neutrality between gratitude and ingratitude. Those who are not grateful soon begin to complain of everything.[10]
>
> (p. 42)

The Dalai Lama gives similar advice in *The Art of Happiness*:

> ... whether we are feeling happy or unhappy at any given moment often has very little to do with our absolute conditions, but rather, *it is a function of how we perceive our situation, how satisfied we are with what we have.*
>
> The second and more reliable method is not to have what we want but rather to want and appreciate what we have.[23]
>
> (pp. 11–18)

Most of the healthcare professionals whom I have met who are discontented with their lot seem to differ more in personal philosophy than in personal circumstance. Many seem to feel sorry for themselves in some way. Perhaps this has to do with the difference between an individualistic approach to life (i.e. looking after number one) and one that finds meaning primarily in relationships with others. Perhaps it is simply a matter of the glass being half-full or half-empty.

Strategies for fulfilment

It follows from what has already been said that striking a balance between good clinical care, adequate financial reward and time off is the key to finding professional fulfilment. Assertiveness will be required. Professionals who can 'never say no' to patients, to colleagues, to family or to themselves are bound to end up short of free time as they hare around trying to please everyone. Spending one's life in permanent fifth gear means that there is no margin for error or for unexpected life events. Illness, bereavement or accident demands an extra effort that is just not available. Trust me on this point, as a particular expert on over-commitment.

Time for oneself

The Western materialist culture has no role for personal reflection – far better for the individual to be either making goods or buying them. If personal philosophy is needed, buy a fridge magnet with a sound bite. If relaxation is required, drive to the video store or purchase a new television. James Drane writes:

> Leisure, which once was a time for self-remembering, has become a form of self-forgetting (not reading and reflection, but distractions and activities).[4]
>
> (p. 140)

Solitude is vital to personal fulfilment. It is the time when we can catch our breath, sort out our priorities and work on understanding ourselves better. It is the time to look through dark glass. Here is Thomas Merton, who dedicated his life to solitude:

> To deliver oneself up, to hand oneself over, entrust oneself completely to the silence of a wide landscape of wood and hills, or sea, or desert; to sit while the sun comes up over that land and fills its silences with light. To pray and work in the morning and to labour and rest in the afternoon, and to sit still again in meditation in the evening when night falls upon that land and when the silence fills itself with darkness and with stars.[10]
>
> (p. 97)

The ability to contemplate is the essence of our humanity. We cannot hope to grow and develop as individuals if we fail to spend time in solitude. We cannot cultivate contentment, kindness and compassion without giving the matter deliberate thought. Merton tells us that contemplation is not an easy ride:

> For inner silence depends on a continual seeking, a continual crying in the night, a repeated bending over the abyss.[10]
>
> (p. 86)

This idea of working in solitude on developing our personal understanding is very much part of religious devotion, particularly Buddhism. The Dalai Lama writes of 'inner discipline' that is required to combat the negative mental states of anger, hatred and greed and to cultivate positive states such as kindness, compassion and tolerance.[23] The discipline involves being honest both with oneself and to oneself. Discarding the goal of perfection and accepting the reality of our shadow in all our endeavours are crucial aspects. We also need to accept our vulnerability and our uncertainties. As Glin Bennet puts it, the wounded healer realises that strength lies in acknowledging one's weakness.[5] He continues:

> If we accept our humanity wholeheartedly, then we can allow ourselves to be more open to the frustrations, disappointments and compromises inherent in clinical work – and perhaps in other aspects of our lives as well.
>
> We have to accept that there is a shadow side to the way we deal with

patients, that we are always in danger of trying to become omnipotent and omniscient, and prone to take control of patients to meet our own needs.[5]

(pp. 262–3)

As the role of faultless saint is ditched, there is more likelihood that we can accept ourselves as we are – human beings prone to error who can only do their best.

Time for oneself is, of course, not solely required for inner reflection. We need to relax. Contemplation can provide time for knowledge and experience to be transformed into creative activity. Our personal interests outside work help to define us and give our lives meaning. They become more central as retirement beckons.

Time for family and friends

The family has a major role in keeping healthcare professionals grounded. Patients may think that we are marvellous, but our loved ones know better! Bennet believes that all of us tend to become idiosyncratic if we are not exposed regularly to criticism and control. He argues that those who seek high status or power in their profession may come to believe that they have special wisdom, insight or competence. In general, patients do not complain about us to our face because it is a clinically risky thing to do, whereas our family has no such reservations. As personal relationships worsen, the professional is in danger of becoming socially isolated and increasingly opinionated and arrogant. As relationships based on equality are shunned, the professional cuts a pathetic and sometimes dangerous figure. Overwork and poor family relationships are therefore intertwined in a vicious cycle.[5] Sometimes overwork leads to a personal illness or crisis that gives the necessary time for reflection and learning to occur and for mistakes to be rectified. Those who have lived only for work can find retirement difficult or even impossible to bear.

The family has more positive roles to play. When adversity strikes, a supportive family may be the only resource that seems to understand and nurture us. As we walk through the front door we can shed the expectations of the public to be professional, sensible and responsible. Life at home allows us the luxury of being relaxed, irresponsible or downright silly.

Time with colleagues

Good relationships with colleagues are a vital part of achieving professional fulfilment. We have already discussed the importance of trying to join a team that shares your personal ethos or 'world view'. Ethos is formed partly by what Drane terms 'the psychic disposition' of the person and partly by the circumstances in which the person finds him- or herself.[4] Much can be learned from senior colleagues, virtuous or otherwise. Clinical laziness or personal dishonesty can quickly be adopted in organisations that either approve of this behaviour or fail to deal with it. Much of our continuing education, particularly with regard to skills and attitudes, will be learned from our colleagues. Good role models have a critical role in fostering virtue.

Joining a small group such as a Balint or trainer's group can be the start of a lifelong habit of confronting difficult issues and personal prejudice. It often takes others to hold up the mirror before we can learn to see through it. For such groups to be really effective, they need to be based in the realm of empathy and compassion rather than in the realm of the purely intellectual or rational.[5] Groups should know, of course, when challenging is appropriate and when on other occasions a member needs support and understanding. The friendship of colleagues can be critical in times of need or uncertainty.

Time with patients

In order to find fulfilment in healthcare there must be enough time to get to know the patient in a human sense. Otherwise the patient becomes merely a bag of malfunctioning organs. Any healthcare system where there is insufficient time to get to know our patient as one human being to another is, by definition, de-humanising and demoralising. It is hard, if not impossible, to develop patience and benevolence in such circumstances. If we take the time to connect at a deep level with our patients, compassion will necessarily follow. This quality of compassion and virtuous action benefits not only our patients but also ourselves. As the Dalai Lama puts it, 'the more you give others warmth, the more warmth you receive.'[23] The patient needs help, and the act of giving it enriches the life of the giver. The good healthcare professional is interested both in the life of the patient and in their views about their experiences, suffering or illness. If the time is available and the healthcare professional is willing, a genuine caring professional friendship is possible. It is at this juncture that the professional moves from treating to healing.

Once a genuine professional friendship has developed, the way is open for patients to educate the professional. We learn vicariously, by the experience of those we care for. As we learn more about their trials and sufferings, our admiration for their courage in adversity follows. If their stoicism or resolve impresses you, take the opportunity to tell them how you feel. Take the time to recognise the beauty of a mother's devotion to her disabled child, or the son's tenderness towards his dying father. Patients who come to trust and respect us bolster our resolve and conviction. With professional friendship may come offers of help or moral support in times of hardship such as personal illness or bereavement.

Fulfilment and personality

Achieving fulfilment in our work contributes to personal growth and improves our self-esteem. Maslow writes:

> Satisfaction of the self-esteem need leads to feelings of self-confidence, worth, strength, capability and adequacy, of being useful and necessary in the world.[20]

(p. 21)

Indeed Maslow goes on to say that, at the highest level of living, duty *is* pleasure, one's 'work' is loved, and there is no difference between working and vacationing. A step too far, one might argue! On the other hand, there is no denying the satisfaction of enjoying one's work and the infectious enthusiasm and creativity that this enjoyment can generate. Working to the best of one's ability is not always possible but, when it does occur, there is no reason why we should not take some quiet satisfaction from it. Thanks from grateful patients can be gracefully received without danger of conceit or arrogance developing. So long as we remain grounded and open to lessons from our next mistake (usually just around the corner), the humility that is essential to maintaining our rapport with patients and our vigilance for the unexpected can remain intact. Like all other human beings, healthcare professionals have a legitimate need to be appreciated, valued and loved. As we develop warmth and affection for our patients, so they will for us. Once healthcare professionals have learned the skill of accepting thanks without embarrassment, more praise will be forthcoming. Our work has more than enough difficulty and sadness, so we need to learn to enjoy the good times when they occur.

Finally, the healthcare professional needs to know when to go. My advice is to plan from the start of your career for an early retirement. In the modern world, it becomes increasingly difficult to maintain the necessary stamina, knowledge and skill to survive as a healthcare professional much beyond the age of 55 years. With luck we may have another 25 years to live, and we need to prepare for a second career doing something less demanding and more fun.

References

1 Osler W (1892, reprinted in 1932) The student life. In: *Aequanimitas, With Other Addresses to Medical Students, Nurses and Practitioners of Medicine* (3e). Blakiston's Son, Philadelphia, PA.

2 Gide A (1970) *Fruits of the Earth.* Penguin Books, Harmondsworth.

3 Kierkegaard S (1962) *The Present Age.* Harper and Row, New York.

4 Drane J (1988) *Becoming a Good Doctor: the place of virtue and character in medical ethics.* Sheed & Ward, Kansas City, KS.

5 Bennet G (1987) *The Wound and the Doctor: healing, technology and power in modern medicine.* Secker & Warburg, London.

6 *The Revised English Bible.* Ecclesiastes 5:10, 6:9.

7 Bauby J (1998) *The Diving-Bell and the Butterfly.* Fourth Estate, London.

8 Toon P (1999) *Towards a Philosophy of General Practice: a study of the virtuous practitioner.* Royal College of General Practitioners, London.

9 Gyatso T (2001) *Ancient Wisdom, Modern World: ethics for the new millennium.* Abacus, London.

10 Merton T (1975) *Thoughts in Solitude.* Burns & Oates, London.

11 Moore T (1992) *Care of the Soul: how to add depth and meaning to your everyday life.* Piatkus, London.

12 Freudenberger H (1974) Staff burnout. *J Soc Issues.* **30**: 159–65.

13 Sanders K (1991) *Nine Lives: the emotional experience in general practice.* Roland Harris Education Trust, Oxford.

14 Hauerwas S (1988) *Suffering Presence: theological reflections on medicine, the mentally handicapped, and the Church.* T & T Clark, Edinburgh.

15 Cassell E (1985) *The Healer's Art.* MIT Press, Cambridge, MA.

16 Berger J and Mohr J (1997) *A Fortunate Man: the story of a country doctor.* Vintage Books, New York.

17 Campbell A (1984) *Moderated Love: a theology of professional care.* SPCK, London.

18 Tonks A (2002) The good doctor: summary of responses.*BMJ.* **325**: 715.

19 McMullin P (2002) Now I am retired ... *BMJ.* **325**: 714.

20 Maslow A (1970) *Motivation and Personality.* Harper and Row, New York.

21 Ignatieff M (1994) *The Needs of Strangers.* Vintage, London.

22 Nouwen H (1979) *The Wounded Healer.* Doubleday, New York.

23 Gyatso T and Cutler H (1998) *The Art of Happiness.* Hodder & Stoughton, London.

Further reading

- Bennet G (1987) *The Wound and the Doctor: healing, technology and power in modern medicine.* Secker & Warburg, London.
- Campbell A (1984) *Moderated Love: a theology of professional care.* SPCK, London.
- Gyatso T (2001) *Ancient Wisdom, Modern World: ethics for the new millennium.* Abacus, London.
- Gyatso T and Cutler H (1998) *The Art of Happiness.* Hodder & Stoughton, London.
- Maslow A (1970) *Motivation and Personality.* Harper and Row, New York.
- *The Revised English Bible.* Ecclesiastes.

CHAPTER 15

Professional virtue

Who put wisdom in depths of
darkness
and veiled understanding in secrecy?

Job 38:36[1]

The art of medicine is rooted in the heart. If your heart is false, you will also be a false physician; if your heart is just, you will also be a true physician.

My true sons and pupils are those who can preserve the lives of others because they have died to themselves.

Paracelsus, quoted in Needleman[2]

It is not the genius that we shall need, not the cynic, not the misanthropist, not the adroit technician, but honest, straightforward men.

Dietrich Bonhoeffer, *Prisoner for God: letters and papers from prison*[3]

Still, yours *was* the last as well as the first great and honourable passion of man – the fusion of two loves, the love of knowledge and the love of man, the fusion of the search for understanding and the impulse to help and serve suffering humanity.

Jacob Needleman, *The Way of the Physician*[2]

Indeed, if we had to choose between learning and virtue, the latter is definitely more valuable. The good heart, which is the fruit of virtue, is by itself a great benefit to humanity. Mere knowledge is not.

Tensin Gyatso, *Ancient Wisdom, Modern World*[4]

Introduction

The philosophy and ethics of virtue is no lightweight affair. Intellectual giants such as Plato, Aristotle, Homer, Kant, Nietzsche, Hume and MacIntyre appear on the guest list. I plan to sidestep much of this, partly because the debate is so complex and partly as a small reward for you, brave reader, who have got this far.

Why is the last chapter dedicated to professional virtue? The essence of humanity in healthcare is that only an impoverished form of practising medicine is possible without it. It is not against the law for healthcare professionals to earn a living and pay no attention to what we have considered thus far in this book. It is possible to punish vice, but you cannot legislate to enforce virtue. This is part of the beauty and mystery of the human condition. Virtue has to do with freedom of choice and personal expression. It is an integral part of our character and inner being.

Healthcare without virtue becomes an industrial process, a medical production line. Healthcare workers feed patients into machines and increasingly begin to resemble them. Machines are not kind and machines do not smile. Virtue cannot be learned from a book nor from a lecture. Aristotle used the term *phronesis* to describe the ability to reason correctly about practical matters. *Phronesis* has generally been translated as 'practical wisdom'. This wisdom may be learned from our role models, and it tends to accumulate with age and experience if the spirit is willing. Rosalind Hursthouse has written:

> ... a virtue is generally held to be a character trait, a state of one's character. The concept of a virtue is the concept of something that makes its possessor good; a virtuous person is a morally good, excellent, or admirable person who acts and reacts well, rightly, as she should – she gets things right.[5]
>
> (p. 11)

One of the problems with virtue ethics is that it relates to moral judgement and, as such, there can be endless discussion and debate but ultimately no right or wrong. Alasdair MacIntyre expresses it thus:

> But moral judgements, being expressions of attitude or feeling, are neither true nor false, and agreement in moral judgement is not to be secured by any rational method, for there are none.[6]
>
> (p. 12)

Definitions

There can be no concrete definitions in the world of virtue ethics, but I plan to use some practical wisdom to help us on our way. In general, employing a virtue makes human beings feel good about themselves. Hursthouse describes a virtue along Aristotelian lines as a 'character trait a human being needs to flourish or live well.' Virtues benefit their possessor and make their possessor a good human being.[5] MacIntyre expands this to say that they also:

> sustain us in the relevant kind of quest for the good, by enabling us to overcome the harms, dangers, temptations and distractions which we encounter, and which will furnish us with increasing self-knowledge and increasing knowledge of the good.[6]
>
> (p. 219)

He goes on to argue that the central features of the modern economic order are at variance with the tradition of the virtues.[6] Virtues relate primarily to how our conduct affects others, and an individualistic culture that encourages 'looking after number one', accumulation of possessions and adoption of market values as the key to behaviour may not foster a virtuous society. On the other hand, human beings seem to have an innate desire for virtue. James Drane writes:

It is the very nature of human beings to do good in the sense of acting according to some standard of goodness, honesty or justice.[7]

(p. 183)

To the same extent, communities tend to respect those who live a virtuous life. Practical wisdom may be learned by asking for, and following, their advice. Hursthouse writes:

> When I am anxious to do what is right, and do not see my way clear, I go to people I respect and admire, people who I think are kinder, more honest, more just, wiser than I am myself, and ask them what they would do in my circumstances.[5]

(p. 35)

Those without virtue are prone to frequent conflict with others and lack inner contentment and a clear conscience. Hursthouse quotes Richard Hare, who argued that without the virtues:

> all our endeavours would miscarry, and all the joy and warmth in life would disappear. Those who do not love their fellow men are less successful in living happily among them.[5]

(p. 178)

If we can define virtue, why is it not simple to teach? Hursthouse argues that the teaching of virtue needs to start in childhood:

> Virtue ethicists want to emphasise the fact that, if children are to be taught to be honest, they must be taught to love and prize the truth, and that *merely* teaching them not to lie will not achieve this end. But they need not deny that, to achieve this end, teaching them not to lie is useful, or even indispensable.[5]

(p. 39)

There are also the lessons learned by example, and these are an important factor in professional training. Here is Hursthouse again:

> We can represent giving pleasure to others, helping, co-operative activity, companionship, harmony rather than strife, truth-telling, even the conquering of fear and the endurance of pain and discomfort, to our children as enjoyable in themselves, as well as being good or praiseworthy or having to be done, in the full confidence that they will indeed come to find them enjoyable, as we have.
>   The virtuous point out that someone who is generous and charitable is likely to enjoy the benefits of being liked and loved, which the selfish and callous miss out on.[5]

(p. 11)

Professional virtue

In the Middle Ages the term 'profession' included only lawyers, doctors and priests, but it has subsequently come to include a wide variety of other occupations. Drane argues that the essence of a profession is contained in the original grouping:

> Historically what priests, doctors or lawyers professed was an ethical reality: to hold themselves bound to do a certain type of good for others. They promised service and the many particular obligations that were listed in codes of professional conduct. A lived ethics, in the sense of a commitment to objective moral standards, constituted the essence of a profession.[7]
>
> (p. 15)

To be part of a profession is to lay claim to special knowledge and skills, and there are both duties and benefits that accrue for the membership. Bennet writes:

> Privilege and power are essential attributes, also a high degree of autonomy with a freedom to define one's working arrangements. All professionals have expertise of some kind, and their profession ensures a monopoly of that expertise which, most importantly, is sanctioned by law. Entry into the profession is strictly controlled and new entrants are likely to endure years of privation and hard work before the full privileges can be experienced. A profession is something like a tribe, or a club, which is tolerant of its members, provided their conduct remains within certain unspoken boundaries, and provided they do nothing to weaken the prestige and authority of the profession. A profession controls its own affairs and the conduct of its members, without any interference from outside.[8]
>
> (p. 62)

There is a conflict within the caring professions in that a member is gaining income, prestige and power from other people's illness, suffering or social disadvantage.[9] The public trust the healthcare professional to put more into their work than simply pursuing wealth or status. In these circumstances we must recognise and deal with the tension that exists between altruism and egoism. The special body of knowledge and skills that we possess requires some detachment, but this should not be used simply as a method of personal defence. Similarly, we need to be careful that the power we wield over patients is not used for abuse or self-aggrandisement.[9]

Alastair Campbell argues that the caring professions operate in a religious sense:

> ... professional helpers represent more than human attempts to care. Their opposition to illness, pain and social disadvantage symbolises the 'impossible ideal' of *agape*, a love which restores full value to every individual, however damaged, however oppressed, however bereft of hope. In this sense the professional commitment is a religious one, though this need not imply that the practitioners see themselves as believers. Their *actions* and *attitudes* look for an ultimate conquest of suffering.[9]
>
> (p. 85)

The special nature of virtue in healthcare becomes clearer as we acknowledge the particular nature of our duties. Here is Drane writing about doctors in particular:

> Every human being, for example, is under moral obligation to respect others, to help them, to keep promises and secrets, and to be truthful, but the doctor is obliged to go beyond normal expectations in relationships with patients. Profession binds the doctor to higher ideals and higher virtues because of the nature of the medical relationship.
>
> Virtue is not disassociated from objective standards of conduct, but higher standards of professional conduct require higher virtue and greater personal effort in character formation.[7]
>
> (p. 18)

Drane rightly draws attention to the close link between character and virtue. He argues that virtue refers to a 'lived personal dimension of morality'. Our professional virtues become an integral part of our clinical character and our *ethos*:

> In this sense, it is correct to say that virtue not only orders the inner life of a person but, like character, influences a person's relation to the whole of existence. After realising that certain forms of moral conduct are indispensable to good medicine, a doctor can learn to be helpful, kind, caring, respectful, promise-keeping, friendly, and the rest.[7]
>
> (p. 159)

This also highlights the shame that is brought upon the professions when healthcare students are exposed to teachers who lack these qualities. The essence of medical ethics and of medical virtue is that healthcare professionals should always act humanely and in the *best interests of the patient.*

Professional character

The term *ethos* relates to the nature and disposition of a person, organisation or community. Ethos is composed of characteristic attitudes. I have previously suggested the importance of working with colleagues who share your own ethos, if at all possible. The ethos of an organisation will be influenced by the virtues and character of those who work within it, and the same applies to professions. There will be changes to aspects of ethos with time, as characters and circumstances change. In healthcare, for example, the tradition of extremely long working hours has been tempered in European countries. How can a virtuous ethos be generated or encouraged? Drane proposes the following:

> Creating an *ethos* always involves commitment to a project. Human beings make themselves not out of nothing, but with the cooperation of both intelligence and freedom. Once an inner ethical being is created, human life becomes something more. It is given new depth, a greater significance, and a reason for hope. None of this is immediately evident on the outside. The inner creation is never demonstrable by scientific criteria. But when it takes place, it makes all the difference in the way a

person acts. It is like that mysterious moment when a seed breaks apart and sinks its roots. It happens in a moment, and yet it permits the moments which follow to have a unity, a direction and an inner consistency.[7]

(p. 150)

This is a critical point in the formation of the virtuous healthcare practitioner. I sense that most healthcare professionals are virtuous, but healthcare institutions can easily become derailed from the noble path. Poor management, inept leadership, undue political interference or unsatisfactory working conditions can all lead to a collapse in morale and a loss of commitment to ideals. The leading characters in the healthcare professions have an important role here. Both Maslow and Kierkegaard emphasise the importance of finding this commitment to an ideal, a meaning system, a model of existence, or a vision of life.[7] Maslow talks of finding 'a calling, the altar upon which to offer oneself'.[10] Drane emphasises the difference between working with and without a purpose:

Deeds repeated one after another lead nowhere and do nothing; but deeds derived from attitudes, informed by a faith and directed towards an ideal can lead to the development of both virtue and character.[7]

(p. 157)

Seven virtues for healthcare professionals

Listing virtues is a personal affair, and some might argue a fruitless task. There is no right or wrong, and no way of resolving disputes. I have compiled a list of seven virtues for the healthcare professional to consider. They appear in no particular order and without a catchy mnemonic.

Truthfulness

The patient has a right to expect truthfulness from healthcare professionals when it is genuinely asked for. This is not to say that the truth must be force-fed to those who have not requested it. As Drane puts it:

The virtue of truth, in the face of mystery, takes the form of silence.
... the good doctor, besides knowing how to talk truthfully, also knows how to be silent.[7]

(p. 54)

He goes on to explain how judgement and consideration of the patient's best interest are central to the task:

A context of benevolence means that the emphasis is placed upon when and how and with what sensitivity the truth is communicated to this particular patient with these unique personal needs.

The doctor's virtue of truthfulness requires both sensitivity and subtlety.[7]

(p. 59)

Breaking bad news is not the only area where truthfulness is called for. Owning up to personal shortcomings or mistakes is important. Patients need to know that actions have been driven by genuine concern, not by financial or political expediency. Honesty in motivation is a central tenet of virtuous healthcare.

Trustworthiness

The healthcare professional needs to be reliable and efficient. Mistakes will occur but great efforts should be made to minimise them, and to learn from them when they do occur. Secrets that are entrusted to our care are buried with us in our graves. Our promises must be honoured. The patient's intimacy and vulnerability must not be abused.

Insight

Insight is an invaluable skill in healthcare. Our decisions are often based upon vague or uncertain information. Insight develops with age and experience, and is more likely if we know the patient well. Human nature can never be fully understood but, with effort over many years, repeating patterns of behaviour become apparent. Sharing our insight with the patient is not always appropriate or beneficial. The point is not to show the patient or the world how smart we are, but to use insight to guide us in the best way to help them. We need insight into ourselves and the relationship that we have with our patients, and we need to be aware of our own needs and failings. We inevitably develop a *persona* in our work, and we need enough insight to be able to leave this *persona* at work when we leave at the end of the day. Here is Needleman again:

> ... the medical mind requires a harmonic balance of thought, feeling and instinct. This balance of three factors in the mind of man is what results in medical virtue, which of course is one expression of human virtue as such, or moral power. Out of the blend of thought, feeling and instinct there arises authentic intuition, courage and will, all of which, taken together, may be given the ancient name *intelligence*.[2]

(p. 32)

Hursthouse also highlights the need for insight in developing virtue when she talks of 'the sensitivity, perception, and imagination necessary for being thoroughly virtuous'.[5]

Respect

James Drane emphasises the role of respect in developing medical virtue. He stresses the importance of maintaining a proper distance in the encounter with the patient:

> Keeping distance restrains an inclination to dominate the other, to take possession, or to use the other for one's own ends.
> The virtue of respect disposes a person, first of all, to recognise the significance, dignity, freedom of the other, and then to keep enough distance to let the other be.[7]
>
> (p. 66)

Respect for the patient helps to ensure that healthcare professionals are not abusing the power that stems from their role. Genuine respect for the opinions of others reduces the likelihood of arrogance. There may at times be a gulf between the world views of the patient and the healthcare professional. Respect for the views of others allows a genuine human dialogue to take place and a plan to be agreed upon that the patient can sign up to. Drane concludes:

> The good doctor helps, talks to and respects those who are weak and defenceless.... only morally flawed doctors do not respect their patients. The virtue of respect is not a frill, but rather an essential of any medical ethics which addresses common, everyday medical acts and not just unusual cases.[7]
>
> (p. 69)

Respect is the virtue that drives the conviction that the patient is the centre of the medical encounter, and that the patient's beliefs, opinions and character must be sought and valued. Here is Drane again:

> The patient's lifestyle, value system, and way of being will often be very different from the doctor's. Consequently, what the doctor believes is best for the patient may not at all agree with the patient's conviction about his or her own welfare. Respect is the virtue which disposes the doctor to handle such differences with sensitivity, avoiding either deceit or manipulation.[7]
>
> (p. 67)

Vulnerability

We have talked at some length about this curious quality. To have the openness to allow others to come close to us, to let our defences down, and to let loose our concern and humanity for those who suffer is to risk personal pain. Without vulnerability life is safe and sterile but, in my view, ultimately meaningless. Vulnerability is to rush into a burning house to save the child inside. There are limits to the amount of pain and suffering that one human being can share with others, and this is the reason why balance is always required. At times of personal crisis or suffering it is perfectly sensible to erect defences and accept that our healing abilities will be temporarily reduced. Remaining vulnerable can be exhausting, and there is a genuine risk to selfhood which should not be underestimated. Maintaining vulnerability is an act of faith and courage.

Compassion

Compassion was considered in detail in Chapter 13. It is an active virtue, demanding personal action. Vulnerability leads to closeness, closeness leads to empathy and humanity, and these in turn lead to compassionate deeds. Some healthcare professionals argue that they cannot afford to be compassionate. They may be working in situations where compassion is difficult, or even impossible. Examples of such situations would include an oncologist facing 50 patients with metastatic cancer in an afternoon clinic, or those working for frontline charities in areas of catastrophic human disaster. These would be situations in which healthcare professionals can merely do their best and try to cope with unreasonable burdens of suffering. Crises will always occur, but having to work long term in situations such as these may lead to dehumanisation and damage to the person, which may be irrevocable. Compassion is what makes healthcare ennobling and ultimately worthwhile. Drane explains:

> By individual acts of selfless caring for the sick, a doctor becomes a caring self. By repeated just acts, he makes himself just. Acts follow one upon another, but gradually they leave something permanent in their wake. That something is a reality which gives unity to acts and keeps life from being a disconnected chaos of behaviours.[7]
>
> (p. 138)

Enthusiasm

Enthusiasm is the lifeblood of any profession. Without enthusiasm, professional effort becomes repetitive and tedious and younger members catch disenchantment like any other infectious disease. Those who lack enthusiasm should be banned from teaching others. Enthusiasm fosters hope and optimism, and these are critical qualities in our quest to help the sick and suffering. Enthusiasm encompasses valuing the traditions of the discipline and learning from past masters. MacIntyre writes:

> Lack of justice, lack of truthfulness, lack of courage, lack of relevant intellectual virtues – these corrupt traditions, just as they do those institutions and practices which derive their life from the traditions of which they are the contemporary embodiments.[6]
>
> (p. 223)

Living a good life engenders enthusiasm. Cutler comments on the ability of the Dalai Lama to 'inspire rather than awe', and attributes this to his belief in 'the fundamental gentleness and goodness of all human beings, a belief in the value of compassion, a belief in a policy of kindness, and a sense of commonality among all living creatures'.[11] Hursthouse also highlights the importance of hope when she writes that 'believing that human nature is harmonious is part of the virtue of hope'.[5]

This is not to argue that healthcare professionals and teachers must always be full of enthusiasm or hope. However, I do suggest that humane professionals strive to adopt an enthusiastic approach, to live good lives and to behave virtuously. An ethical and virtuous life takes time and practice. Commitment to a cause or belief greater than merely looking after oneself is essential. Drane believes that this commitment is central to ethical behaviour in medicine:

> Some ethical failures in medicine derive from the doctor's never having been committed seriously to anyone or any ideal beyond his or her well-being. Far more commonly, ethical faults result from a weakening of an original commitment, and its associated ethical ideals.[7]
>
> (p. 148)

As Drane has provided us with the main framework of this chapter, it seems only fair to let him have the last word:

> Because maturing or perfecting one's character takes time, patience is required to become ethical. No one can force the circumstances which call for critical response of the inner self which in turn solidifies a character. On the other hand, we only have a certain limited time to carry out our ethical enterprise. Death fixes forever the *ethos* we have created.[7]
>
> (p. 148)

We live, dear reader, in strange but exciting times. For those who have managed to plough through this book, I feel a warm companionship. May your careers be long, successful, enjoyable, rewarding, compassionate and virtuous. If this doesn't happen all of the time, may it at least happen some of the time.

References

1   *The Revised English Bible.* Job 38:36.
2   Needleman J (1992) *The Way of the Physician.* Penguin Books, Harmondsworth.
3   Bonhoeffer D (1958) *Prisoner for God: letters and papers from prison.* Sheed & Ward, Kansas City, Missouri.
4   Gyatso T (2001) *Ancient Wisdom, Modern World.* Abacus, London.
5   Hursthouse R (2001) *On Virtue Ethics.* Oxford University Press, Oxford.
6   MacIntyre A (1985) *After Virtue* (2e). Duckworth, London.
7   Drane J (1988) *Becoming a Good Doctor.* Sheed & Ward, Kansas City, KS.
8   Bennet G (1987) *The Wound and the Doctor.* Secker & Warburg, London.
9   Campbell A (1984) *Moderated Love: a theology of professional care.* SPCK, London.
10 Maslow A (1987) *Motivation and Personality* (3e). Harper & Row, New York.
11 Gyatso T and Cutler H (1998) *The Art of Happiness.* Coronet, London.

Further reading

- Campbell A (1984) *Moderated Love: a theology of professional care.* SPCK, London.
- Drane J (1988) *Becoming a Good Doctor.* Sheed & Ward, Kansas City, KS.
- Hursthouse R (2001) *On Virtue Ethics.* Oxford University Press, Oxford.
- Needleman J (1992) *The Way of the Physician.* Penguin Books, Harmondsworth.

Index